Understanding the Music Industries

Understanding the Music Industries

Chris Anderton, Andrew Dubber
and Martin James

Los Angeles | London | New Delhi
Singapore | Washington DC

Los Angeles | London | New Delhi
Singapore | Washington DC

SAGE Publications Ltd
1 Oliver's Yard
55 City Road
London EC1Y 1SP

SAGE Publications Inc.
2455 Teller Road
Thousand Oaks, California 91320

SAGE Publications India Pvt Ltd
B 1/I 1 Mohan Cooperative Industrial Area
Mathura Road
New Delhi 110 044

SAGE Publications Asia-Pacific Pte Ltd
3 Church Street
#10-04 Samsung Hub
Singapore 049483

Editor: Mila Steele
Editorial assistant: James Piper
Production editor: Imogen Roome
Copyeditor: Kate Harrison
Proofreader: Louise Harnby
Marketing manager: Michael Ainsley
Cover design: Francis Kenny
Typeset by: C&M Digitals (P) Ltd, Chennai, India

Library of Congress Control Number: 2012938831

British Library Cataloguing in Publication data

A catalogue record for this book is available from
the British Library

ISBN 978-1-4462-0794-9
ISBN 978-1-4462-0795-6 (pbk)

CONTENTS

BOXES AND FIGURES

LIST OF BOXES

LIST OF FIGURES

NOTES ON AUTHORS AND CONTRIBUTORS

Chris Anderton

Chris Anderton is a Senior Lecturer in Popular Music Studies at Southampton Solent University and is the Course Leader for BA (Hons) Music Promotion. He has published scholarly articles and book chapters examining not-for-profit bootlegging, progressive rock, and the history, geography, cultural economy and marketing of British music festivals. His other research interests include the future of the music industries, creative audiences, artist–fan interactions, and alternative distribution and copyright regimes.

Andrew Dubber

Andrew Dubber is Reader in Music Industries Innovation at Birmingham City University and is Award Leader for the MA in Music Industries and the MA in Music Radio. He is a member of the Centre for Media and Cultural Research, an advisor to Bandcamp and Planzai, and the founder of New Music Strategies – a pan-European music think-tank and strategy group. His research interests include digital media cultures, online music enterprise, radio in the digital age, music as a tool for social change, and music as culture.

Martin James

Martin James is a Senior Lecturer in Popular Music Studies at Southampton Solent University and is the Course Leader for BA (Hons) Popular Music Journalism. He worked as a music journalist on the editorial teams of a variety of market-leading titles, and contributed to almost every major music and lifestyle magazine in the UK and US. He has written several critically acclaimed books and biographies, including *State of Bass – Jungle: the Story so Far* and *French Connections: from Discotheque to Discovery*.

Holly Tessler

Chapter 3: Songwriting and Publishing (co-author)
Chapter 10: Contractual Agreements and Relationships (co-author)
Holly Tessler is a Senior Lecturer in Commercial Music in the School of Creative and Cultural Industries, University of the West of Scotland. Areas of research include the music industries as creative industries, the relationship between music, culture and technology, music and branding, the mediation of popular music, and the role of narrative in popular music/music industries practices.

Andy West

Chapter 3: Songwriting and Publishing (co-author)

Andy West is a Principal Lecturer at Leeds College of Music. He was previously a Teaching Fellow of Bath Spa University where he designed and directed the world's first MA in Songwriting from 2007–11. Andy has taught at songwriting festivals and his songs have been used in numerous television shows including *Heroes*, *Lost* and *In Cold Blood*. His PhD examines the teaching and learning of songwriting in higher education.

INTRODUCTION

When we talk about 'the music industry' or 'the music business' in day-to-day life, it is assumed that we all agree about what it is we are talking about. Likewise, when newspaper columnists discuss 'the death of the music industry' or use phrases like 'the music industry believes that ...' there is an underlying presupposition that the music industry is a single, unproblematic, corporate entity that shares values, strategies and methods. In fact, nothing could be further from the truth.

The music industries exist in a multitude of forms: a network of businesses that vary from the very small to the very large, and represent a wide range of commercial activities. They produce goods and services of many different kinds, from a monthly night of DJs playing a local venue to a music royalties collection agency with 800 employees, or from a large merchandise company making band posters and t-shirts to a single individual providing musical score transcription services for composers and orchestras (to describe just a few). Many music businesses do not appear to be especially business-like in their style, and some may even have the appearance of a group of friends working together on a hobby project that they love. Indeed, they may be just that. Collectively, the economic weight of the smaller businesses may not match that of the major recording and publishing companies, but their activities are still significant and are worthy of our attention.

QUESTIONING 'TRADITIONAL' MODELS OF THE MUSIC INDUSTRY

The 'traditional' music industry model for aspirant artists/performers starts with writing or choosing songs, playing live to build a following, seeking publishing and recording deals, and then recording in a professional studio with the resultant record manufactured and promoted through magazines, radio and television to drive retail sales. Every aspect of this flow model has been disrupted by the digitalization of the music industries since the 1980s. Digital recording, distribution, marketing and sales have become commonplace as have financially affordable tools for achieving a professional product.

This does not mean the traditional model is in danger of being entirely replaced or that the major record labels and publishers will necessarily lose their predominant position. But it does mean that the model is being actively reconfigured at all scales of the music industries, and those interested in studying and working in those industries must keep abreast of the changes and possibilities that are emerging. This book supports this by examining several sectors of the music industries in light of technological developments and in relation to both major and independent artists and companies. These chapters discuss the sectors in separation from each other in order to impose some clarity and order. However, in reality, there are numerous linkages in what is a highly interdependent set of business responsibilities, roles and activities. Readers are encouraged to make creative connections between the chapters in order to further understand how the different areas impact each other.

STRUCTURE OF THE BOOK

This book addresses the rich variety and scale of the music industries by examining the most important aspects of those industries, and considering the effects of technological, social, cultural and economic change upon them. To help frame those considerations, the first chapter outlines some of the key research approaches used by scholars for understanding the historical development of the music industries and the contemporary issues that face them. Chapter 2 moves on to discuss the structure and strategies of the recorded music industries at every level – from major transnational media conglomerates to the micro-independent bedroom labels and independent artists. Critical to this chapter are the effects of technological developments and the need for record companies of all sizes to deal with the changing and uncertain tastes of the public.

Chapter 3 focuses on songwriting and publishing, and helps readers to understand the creative and the industrial contexts and issues involved in writing and making money from songs. Chapters 4, 5 and 6 explore, in turn, the workings of record production (specifically record production), music distribution, and music promotion. These are crucial areas of the recorded music industries and ones that have been subject to considerable innovation in recent decades as digital technologies have developed and transformed their operations. Chapter 7 turns attention to the live music industry. This sector has seen sizeable growth in the 2000s and now outperforms the recorded music business in the UK in terms of income generated. The emerging inter-relationships between the live and recorded music sectors are unpicked, as are changes in primary and secondary ticketing. Chapter 8 then considers consumption practices based around music and how music is made meaningful by audiences.

The final two chapters of the book examine legal aspects of the music industries. Chapter 9 explains and reviews copyright law in the UK and the US and the historical and philosophical framework that underpins it. The chapter also assesses the differing responses and tactics of the music industries and artists to the issue of music piracy. Chapter 10 discusses some of the contractual agreements and relationships through which the music industry operates, with an emphasis on artist management, music publishing and music recording.

Taken together, the chapters of this book offer a framework for developing a deeper understanding of the many aspects of the music industries and their inter-relationships with each other. It helps to make sense of them in historical, cultural, technological and economic terms, and to provide a critical focus on the processes that lead to change. By adopting a research-centred and analytical approach, readers can keep track of the ongoing development of the music industries and place themselves in the front line of innovation and entrepreneurship in the future.

ACKNOWLEDGMENTS

The authors would like to thank all of the music industry personnel that contributed their time and feedback to the preparation of this book; our colleagues at Southampton Solent University and Birmingham City University; Andy West and Holly Tessler for their timely contributions and expertise; Louise Morrell for graphic design; Mila Steele, James Piper and Imogen Roome at Sage; and all of our families for their support.

1

STUDYING THE MUSIC INDUSTRIES

This chapter explores several ways of unpicking and analysing the complex web of practices, strategies and narratives that characterize the music industries, from political economy and the culture industry to sociological and historical approaches. It also highlights the transformations that digital technologies have brought to all areas of the music industries.

KEY FINDINGS

- The music industries may be explored from a variety of research perspectives.
- Technological developments have had, and continue to have, significant impacts on the structure and work of the music industries.
- Interdisciplinary approaches may offer new insights into the music industries.

GETTING STARTED

The study of the music industries is not a uniform endeavour. There are many and varied approaches that yield valid, interesting and important understandings about those industries, their cultural and economic impacts, and their effects on the lives of those who work in and interact with them. These studies can happen at a macro level, in which scholars examine the effects, economic impacts and practices of the music business as a whole, and their inter-relationships with other businesses, laws and social forces. They can also happen at a micro level, where they centre on the activities of individual businesses or, indeed, individuals. Some research focuses on areas between these two extremes or examines specific sectors of the music business. One approach is never more significant than, or entirely separate from, all of the others, and a rounded understanding of the music industries as a whole demands a grasp of the various ways that these approaches may reveal insights into the business of music. This chapter begins this process by introducing a range of research approaches, starting with organizational structure.

ORGANIZATIONAL STRUCTURE

One useful way to understand the activities of a business, whether a small-to-medium enterprise (SME) or a multinational corporation, is to examine its organizational structure. In the music industries, there will be areas of responsibility for product (or artist) development, finance, legal, technical and general organizational planning, operational and administrative staff, sales and marketing personnel and so on. In larger businesses, each of these areas will have people or entire departments who specialize in just one aspect of the business. In contrast, smaller companies may give responsibility for several, many, or even all of those roles to just one person. And of course, the roles that exist within a music organization will depend to a large extent on what particular task that organization is performing, or which sectors of the music industry that business represents and connects with.

A music business, just like any other business, does not operate in a vacuum, but has suppliers and industry partners that allow it to function without having to perform every specialist role. What is important to examine when considering a music organization is not merely the roles and responsibilities within that organization, but crucially, the relationships that that business has with outside agencies. Drawing and mapping those internal and external connections helps us gain a better understanding of the workings of these organizations and their place within the broader political economy and creative industries context.

When investigating the music industries, understanding the organizational structure of a particular business (or of more than one) can offer critical insights into how that business works, and provide useful knowledge in terms of practical applications. For example, discovering repeatable procedures for music business success (or systems and approaches to be avoided), identifying problems within the structure and linkages of an organization, or simply generating new knowledge about the ways that music organizations can and do work, can provide clues as to how they might potentially do so more profitably.

POLITICAL ECONOMY

Work in the field of political economy examines and explores the relationship between music organizations and the political and economic frameworks within which they operate. In other words, political economy is interested in power relationships and flows of capital. At its broadest, and particularly with respect to policy, this is generally understood at the level of the nation-state, and the political infrastructure into which the larger industry as a whole plays a role.

Political economy studies are primarily interested in macro-level examinations of industries and how their goods and services, production practices and management relate to and are informed by the legal and economic climate in which they operate. Accordingly, a political economy approach to analysing the music industries will be concerned with how music businesses make money, how they may affect policy, and how broader policies may in turn influence the kinds of activities in which music businesses engage. Exploring and understanding the music industries in these terms reveals the significant impact that the music industries may have to a nation's economy.

The industries not only contribute to the economic well-being of a nation and employ a great many people, but are also strongly linked to the wider political environment, and reflect the economic conditions of the times. The corporate record industry, for instance, relies upon a system of capitalism as a political framework for its activities. The division of labour, distribution of scarce resources, and dependence on financial infrastructures are, therefore, of particular interest to political economic analysis.

Economic infrastructure

Political economy approaches may examine the ways that the economic infrastructure of a business sector or organization is structured and works in practice. For instance, record labels have tended to work in a particular way over the past decades – with a few hits providing the revenue required to prop up the business, which often takes losses elsewhere on many more unsuccessful releases. Indeed it is a commonly held belief that eight out of ten releases fail to recoup costs. This is, in part, because the recorded music business has traditionally been based on a model of high fixed costs and low marginal costs. That is to say, it is (or rather, was) expensive to record an album (fixed costs), yet relatively cheap to manufacture each individual copy (marginal costs). Hence, the more copies that are sold of a particular release, the higher the profit margin on each sale made. From a record company's perspective, it is preferable to make one album that sells a million copies than to make 100 albums that sell only 10,000 copies each. The same overall number of records would be sold in both cases, but the fixed costs of producing those 99 other albums would significantly reduce the profit margin. This economic principle explains the importance of hits and hit-makers to the recorded music industry: an artist who can sell 20 million copies of a record (as Michael Jackson did with his *Thriller* album in the 1980s) is a far more valuable asset to a major recording company than an entire catalogue of artists that may collectively sell more copies between them.

Oligopoly and the star system

The political economy approach is also interested in the form that the industry takes as a whole. The recorded music business is, arguably, an oligopoly: an industry in which very few players dominate the market. This is certainly true in sheer financial terms, as three major multinational companies (known as the 'majors') command the majority of revenues within the globalized music industry, whether under their own label names, or as owners of many of the larger, so-called independent labels (see Chapter 2). This oligopolistic market concentration is of significance for scholars, since it not only impacts upon the organization of capital and political impact of the majors, but also affects how culture is produced and disseminated. That is to say, the political and economic structure and organization of the major recording companies can have a direct bearing on the kind of music that gets made and heard. For instance, the predominant economic model of the recording industries is based on the 'star' system, in which a relatively small number of artists provide the vast majority of revenue. This model guides the strategy and thinking of the major record companies, so affecting the choices that record company personnel make regarding which artists should be released and promoted to the buying public.

The political economy approach may, then, reveal how and why unequal power relations can have an effect on the music that gets created, promoted and released. Not only do patterns of corporate ownership affect the selection and availability of music that gets broadcast and sold in stores, but similarly, commercial pressures can impede and suppress oppositional forces. The purpose of multinational corporations is not to distribute works of art, but to maximize profit (not simply 'make money') – and political economists stress that it is the maintenance of control over the means of production and distribution that is paramount to the interests of the corporate music business world.

The music industries as copyright industries

The political economy approach revolves around an understanding of the numerous ways that money can be made from music, and how that money is then distributed. The central mechanism for revenue generation in the music industries (at both a macro and a micro level) has been copyright, which is a form of intellectual property. In fact, Patrik Wikström (2009) goes so far as to assert that the music business is fundamentally a copyright industry, which marks it out as distinct from other kinds of industries that deal in goods and services. Copyright ownership, and control over intellectual property assets, serve to create wealth in different ways to that seen when, for example, buying and selling commodities (sugar, wheat, copper and so on) or providing services (financial, legal, personal and so on). Copyright is so central to the music industries that it will be discussed in much greater detail in Chapter 9, but it is worth mentioning here that copyright exploitation is central to the political economy approach to understanding the music industries.

Perhaps most importantly, it is crucial to remember that the political economy of the music industry is always changing, and that this is affected by a wide range of forces. Changes in public policy brought about by a change in government or the changing of hands of a portfolio between different political representatives can have wide-reaching influences. The sale or purchase of record companies by other organizations can affect the whole of the music business. Changes in public taste can also impact the fortunes of whole sectors of the music industries. Even changes in other, related industries can have a huge impact, for instance, radio station formats change over time and the consumer electronics industry continually experiments with new devices and ideas. Technology can, of course, have a major role in the changing fortunes of the music industries, and this will be examined in more detail in later chapters.

CULTURE INDUSTRY

The music business is commonly referred to in the literature and in public policy as one of the 'cultural industries' or 'culture industries'. These are usually described as those industries that create, produce and distribute goods and services that are cultural in nature, and may be further defined by their relationship to copyright as a primary means of control over the economic functions of those industries. In one sense, to study the music business as a culture industry is little different to the study of the music business in terms of its political economy, but the critical focus as well as the key thinkers and core texts tend to have some significant differences.

Commodification and standardization

The term 'culture industry' was first coined by Theodor Adorno and Max Horkheimer in *Dialectic of Enlightenment* (2002, originally published in German in 1944). They argued that industries that create and distribute artefacts of popular culture are in essence no different from factories producing standardized goods, and that the simple gratifications produced by mass culture consumption have the net political effect of calming and appeasing the public at large. Their critique of the music business suggests that the commodification and standardization of popular culture creates a single marketplace in which the most popular works succeed, regardless of their 'artistic merit' or 'cultural worth' (both entirely problematic terms that require some unpacking when working in this area of critical theory).

In addition, Adorno and Horkheimer suggest that the vast majority of this standardized fare is owned and controlled by a very small number of major corporations that claim to serve consumer needs by supplying what audiences want – and that point to the popularity of their successes as evidence that they are serving this need. However, by both creating and meeting demand for standardized products, the culture industries are described as manipulating the public, so that the identities and individual tastes of consumers are minimized. In this way, the music business can perpetuate the 'star' system that, as noted earlier, is the most effective profit-generating method for the recording industries: producing more copies of fewer and fewer items.

Creative work and everyday practice

In *The Cultural Industries* (2007) David Hesmondhalgh suggests that cultural and creative businesses create and disseminate texts that 'have an influence on our understanding of the world' (2007: 3). As such, these industries help shape and define what our culture is and how we relate to it. It is, therefore, crucial to have an understanding of how these texts are arrived at and selected, and how these decisions are made with respect to the corporate desire to not just make profit but to maximize it. A culture industries analysis of the music industries will also pay attention to the 'work' that is done in that context, and how cultural workers spend their time. Hesmondhalgh's more recent book with Sarah Baker, *Creative Labour: Media Work in Three Cultural Industries* (2011), goes into some depth on the work that employees of the cultural (or creative) industries, including the music business, actually do, the extent to which it can be considered creative work, and what it is that constitutes 'good work' in that context.

Similarly, Keith Negus offers a more nuanced examination of the recorded music industries in *Music Genres and Corporate Cultures* (1999). He argues that it is difficult to apply Adorno and Horkheimer's critique equally across all cultural industries: that there are significant differences between (for instance) the film industry and the recorded music business. He also problematizes the relationship between industry and 'creativity' – that is to say the tension between what artists want to create and what their record companies wish to produce, promote and release. Furthermore, Negus explores the idea that not only does industry produce culture, but culture produces industry. In other words, music businesses capitalize on and exploit existing cultural practices and scenes as much as they seek to create them. As with Hesmondhalgh's later work, Negus is concerned with understanding the role of workers within recording companies. He finds that, while the term has a somewhat different meaning in the corporate context, record companies can be discussed in terms of an internal 'culture' that informs and shapes practices and decisions made by personnel working within them (Negus, 1999; see also Negus, 1992). Indeed, understanding and analysing what people do within the music industries is an important approach to the scholarly study of the music industries and offers insights that may not be gained with an abstract political economy approach to that same business or sector.

SOCIOLOGY

The study of the music industries as a function of culture and society is another popular approach to understanding the music industries. Music is culture, and industries are formed from aspects of cultural engagement. It is too easy when studying music as an industry to fall into the logical trap that suggests that people are simply consumers that are marketed to, and who purchase undifferentiated products from footwear to chocolate bars to pop music. In fact, people are complex, diverse and interesting – and their engagements with the music industries are rich, nuanced and complicated.

Symbolic meaning

In short – music creates symbolic meaning for people, and that meaning is expressed in all sorts of different ways. People do not simply discover, buy and listen to music. They dance to it, they gather with others who enjoy the same music, they collect and organize music, and they create new knowledge around that music. Subgenres form, and scenes are created that support and reinforce those subgenres. Clothing and personal styles represent a kind of tribal affiliation with different kinds of music (note, for instance, the differences between emo attire, hip hop fashion, skater punk clothing and club wear for house music fans) and identity is formed and expressed through music, particularly – though hardly exclusively – by young fans (see Frith, 1996).

Moreover, the culture of music is expressed in many varied ways, all of which are worthy of study. Examples include the venues attended by music fans, and how those venues form the basis for social cohesion and the formation of scenes, the musical heritage of cities and nations and their impact on cultural identity, and the broadcast of local music and its effect on both civic pride and the development of local music industries. There is also the relationship between music, race and gender, and the ways that our personal daily routines are integrated with music listening in supermarkets, shopping malls, health clubs and other places where people perform social and cultural activities.

The study of music as culture and as a social force allows for a deeper understanding of how musical meanings are created and communicated. It also sheds light on how these meanings form the basis of the music industries and the opportunities that exist for businesses to engage with subcultures, scenes, and daily activities. As such, what people do with music in a broader sense, other than simply listening to it, can reveal fascinating insights and great potential for research. For a deeper understanding of the study of popular music culture, see Tim Wall's (2003) *Studying Popular Music Culture.*

MUSICOLOGY

Musicology is the study of musical works as texts for critical analysis. Arguably, there is very little overlap between the world of the musicologist and the student of the music industries. Yet, there is considerable scope for interdisciplinary research, study and teaching across these fields in relation to the creation, performance and reception of musical works. Knowledge of the specialist language of musicology (or the musicological study of musical texts) is not strictly essential for studying the music industries, but an awareness of the terminology and an appreciation of how the musical 'text' (whether on paper, on record or in performance) works will offer a broader and more grounded understanding of the art, expression and culture at the heart of the field. A broad musical palate, a wide range of listening, an understanding of a variety of musical genres, and the ability to talk about music in a way that communicates with musicians and music professionals is a good basis for professional conduct within the music industries. In other words, while it is not necessary to be able to compose a song, write an arrangement, transpose a work to another key or be able to play the drums in a 6/8 time signature, it is a good idea to know what such things are when studying the field or working with musical people.

Taking popular music seriously

The serious study of popular music works as texts has been a fairly recent development, in part because many musicologists have been slow to accept popular music forms as worthy of scholarly attention. It has been pointed out, for example by Simon Frith and Andrew Goodwin (1998), that many rock musicians and rock critics lack the specialist vocabulary and techniques of musical analysis that academic critics of 'serious' music forms command. However, popular music forms are increasingly garnering the attention of musicologists. For instance, the International Association for the Study of Popular Music (IASPM) is an interdisciplinary organization established in 1981 to connect scholars working on different aspects of popular music business and culture, and has over 600 members worldwide. At an IASPM conference, you are as likely to hear people talk about polyrhythm in jazz or the relationship between Frank Zappa and Third Stream music as you are to discuss the marketing strategies of major record labels or electronic ticketing at music festivals.

When understanding and analysing the music industries, it is a good idea to bear in mind that there are other things at stake than just the commercial infrastructure and political economies of labels and distributors. To many people within both academia and the broader music industries, the artworks at the centre of those industries are of paramount interest. Musicology provides the language by which those works can be discussed with clarity and an agreed set of terms. Fundamental concepts and modes of analysis can be found in Allan Moore's *Rock: the Primary Text* (2001) and David Machin's *Analysing Popular Music* (2010).

METANARRATIVE

A metanarrative is 'a global or totalizing cultural narrative schema which orders and explains knowledge and experience' (Stephens and McCallum, 1998). It is a grand, unifying story that makes sense of all of the little stories that happen along the way – by making them part of a bigger, universal picture. The term was originally introduced and critiqued by the French philosopher Jean-François Lyotard (1984) and was used in relation to such metanarratives as Marxism and religious doctrine, where the unifying story is understood as embodying universal truth. It has since been used more narrowly within literary criticism and communication studies to examine specific narrative fields (for example, see Baringer, 2004), and it is in this more limited sense that we use the term here. By examining metanarratives we can unpick the simplistic cause and effect explanations provided for often complex inter-relationships and conflicts, and investigate the purposes to which they are used. Two examples of metanarratives are given here, each of which offers an all encompassing way to think about historical change within the music industries.

Music industry responses to socio-technological change

First, we can understand major recording company campaigns to sue file-sharers and digital pirates as part of a bigger story about the ways in which large, incumbent organizations who have been doing well for a long period of time react defensively when they perceive that their way of life and means of income generation are under threat from a changing environment. As a common thread through the larger narrative of the music industries, this is a recurring theme. For example, broadcast radio was perceived as a major threat to the recording industry when it was introduced in the 1930s: if audiences are able to listen to music for free on the radio, why would they buy it? A parallel with the current situation regarding illegal downloads and streaming services is clear, with the metanarrative of an industry under threat being used to lobby for stronger copyright legislation and enforcement.

'Read–write' vs 'read-only' culture

A second example of a music industry metanarrative is the tension between what is often referred to as 'read–write' culture versus 'read-only' culture. The professionalized, broadcast-centric, one-to-many infrastructure of the recorded music business changed people from being active participants (purchasing a score in order to play it on an instrument at home) to passive recipients whose relationship to the music was merely as listeners. It can be argued that this narrative is seeing a long-overdue return to a read–write culture in which digital technology facilitates active engagement with musical content: passive consumers are once again becoming active participants in the music creation process (see Chapter 8). Thinking of consumers in this way places power in the hands of music users rather than music producers and is related to the wider metanarrative of the freedom of information on the internet, and those seeking either the relaxation of copyright laws or the enhancement of fair dealing provisions and protection of the public domain (see Chapter 9).

HISTORICAL ANALYSIS

Historical analysis allows researchers to offer detailed examinations of very specific aspects of the music industries in ways that may not be accessible otherwise. Here, metanarratives are replaced by small, local narratives (Lyotard, 1984) and, if handled well, an historical approach to a particular musical figure, recording studio, record label, promoter, city scene or genre can reveal details and subtleties that explain or express aspects of the music industries that would otherwise be invisible. Examples of these popular music histories abound, and fill not only the pages of academic journals and scholarly books, but also the shelves of popular bookstores in the form of biographies and other works aimed at a general readership.

Popular music history is also increasingly found in the form of radio and television programmes. National Public Radio (NPR) and the Public Broadcasting Service (PBS) in the United States have many popular and acclaimed series that explore the origins and the events that have shaped the business, while the BBC and other broadcasters offer similar coverage in the United Kingdom. Many of these shows are demarcated by musical genre, such as the BBC 'Britannia' series of documentary programmes (including *Jazz Britannia*, *Pop Britannia*, and *Folk Britannia*). There are also programmes that focus on specific artists and record companies or on the production of particular popular music artefacts or events, most notably the *Classic Albums* television series where each episode examines a specific record as an item of historical significance.

It may be argued that the history of popular music industry and culture is, in and of itself, a music industry form. The publication and production of popular music history books and documentaries meets a consumer desire for a closer connection with and understanding of music and musicians. There are, for instance, hundreds if not thousands of books about The Beatles alone, and this not only provides an incredible wealth of material for someone investigating that band and its influence on the course of popular music business, but is in itself a phenomenon worthy of study.

Historiography

The music industries are, at the simplest level, people being industrious with music, and stories about people and their work contribute greatly to the knowledge we have about how the industries operate. Furthermore, through the critical practice of historiography, we are able to study how and why those histories are told in the ways that they are: to examine their discourses, reliability and methods of enquiry, as well as to understand the critical (and political) frameworks and biases that underlie them. What guides the choices of important dates? What information is included or excluded? Which albums and artists are lauded and which ignored? Sarah Thornton (1990: 89) notes that the subject matter of music histories is often rooted in 'sales figures and personality' or in 'aesthetic/political radicalism and ... sustained media attention'. In essence, history is 'written by the victors' and so a great deal of history is ignored. The strategies identified by Thornton may lead to the canonization of music histories into discrete cultural narratives that serve to exclude the cultural experiences of people whose music tastes do not match those of cultural and media critics. Such canons should be examined and critiqued through historiography (for example, see Kurkela and Väkevä, 2009) in order to understand the processes by which they come to form, or to offer alternative voices and stories.

TECHNOLOGICAL DEVELOPMENT

When studying the music industries, it is difficult – perhaps impossible – to overlook the impact and influence of developments in technology. It is possible to chart the progress of the sector in direct relationship to the development and dissemination of different technologies of music composition, production, distribution, promotion and consumption. In fact, it is possible to argue that the emergence and widespread acceptance of different technologies (within the recording industries and in the hands of consumers) have driven change in both the music business and in popular music culture.

It goes without saying that musical instruments – from the violin and the harpsichord to the synthesizer and the electric guitar – are themselves technologies. That is, they are tools created and fashioned by human beings to perform specialist tasks. Different types of musical instrument have allowed for different types of music to be created, different genres of music to be established and new types of musical creation to emerge. Through the development of amplification and electrification, different sounds and effects have been made possible. The cultural impact of these changes is difficult to over-estimate, as Bob Dylan discovered when he switched from the acoustic to the electric guitar only to be confronted with boos and cries of 'Judas!' in the mid-1960s (Shelton, 2003).

Technologies of production

One of the first technologies to revolutionize and create the music industries as we know them today is audio recording. Thomas Edison's 'talking machine' was invented during the final years of the nineteenth century, yet it was in the early parts of the twentieth century – and significantly, after the First World War – that audio recordings of music became a mass-produced phenomenon. The impact upon the dominant form of music business at the time – the printed sheet music industry – was understandably devastating. In fact, at the time of that change, many musicians and members of what was then 'The Music Business' (in the same way that the record companies are considered 'The Music Business' today) resisted the new technology strenuously. The notion of singular idealized performances of popular songs recorded by international artists that could be played over and over again without the involvement of live musicians must have seemed a major threat to the success of the mainstream industry of the time, though of course that industry soon adapted.

For a long time, the vinyl 7" single was the defining medium and format for popular song. As a physical disc of a particular size that revolved at a certain speed – 45 revolutions per minute (or 45 rpm) – the single could only contain songs up to a maximum running time of around four minutes. Consequently, what we know today as the 'perfect 3-minute pop song' has its roots in the physical characteristics of a recorded medium, rather than in some abstract ideal of what music should sound like. Similarly, the widely understood concept of the 'album' – a collection of songs by an artist that represents a single body of work – also has certain characteristics based on the physical attributes of the recorded medium – whether the 12" 33 1/3 rpm Long Play (LP) vinyl record, or the longer compact disc format. In fact, certain genres of music, such as progressive rock (which included longer, more ambitious tracks and the idea of the 'concept album'), grew in part from the artistic and creative exploration of the physical characteristics of the LP. More recently, technologies such as the Apple iPad have allowed musicians to experiment with and expand the potential of the album even further using apps (which are computer programs that run on tablets, smartphones and similar devices) (see Box 1.1).

Box 1.1
Björk's *Biophilia* (2011)

Biophilia (2011) was Björk's seventh studio album release as a solo artist. It was presented as a multimedia experience across a range of technologies including CD, vinyl, digital download, digital book, live performances and the Apple iPad/iPhone. Described as the first proper 'app album' for the iPad, it features a free 'app box' that displays a series of constellations in a three dimensional universe. Each constellation represents one of the album's ten songs and each song is purchasable separately as an app that offers audio-visual experiences (essays, animations and so on) and opportunities for user interaction. For instance, the track 'Crystalline' includes an interactive animated game in which users navigate tunnels and collect crystals, with their gameplay affecting the structure of the music as it plays. The publicity that surrounded the album and its claim to be 'the first' of its kind was helpful for its promotion and marketing campaign, but we might question how many other music artists will follow suit. Few have the financial backing to create an elaborate package of this sort, while many more might prefer to focus on making music than working with interactive artists and app developers.

There are a number of other technologies that have also significantly affected the production and potential of recorded music as a creative form (see Katz, 2010). These include: magnetic tape and multi-track recording, which allowed editing, splicing and overdubbing of musical recordings, electronic effects, effects pedals and samplers, which added new and previously unheard sounds to the palette of musical performance, and the computerization of recording and composition. This latter example allowed for non-destructive editing, 'step programming' and sequencing, and – perhaps most significantly – the opportunity to record professional-sounding works in non-professional situations such as 'bedroom studios' (see Chapter 4).

Technologies of consumption

Consumer technologies have also revolutionized the experience of music. Numerous recorded music formats have been introduced – some more successfully than others – such as quarter-inch reel-to-reel tapes, compact audio-cassettes, 8-track cartridges, mini-disks, digital audio tapes (DATs), compact discs (CDs), DVD-Audio, and USB flash drives (amongst many others). Each of these media forms had specific characteristics that gave them a distinctive and sometimes competitive edge at various times. These include audio fidelity, the length of the recorded media, the ability to rewind and fast-forward tracks or have instant access to them, and the size, shape and content of the packaging and artwork. Such characteristics impacted upon the success or otherwise of each medium, as did marketing, timing and pricing. Yet, when we read about recorded media, it is only usually the successful formats that are mentioned – as if the record industry moved smoothly from records and cassettes to CDs, and now from CDs to MP3s – when in fact the transitions were far more complex, problematic and worthy of study than such a simplified narrative suggests.

MEDIA ECOLOGY

Media ecology examines the far-reaching impact of a changing technological environment, and regards technologies as environmental forces that exert influence over human affairs. At its simplest, it explains the differences between technological ages, and how the activities, industry, communication and ways of thinking that are found in those ages are influenced by technology. Applying this approach to the study of the music industries helps us to understand the changing fortunes of the sector in relation to the rapid and accelerating technological change seen over the past 100 years. These changes can be studied at a paradigmatic level – large-scale developments such as the shift from print culture (sheet music) to electric culture (recorded music and broadcasting) – and at the level of specific technologies, such as the introduction of stereo recording and the development of transistor radios or MP3 players for portable and individual listening.

From the electric to the digital age

Arguably, the music industries are experiencing a paradigmatic change in the early twenty-first century. Just as the music industries were profoundly and irrevocably changed in the shift from the print age to the electric age, so too are we seeing a profound reconfiguration of the music industries as we shift from the electric age to the digital age. Digital technologies have continued to transform every aspect of the music business from composition right through to consumption. Consequently, the predominant (electric) music industries of the late twentieth century appear to be under threat in much the same way as the print music industries were a century ago. And this is where the media ecology approach is so important and timely: because if that is the case, then the shift to digital and online music is not merely a change in format (as was the shift from vinyl records to CDs) but a complete change in the media environment and a radical restructuring of the whole industry. In other words, the sale of recordings, like the sale of sheet music, may well become a proportionately minor aspect of popular music consumption, and industries that fail to adapt run the risk of becoming an increasingly niche proposition.

Technological determinism

It is important to raise one particular warning about the media ecology approach – and that is the ease with which it is possible to fall into a position of technological determinism. Technological determinism is the notion that technology is the driving force of a society's history and culture. That is, the idea that technology is something that happens to culture and business, and that we are powerless to control or choose our reactions to it. And while it may seem that a media ecology approach demands that conclusion, in fact the ecological framework offers a more subtle relationship than mere cause and effect. As with any environmental shift, it is necessary to adapt in order to survive and thrive when the technological environment shifts. However, adaptations are not caused by environmental change, but are developed in response to them. That is to say, we choose our responses and so our uses of technology are socially negotiated.

For instance, when wireless telegraphy was first used for commercial purposes by Marconi, it was intended as point-to-point communication over distance – and in particular, ship-to-shore. When telephones were first introduced into the home, the imagined consumer use was to pick up the receiver at a particular time (and to this day we still call it a receiver, and not a transmitter) and listen to a public performance from the concert hall at the end of the street. In fact, users and entrepreneurs of the media decided to use the telephone for two-way point-to-point communication, and conversely, wireless telegraphy (or radio, as it became known) as a means of disseminating musical performances to geographically dispersed audiences.

So while it is true that a refusal or inability to adapt and change to a transformed media and technological environment is analogous to the dinosaurs' inability to adapt to a changed physical environment, the environment itself doesn't force a single and predictable change: we can select and negotiate our responses to that change. In other words, the technology 'affords' a certain range of possibilities, and we have agency in choosing our responses within that process. For more on media ecology, Marshall McLuhan's seminal work *Understanding Media* (1964) is an ideal place to start.

DIGITAL TECHNOLOGIES

It is fair to say that digital technologies have already transformed or are in the process of transforming the entirety of the music industries, and there are dozens, if not hundreds of ways that digital technologies have affected the music industries: from their impacts on copyright and distribution to those upon composition, production, distribution, promotion and consumption. There is also a rich vein of research that examines how digital technologies influence music business activities, and great scope for future study.

Digital media technologies have been in use since the 1970s, so to speak of them as 'new technologies' or 'new media' can be somewhat misleading. Digital media are different in many ways from physical media, and the differences are of considerable consequence for the future of the music industries. There are a number of different approaches and areas of investigation that can, and should, be given serious critical analysis, though we must continue to be wary of technological determinism in our discussions. Of particular importance is the need to consider those characteristics and aspects of digital media that mark them out as different from analogue and physical media (though it must be remembered that some technologies, such as the CD, are actually a combination of physical format and digital content).

Digital is discrete

The first thing to note about digital media is that while analogue audio recordings capture and reproduce sound as a continuous wave, digital recordings sample sound in discrete audio 'snapshots', where each snapshot is described by digital information in the form of binary digits (1s and 0s). In the case of the CD, the sound is sampled 44,100 times per second. From this very finely granular data, the CD player can convert the captured sound back into waveforms, but even at this very accurate level, this is merely an approximation of the original analogue data.

Digital is perfectly replicable

The second thing to know about digital media is that the relationship between original and copy, as seen in the physical world, does not apply in the same way to the digital world. A physical copy of an artefact is always imperfect in comparison to a physical original, as anyone who has taped from cassette to cassette can tell you. In contrast, a digital copy of a digital 'original' is fundamentally the same as that original, and does not deviate in any observable way from it. Digital media can be infinitely replicated and distributed in a near frictionless manner, and the copied files are indistinguishable from the original to the extent that they might as well be the original. Put another way, the original is simply another copy. They can be described, to draw on Jean Baudrillard (1994), as simulacra: copies for which no original exists. In some cases, such as MP3, file-conversion programs are used to create smaller ('lossy') files by removing some parts of the audio information, but once converted, each MP3 copy is perfectly replicable without further loss of quality.

Copying could, in fact, be said to be the natural state of digital media. When files are moved (uploaded/downloaded) from place to place in the digital realm nothing physically moves, so when you download a song from an online retailer that song never actually leaves the store. Instead, your computer is issued with instructions as to how to make a perfect copy of it. The implications of this for copyright and the music industries in general are profound, and the philosophical, economic and legal ramifications are significant. If there is infinite supply of an item, how can pricing be agreed? If no loss incurred when unauthorized duplication takes place, can there be theft? While the answers to these questions are far more complex than might appear at first glance, there is certainly more than one 'obvious' answer, and these answers have been central to debates within the music industries since the advent of digital media – and certainly since the rise of online transmission and replication of audio files.

Digital transformations: production

One of the most significant impacts of the development and rise of digital technologies over the past 25 years or more is the extent to which the composition and production of music has been made more accessible. Not only has the creation of recorded music become 'democratized' (quotation marks included to signify the deeply problematic nature of that term), practices such as sampling, remixing and the production of music videos have become affordable and achievable for much wider participation. In a way, the de-professionalization of certain areas of music production – due to massive reductions in the cost of entry and the ease with which quality results can be achieved without years of training and the mastery of specific skill sets – has created both a serious problem for the music industries, and a significant opportunity.

Digital transformations: consumption

Digital media have also affected the ways that people consume music. Examples include the rise of portable MP3 players for personal music playback, the development of video games such as *Guitar Hero* and *Rock Band*, and the emergence of streaming 'cloud' music services such as Spotify, Last.fm and Pandora that challenge the traditional (at least for the last century) system of purchasing or owning recordings. Likewise, collecting, organizing and creating knowledge about music has transformed through the use of online fora and community discussion groups centred on specialist interests and niche music. Deleted and out-of-print recordings are shared amongst fans, and recordings of concerts and demos can be centrally stored but accessed globally.

Digital transformations: distribution

The impact of digital technology upon the distribution of music – through 'legitimate' means as well as via unauthorized, peer-to-peer file-sharing sites – is worthy of ongoing investigation, as is digital's role in the decline of the independent and chain retail music store. The long-tail effect observed by Chris Anderson (2006) has important ramifications for the economics of music retail in the online environment, as it challenges the notion of the 'hit' as the central mechanism for revenue generation, or as the only framework for business success at a mainstream corporate level (see Chapter 5). Yet the impact of digital technologies goes deeper than simply the sale of recordings to consumers. For instance, major record labels have made considerable inroads into business-to-business (B2B) strategies and markets with respect to mobile handset manufacturers, soft drink companies, and other corporate entities wishing to supply music as a value added feature to attract their own prospective customers.

Digital transformations: promotion

Promotion of music is also affected by digital technologies. Rather than relying on opinion leaders and taste-makers authorized by the mainstream press and electronic media, digital technology affords the potential for publishing and distribution of opinion through social media sites and blogs. Independent companies and so-called 'unsigned' artists have taken to giving their recordings away as a method of removing barriers and developing a fan base. Author Kevin Kelly wrote on his blog that the independent artist could make a decent and sustainable living from a base of just '1,000 true fans' (2008). He argued that artists should focus on increasing the annual spend of their most enthusiastic fans, rather than attempting to increase the number of individual sales to an anonymous and transient audience.

ISSUES

As we have seen throughout this chapter, the study of the music industries can take on many and varied forms and may emerge from a range of critical positions. As a result, it lends itself to cross-disciplinary approaches. Sociologists, business scholars, musicologists, psychologists, engineers, media academics and scholars from many other disciplines besides all have good cause to study the music industries as a natural part of their field. But of course, this raises some issues for the music industries scholar (from whatever field they may come).

The problem of specialism

For a start, each specialism has its own language. Musicologists freely use terms that are often obscure to sociologists, and vice versa. This can have the effect of fragmenting the field, and making some works that would be of interest and of benefit to some scholars inaccessible because they are unfamiliar with the terminology that has been developed and used by their neighbouring field over a period of decades. At academic conferences, such as those of IASPM, it is possible to attend presentations that explore the technological, social, textual, historical, cultural, or business aspects of music, based on research and studies carried out by scholars from as many different fields. The issue of communicating across disciplinary language barriers can be problematic in such contexts, yet interdisciplinary study and new, integrated and 'joined-up' avenues of research can emerge that offer cross-pollination and collaboration, and new insights into the music industries.

The problem of fandom

One tendency to be cautious of – and it is a trap that many music industries students immediately fall into when commencing their studies – is the temptation to focus one's scholarly attention on some variation of the topic: 'Why my favourite band is so great.' There is, of course, a difference between research and advocacy, and between scholarly activity and fandom, though that is not to say that one should not shine an academic light on something you are enthusiastic about. In fact, for many scholars, the relationship between academic and fan, or Aca-Fan as scholar, blogger and author Henry Jenkins describes himself (2006) – can be very close (see also Jenson, 1992). Having the advantage of a wealth and depth of knowledge about a subject can be a very good starting point, and involvement in a scene or aspect of the business can be a very useful entry point into the study of that scene or organization. Nevertheless, it is important to separate the enthusiasm of a fan who wishes to convert prospective readers to the wonders of their favourite type of music or artist, and scholarly research that analyses and sheds light on the meanings and implications of that object of study.

CONCLUSION

This chapter has provided a number of theoretical frameworks through which students of the music industries can approach the analysis of their chosen subject. We have demonstrated that there are multiple ways of examining and interpreting meanings within the field. In addition, the purpose of this chapter has been to highlight the complex and discursive nature of the music industries and to show that describing 'The Music Industry' as if it is a simple, coherent or indeed explainable object of analysis with commonly held and universally shared characteristics misunderstands or over-essentializes the field. The music industries exist within a wide range of geographic, temporal, legislative, technological, economic, media and cultural contexts that influence how they operate, and the cultural meanings that they contribute. Finally, the chapter has suggested that an approach which brings together a range of different academic disciplines has the potential to reveal more nuanced and integrated insights about the different sectors of, and issues within, the broad-based music industries.

FURTHER READING

David Hesmondhalgh's *The Cultural Industries* (2007) and Tim Wall's *Studying Popular Music Culture* (2003) are each highly recommended for thinking further about how industries work with cultural artefacts such as music. Keith Negus' *Popular Music in Theory* (1996) is similarly recommended for its useful guidance on reading popular music histories critically, while Tim Wall and Paul Long's 'Jazz Britannia: mediating the story of British jazz's past on television' (2009) offers a useful example of how music history is presented and interpreted through television. Discussions about the impact on the music industries of digital technologies and the internet may be found in Andrew Leyshon's 'Time-space (and digital) compression: software formats, musical networks, and the reorganisation of the music industry' (2001), Chris Anderson's *The Long Tail* (2006) and Patrik Wikström's *The Music Industry* (2009).

2

THE RECORDED MUSIC INDUSTRY

This chapter explores the history of the recorded music industry and shows how it has been subject to considerable highs and lows since its emergence at the end of the nineteenth century. It details the overall structure of the sector before examining the various strategies that record companies employ to deal with the risks and uncertainties of changing popular tastes. Critical to our discussions is the past and continuing impact of technological development upon the functions, business practices and fortunes of the industry.

KEY FINDINGS

- Technological change has had, and continues to have, profound impacts on the development and fortunes of the recorded music industries.
- The recorded music industries are dominated by a small number of global record companies, but there is a thriving independent sector characterized as local, innovative and authentic.
- A number of strategies have been adopted for dealing with the uncertainty of public tastes.
- Media rights and artist–fan interaction are of great importance to the future success of the recorded music industries.

THE STRUCTURE AND SIZE OF THE RECORDING INDUSTRY

Historically, the vast majority (70 to 80 per cent or more) of recorded music released in any given year has been produced and released by a relatively small number of transnational companies, collectively referred to as 'majors', that each operate in over 70 countries. This disproportionate control of the market is known as oligopoly and in the late 2000s comprised the 'big four' of Universal Music Group, Sony Music Entertainment, Warner Music Group and EMI Music. The constitution, ownership and names of these 'major' companies shift continuously over time. For instance, agreements were made in late 2011 to sell both EMI Music and EMI Music Publishing (see Box 2.1).

Box 2.1
The major transnational recording companies

Universal Music Group

In the late 2000s, the largest share of the recorded music market was regularly attributed to Universal Music Group, which incorporates well-known record labels such as Verve, Decca, A&M, Island and Motown. Headquartered in the USA, Universal is a division of the French media conglomerate Vivendi SA. Vivendi also owns or has stakes in pay-TV and cinema (including the Canal+ Group and NBC Universal), computer games developers (Activision|Blizzard), mobile phone/internet service providers, and concert ticketing companies. In 2011 Universal agreed to purchase EMI Music.

Sony Music Entertainment

Sony Music Entertainment is a wholly owned subsidiary of the Sony Corporation of America, which is itself a subsidiary of the Sony Corporation (a Japanese media and electronics conglomerate). Its record company operations encompass well-known labels such as RCA, Columbia, Epic and Arista. Parent company Sony Corporation is active in a wide variety of fields, including consumer and professional electronics manufacturing, computer games/entertainment, motion picture/television production and mobile phone services. In 2011, Sony agreed to purchase EMI Music Publishing.

Warner Music Group

Warner Music Group encompasses well-known record labels such as Atlantic, East West, Roadrunner and Warner Bros. It owns the music publisher Warner/Chappell Music and operates three major music distribution companies. It has also expanded into ancillary services such as artist management, live music, merchandising, sponsorships and brand endorsements. It has done this through organic growth within the group, and by entering into joint ventures such as Brand Asset Management (in association with Violator Management). In 2011, WMG was sold to Access Industries for an estimated US$3.3 billion. Access Industries also invests in the chemicals industry, emerging technologies and media/telecommunications companies.

EMI Music

EMI Music dominated the recorded music market in Britain and Europe prior to the Second World War (Burnett, 1996: 53) and counts Blue Note, Capitol, Parlophone and Virgin amongst its labels. The financial fortunes of EMI have been in decline since the early 2000s, which led it to being purchased by the private equity firm Terra Firma in 2007 for £2.4 billion (financed by Citigroup). Terra Firma restructured EMI into three business units: a New Music division to sign new talent from around the world; a Catalogue division to maximize revenues from its extensive vaults of recorded music; and a Music Services division to expand the company's activities into merchandising, licensing, branding and sponsorship. Despite the changes, EMI continued to post losses. Citigroup Inc. responded by offering the company for sale in 2011.

Market shares

In 2010 the 'majors' shared 76.8 per cent of the global market in physical and digital recorded music sales, with Universal having the greatest market share, followed by Sony Music, Warner and EMI (see Figure 2.1). This general pattern has been seen throughout the 2000s, with Sony Music and Universal vying for the top spot, followed at some distance by Warner and EMI. The remainder of the recorded music market consists of many thousands of smaller record companies referred to as 'independents', 'indies' or 'minors'.

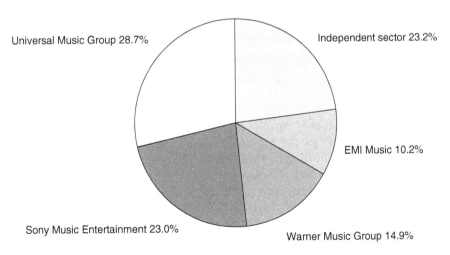

Figure 2.1 Global recorded music industry market shares 2010 (Data source: Informa Telecoms and Media, 2011)

It is important to be critical of such statistics since market shares tend to be calculated using sales data that favour the majors. First, the statistics are based on retail sales data that excludes many direct-to-consumer (D2C) sales by independent labels and artists (whether as digital downloads or mail-order), as well as direct sales in the form of concert merchandise. Second, the data is compiled on the basis of ownership and classification of a record's distributor. If the distribution company is owned by a major recording company, all sales made through that company are recorded as major label sales, even though it may also be distributing the products of numerous independent companies. Distribution will be discussed in further detail in Chapter 5.

The recording industry and the music industry

The recorded music industry is central to the music industries and is often discussed as if it stands for the music industries as a whole (see Williamson and Cloonan, 2007). Changes in record company strategy compound this, since 'multiple rights' recording agreements (also known as 360-degree deals) greatly extend the business roles and revenue streams that record companies are concerned with. These will be discussed further below, but to begin this chapter it is useful to examine the recording industry in terms of its broad history and business structure. This will help us to understand the nature of the companies involved, and the technological, social and economic changes that have produced a century of massive financial successes and near disasters. The chapter will then look at the key characteristics and ideas that define the recording industry, and examine strategies that have been adopted for dealing with uncertain market demand.

A BRIEF HISTORY OF THE RECORDED MUSIC INDUSTRY

The recorded music industry emerged at the end of the nineteenth century when the phonograph and gramophone industries led by Edison, Victor and Columbia began to displace the printed sheet music industry as the central method for disseminating popular music (Millard, 1996; Garofalo, 1999). The first decade of the twentieth century saw rapid improvements in the technologies of recording, duplication and reproduction as shellac-based 78 rpm (revolutions per minute) discs were introduced and affordable domestic record players produced. By 1909, the wholesale value of recorded music in the US market (the key market at the time) was estimated at nearly US$12 million (Sanjek, 1988: 23). Over the following decade, the recording industry expanded rapidly with gross revenues in the United States reaching US$106 million by 1921. This boom in sales allowed new recording companies to emerge, catering to niche markets such as blues and country (Garofalo, 1999).

The boom did not last: the introduction of commercial radio broadcasting and talking pictures, together with global economic recession in the 1930s, led to a catastrophic fall in record company revenues – to just US$6 million in 1933 (Garofalo, 1999). This leads Simon Frith to suggest that 'For anyone writing the history of the record industry in 1932, there would have been very little doubt that the phonograph was a novelty machine that had come and gone' (1992: 55). One consequence of the slump was that smaller record companies closed, leaving the marketplace to a handful of large companies (the 'majors') that became more wide-ranging in their business and music interests (1992: 56). At the same time, broadcast radio became the predominant medium for music and a cross-media star system developed, typified by the singer Bing Crosby, which was dependent on marketing tie-ins between the radio, film and recording industries (1992: 56–7).

The rise of rock 'n' roll

A shellac shortage during the Second World War led to two main developments. First, the majors cut their costs by pulling out of African American music. This market was soon met by new independent companies such as Atlantic Records and Chess Records, which discovered and recorded artists including Ray Charles and Chuck Berry. Second, CBS and RCA developed new consumer formats based on vinyl rather than shellac. These formats became the standard products of the recorded music industry until the 1980s and were the 33 1/3 rpm LP (Long Play) record, and the smaller 45 rpm 'single' respectively (Garofalo, 1999).

Further technological, social and musical changes wrought major changes to the structure of the music business in the 1950s. For instance, transistor technology led to the creation of portable and in-car radio, television became a mass media phenomenon, and post-war economic and social change led to the emergence of a new cash- and time-rich youth-centred market for music: the 'teenager'. The net result of these changes was the rise of a new genre, rock 'n' roll, which expanded its market share from 15.7 per cent of sales in 1954 to 42.7 per cent in 1959 (Garofalo, 1999). Typified by Elvis Presley, the genre mixed elements of soul music and country music and was the source of a moral panic in mainstream America that accused the music of corrupting the nation's youth.

The majors did not initially support rock 'n' roll (seeing it as a temporary fad), which left the independent sector to reap the benefits: record company revenues rose from US$213 million in 1954 to US$603 million in 1959, and by 1959 66.3 per cent of the popular music market was shared between numerous independent record companies (Peterson and Berger, 1990; Garofalo, 1999). The majors later responded by buying the recording contracts of successful independent rock 'n' roll stars, including Dion, Duane Eddy and Paul Anka, and then signed new talent of their own in the early 1960s, such as The Beach Boys and Bob Dylan (Peterson and Berger, 1990: 151). The phenomenal success of The Beatles in the mid-1960s then demonstrated that 'teenage' music could appeal to a much broader audience, and led the US majors to establish offices in London as they sought the 'next big thing' in British music (Frith, 1992: 63–4).

The emergence of rock and the dominance of the album

By the end of the 1960s, the American recorded music industry was achieving annual sales figures of over US$1 billion. Multi-track recording, electronic instruments and stereo reproduction – alongside musical and socio-political changes amongst musicians and audiences – created a period of excitement and diversity in music that led annual sales to double by 1973 and to double again by 1978 (Frith, 1992: 64). The LP became the predominant artefact and revenue stream of both major and independent recording companies with live performance regarded as a promotional tool to drive album sales, rather than an income stream in itself (1992: 64). The industry was supported by the emergence of FM radio, a burgeoning popular music press, and the expansion of higher education – providing a new market for live and recorded music, as well as a source of new artists. Simon Frith suggests that the success of the LP format, and of rock music in particular, fostered other changes within major recording companies. They became more professional in their management style and 'began to be dominated by lawyers and accountants' (1992: 66). In the process they became more conservative in their business strategies and musical choices and market concentration increased as they bought up successful independents (Frith, 1992; Garofalo, 1999).

In Britain, the punk movement of the mid-late 1970s is cited as shaking up or disrupting the status quo of the majors, due to do-it-yourself strategies, anticorporate ideologies, and the growth of an independent sector that succeeded in creating alternative distribution systems. Yet punk musicians and labels offered little commercial threat to the majors, and the more successful punk artists soon signed recording deals with the majors to further their careers (Frith, 1992: 66).

Contraction and recovery in the 1980s

A more serious threat to the recording industry developed at the end of the 1970s (see Frith, 1992: 67). First, demographic shifts in America and Western Europe meant that there were fewer teenagers year on year, hence the primary market for popular music was shrinking. Allied to this was massive growth in youth unemployment caused by worldwide economic recession, and resulting in lower disposable incomes. Second, a range of competitive technology-based leisure activities emerged, including computer games consoles, domestic video recorders/players, and audio home taping.

Global sales fell from 'an all-time high of US$11.4 billion in 1980 ... to US$9.4 billion in 1983' (Garofalo, 1999). The majors responded by dismissing personnel, limiting the overall number of new album releases, and reducing the number of artists signed (Garofalo, 1999; Tschmuck, 2006). They also embarked on a major publicity campaign, 'Home taping is killing music', arguing that copyright piracy was responsible for the industry's problems: a claim that echoes contemporary arguments about the impact of unauthorized file-sharing online.

In the wake of Michael Jackson's enormous sales success with the album *Thriller* (1983), a new strategy was adopted that focused attention on superstar artists and the promotional possibilities of the music video. As Reebee Garofalo (1999) argues: 'If a single artist can move 40 million units, they reasoned, why shoulder the extra administrative, production, and marketing costs of 80 artists moving half a million units each?' Artists such as Prince, Madonna and Bruce Springsteen saw huge marketing support for their albums, which turned into massive sales and the recovery of the music market in the mid-1980s. The majors started to reinterpret their role as 'exploiters of rights' rather than 'producers of records', with music videos linked to movie soundtracks and advertising campaigns in order to exploit their copyrights and gain cross-marketing support (Garofalo, 1999). In essence, music video helped to create a new version of the cross-media star system seen in the 1940s and discussed earlier. Yet, it was the introduction of another new technology that was to really turn the fortunes of the recording industry around: the compact disc.

The compact disc and changing fortunes in the 1990s

The compact disc (CD) was developed by two electronics manufacturers, Sony and Philips, which each owned major recording company subsidiaries. The CD was promoted for its durability, sound quality and ease of use, and priced significantly higher than vinyl – even though the cost of manufacture was about the same (Garofalo, 1999). As vinyl slowly declined in popularity, revenues increased due to simple substitution. However, it was the repackaging of back catalogue recordings that provided a significant boost to record company income in the late 1980s and throughout the 1990s. Consumers were persuaded to purchase back catalogue albums on CD that they already owned on vinyl. Often these recordings were transferred directly from the LP master with little additional work on improving sound quality for the new medium. Since then, some albums have been digitally remastered once, twice or even more times in order to take advantage of improving technologies (including surround sound mixes of albums originally produced in stereo), or with added bonus tracks or additional discs containing live concerts recordings, interviews and other material. Such remastered, re-packaged and 'collectors' edition' CDs are part of marketing and business strategies aimed at producing profit from albums that require considerably less investment than the development of new product.

The CD placed the recording industry on a path of steady growth, with the IFPI reporting that global sales had risen to US$30 billion by 1993 (Garofalo, 1999). This success led to broad changes in record company ownership. For instance, Sony Corporation paid US$2 billion for CBS Records in 1988, while

Matsushita (another large Japanese electronics manufacturer) paid US$6.6 billion for MCA in 1989. Superstar artists could also command highly lucrative recording agreements when re-negotiating contract terms or moving between labels. Prime examples include The Rolling Stones, who were signed to Virgin Records for US$40 million, and Mötley Crüe, who stayed at Elektra Records for a US$25 million deal (Garofalo, 1999).

By the mid-1990s the market had begun to stagnate again as back catalogue CDs saturated the market (Tschmuck, 2006: 160) and consumers turned to hip hop, grunge, Britpop and electronic dance music (often championed by independent record labels). The late 1990s saw a shift in emphasis by the majors, who focused on 'short-run profits from "hit singles" rather than building careers through album sales' in a strategy linked to cross-media marketing and the promotion of 'manufactured' artists-as-brands (Connell and Gibson, 2003: 254). Examples include the Spice Girls, *NSYNC and Christina Aguilera, former television stars such as Kylie Minogue and Natalie Imbruglia, and in the 2000s numerous contestants from reality-based television formats such as *Pop Idol*, *American Idol* and *X Factor*.

Contraction of the market in the 2000s

IFPI figures clearly show a reduction in recorded music revenues since the turn of the millennium. For example, in 2000, the global retail value of the industry was estimated as US$36.9 billion, declining to US$30 billion by 2007 (IFPI, 2001 & 2008). A variety of reasons may be proposed for this post-millennial downturn in revenue. These include global economic recession and the introduction of new leisure technologies that compete for consumer spending and time: DVD/home cinema, mobile phones, browsing the internet, and playing computer games. The decade also saw a rise in physical music piracy, such as pirate and counterfeit CDs produced in Eastern Europe, South America and China, and in online music piracy, most notably the swapping of MP3 files through the internet (see Chapter 9).

The revenue figures produced by the IFPI may be somewhat misleading. The post-millennial period also saw a surge in music production and sale through a variety of online routes that lie beyond the purview of the IFPI, and there are considerably more albums released globally each year than at any point in the history of the recorded music industry. These albums cater to a wide set of niche markets, and this fragmentation may partly explain why the majors, which have historically relied on mass-market sales to produce their highest revenues, may be struggling. It is also why television and film tie-ins, as well as magazines devoted to 'celebrity' culture, are so important to the mainstream popular music industries: they help to create mass-market interest and sales.

THE MAJORS: BUSINESS STRUCTURES AND CHARACTERISTICS

Major record companies dominate the market, and while there are many ways for artists to reach their audiences without needing a major record company, many seek a major label deal because they believe it will help them achieve or extend their earning power and marketing reach. The majors operate on a global scale, yet we must be careful not to think of them as monolithic organizations. They are composed of various divisions, departments and wholly or partly owned subsidiaries and record labels that often act in semi-autonomous fashion. Major corporations will, for instance, encompass music recording, publishing and distribution arms, plus a variety of non-music divisions (merchandising, television, telecommunications and so on) as noted earlier in Box 2.1. Within the recording arm, each major owns or part-owns a wide range of record labels. Tim Wall refers to these as 'brands' (2003: 85) since they have a strong sense of identity and release records under a specific name and logo. The structure of these labels varies, but each fulfils the basic tasks of finding new artists, producing and distributing recordings, and promoting those recordings to the public. Production, distribution and promotion are discussed in detail in later chapters of this book, but it is worth reflecting on the A&R role here, prior to examining the characteristics that distinguish the majors from the independent sector: horizontal, vertical and lateral integration, and global distribution.

Artist and Repertoire (A&R)

The term 'Artist and Repertoire' (A&R) owes its existence to the Tin Pan Alley tradition of the first half of the twentieth century, when it was common practice for songwriting and performing to be separate roles. At that time, the A&R department was responsible for finding appropriate singers for songs and appropriate songwriters for popular singers. Today, the A&R function is much broader than this, and while many people still think of it as primarily about finding and signing new talent, A&R personnel actually spend more of their time developing artists who have already been signed, including 'aspects of rehearsals, recording, marketing, promotion and video production' (Negus, 1992: 38). Instead, the role of 'talent spotter' is more often devolved to talent scouts who are younger staff employed because of their extensive networks of contacts and in-depth knowledge of musical trends and scenes. They keep abreast of these by reading blogs, trade magazines and social media, and by attending gigs and club nights, listening to demos, talking to musicians and promoters, and browsing video sharing sites and so on. They often have relatively little responsibility within the company, and may work for little or no pay since the role is regarded as a 'foot in the door' to a future career. For the record companies, these personnel are useful not only in finding potential new artists, but also in convincing those artists that the company will be supportive of their particular musical direction and interests.

Falling revenues since the turn of the millennium have led many companies to change their A&R strategies and cut back on the numbers of new artists signed each year. Rather than seeking, nurturing and developing new talent, it is more cost-effective to seek out artists who are already 'developed': in other words, those with a strong image, distinctive sound, good songs and a growing fan base. In consequence, traditional A&R roles within the majors have reduced in number, while production companies, management companies and smaller independents have increasingly taken on the function (discussed further below). An alternative form of A&R is the television talent show where the public decides who they will support, and where a number of acts will gain levels of exposure that would otherwise have been difficult to achieve. The logic of cross-media promotion underpins the success of shows such as *American Idol* and *X Factor*. The public sees the personal and musical development of contestants and learns about their lives and interactions with others on the show – thus building a degree of interest, trust and fandom even before the acts have started their recording careers. The winner gains a recording agreement and is almost guaranteed a hit single (and often album) following the climax of the show, even if that fame and success is short-lived. Some runners-up have also found deals and opportunities on the basis of their participation in the shows.

Horizontal integration

The major recording companies are horizontally integrated, which is to say that they have expanded their businesses by merging with or acquiring other record companies (Negus, 1999: 45). This is an efficient method of increasing market share, since it simultaneously reduces competition in the marketplace. It also explains why, when examining the corporate structure of the majors, we find numerous company names attached to individual divisions, subsidiaries and labels. In many cases the names derive from former independent companies that sold all or part of their businesses to the major, and their strength lies in their strong cultural and musical associations. Examples include Motown (soul), Island (rock and reggae) and Def Jam (hip hop), each of which is wholly owned by Universal Music Group. The complex web of divisions, companies and labels seen in the majors is complicated further by frequent structural re-organizations and by the sale of labels between the majors (Negus, 1999: 36). Irrespective of this, each element of the organizational structure is, ultimately, under the control of a 'parent corporation' that 'owns all or most of the shares' in each of its record companies/labels and 'controls the major strategic direction' of them (1999: 36).

Vertical and lateral integration

The major recording companies are also vertically and laterally integrated. Vertical integration means that they own (in full or in part) a range of firms that specialize in other areas of the music industries. Examples include recording studios, pressing plants, and distribution companies. Lateral integration means that they own, or ally themselves with, companies in non-music fields like media, marketing and merchandising. This integrated business model allows the majors to retain control over as many aspects of the production chain (from recording to sales) as possible, leading to reduced costs, increased profits and the assurance that their products can be made available at the right place at the right time and with the right promotion. Advertising, marketing, promotions and personal appearances through linked media companies cannot ensure an artist's success, but they can give an artist valuable exposure to a mass-market audience.

Global distribution

Global distribution is one of the defining characteristics of the major recording companies. Unlike the independent sector, each major owns at least one music distribution company and is able to directly service mass-market retailers and consumers of physical products worldwide (see Chapter 5). As the major-owned distribution companies also deal with the products of the independent sector, the majors have historically been able to exert control over the independent sector's access to the marketplace. The internet has revolutionized this situation, with independent labels and artists now selling both digital and physical copies of albums direct to consumers rather than through intermediary companies. Yet inequalities remain, since the majors are able to run international marketing campaigns to raise product awareness in other countries and across a range of often part- or wholly owned media. The majors also own or control subsidiary companies in numerous countries enabling them to distribute and promote artists and albums worldwide, cater to local markets, and find new talent that might be brought to the world stage. In contrast, the independents have historically focused on their home countries for the bulk of their sales, while signing licensing deals with other record companies to access foreign markets (see Chapter 10).

THE INDEPENDENT SECTOR: DEFINITIONS AND TYPES

The term 'independent' (or 'indie') refers to companies that sign artists and release music independently of the financial and business structures of the majors (including promotion, pressing, and finance). To be truly independent of the majors, a company must use independent distribution networks (ones not owned by a major corporation). An example in the UK is the Beggars Group, which distributes its own labels (Beggars Banquet, 4AD and XL) as well as many others, including the US label Matador Records.

The reality for many independent companies is often quite different. The Association of Independent Music (AIM UK) and the American Association of Independent Music (A2IM) offer a less strict definition. For these organizations, an independent record company is one where 50 per cent or more of the business is owned independently of a major, even where that major has a 49.9 per cent share of the company or the independent is distributed by a major-owned distribution company. For instance, Razor & Tie (whose signings include Joan Baez, Foreigner,

Vanessa Carlton and Richard Ashcroft) is distributed by Sony, while Mute Records is distributed by EMI (see Box 2.2). To complicate matters further, the late 1980s saw the development of pseudo- (or crypto-) independents. These are labels created and wholly owned by majors yet distributed by independent distribution companies (Negus, 1996: 16). Pseudo-independents allow major-label releases to appear on the independent album and singles charts (Fonarow, 2001: 30), which is a significant promotional route for some musical niches, and one that lends an air of authenticity and credibility to an act (Negus, 1996: 16).

Box 2.2
Mute Records

Mute Records was founded by Daniel Miller in 1978 when he released a single as The Normal. By 1980, Mute was signing experimental industrial and electronic music acts such as DAF and Fad Gadget, before finding chart success with electronic pop pioneers Depeche Mode, Yazoo and Erasure. The success of these latter bands allowed Miller to continue supporting experimental and electronic music acts, such as Einstürzende Neubauten and Nitzer Ebb, and the label's albums and singles were licensed to numerous companies across Europe and North America. In the 1990s, Mute signed Moby, whose album *Play* (1998) sold over eight million copies. The success of Moby led, in part, to Miller's decision to sell Mute to EMI in 2002 in a deal worth around £42 million: a deal that allowed Miller to retain creative control of the label, and Mute to continue distribution through independent channels, whilst benefiting from the finance and support structures of the major. In 2010, Mute became independent again, though EMI retained a minority stake in the company, ownership of the brand name, and the recording agreements of several former Mute artists including Depeche Mode, Goldfrapp and Kraftwerk. Mute also has a deal with EMI Label Services for distribution, merchandising and licensing in the UK and North America (Talbot, 2002; Paine, 2010).

For the independent sector, an alternative to seeking funding and support from a major label is to attract the private equity/venture capitalist sector – financial companies that specialize in high risk investments. Relatively few deals have been completed in this fashion, though an early example is Ministry of Sound, which sold a minority shareholding to the private equity firm 3i in 2001. In 2011, Cooking Vinyl formed a partnership with the venture capitalist company Icebreaker Management to fund a number of projects, including an album by Marilyn Manson. The label had previously worked with another venture capitalist firm, Ingenious, on an album project for The Prodigy in 2007. Nevertheless, the bulk of the independent sector operates without such external funding and with artists that do not have a mainstream profile or high sales figures. A variety of business models have been adopted and are discussed below, prior to examining some of the stereotypes that are so often attributed to the sector.

Production companies

Production companies may be operated by managers, record producers, studio owners, artists, fans, and others, and can be regarded as 'nursery' or 'feeder' companies. Their aim is to locate, develop and (sometimes) record artists before attempting to garner the interest of an independent or major record label (Harrison, 2008). Recording budgets and advances are generally rather small, and typically used to produce a demo EP that will be promoted to larger record companies and/or live music promoters. In some cases, these EPs (or even full albums) may be released and sold independently. The production company agreement is often a simple 50/50 split of net profits (once all costs are recouped), rather than one based on royalties. For a production company to succeed it must buy low (by signing relatively cheap deals with unknown artists) then sell high to a larger record company by negotiating a licensing agreement for its recordings or by selling the recording contract outright.

Pressing and Distribution (P&D) deals

A pressing and distribution (P&D) deal occurs when an independent record label pays another record company to manufacture and distribute its records, but retains control over its own production, marketing and accounting. P&D deals are very common in the industry, and may even include some marketing services, but there are downsides. The label loses control over how its products are distributed, such as the choice of physical and online stores that will stock it, and the level of effort that is expended by the distributor in selling the product to those stores. The independent also has to share the sales revenue with the distributor and is reliant on the distributor posting profits in a timely and equitable fashion.

Licensing agreements

Rather than taking a P&D deal, a production company may grant a licensee (a larger record company) the exclusive right, for a specified period, to do certain things with a recording, such as issue it to the public (Harrison, 2008: 57). When the licence expires, the recording reverts back to the copyright owner, who can then license the recording to another company or, if the original deal was successful, renegotiate a higher royalty to extend the licence period. Successful artists who can afford to record their own master sound recordings have increasingly established production companies in order to sign such deals as they offer the prospect of far higher returns and artistic control than would be available under most traditional royalty-based recording agreements (see Chapter 10). Because the licensee record company did not fund the recording costs, it will have a lower risk profile and may be willing to grant higher royalty rates to artists. On the other hand, the company gains control over promotion, marketing and distribution and will reap the benefits of any sales success.

Micro-independent record labels

Micro-independent labels (see Strachan, 2007) are small-scale businesses run from home by musicians and/or music enthusiasts. They are often linked into national or international networks of labels, fanzines and distributors that exist outside of the mainstream music industries. For many within these 'underground' or 'do-it-yourself' (DIY) networks, separation from the mainstream industries is a way to ensure that artists can make the music they wish to make without the commercial pressures so often imposed by larger companies. Micro-independent labels are generally self-funded or supported by donations/loans from friends and family. By maintaining financial as well as artistic control, artists are able to retain their copyrights and any profits made, while fanzine networks and the internet present them with potentially significant marketing opportunities for mail-order sales and/or MP3 downloads.

Internet-only record labels

There are now many thousands of internet-only labels around the world that offer aspiring artists the opportunity to release and distribute their music online. Some of these internet-only labels are free for artists. Others may ask for set-up costs or commission fees, or attempt to sell additional services such as website hosting for further fees. Advances are rarely paid to fund the creation of new recordings, and the artist is often free to sign distribution deals with other online labels. Some labels will make recordings available through their own online portals, while others distribute through digital aggregators to stores such as iTunes and eMusic (see Chapter 5). Net profit share or commission agreements are more common than royalty agreements for these labels as their overheads are much lower than for companies working with physical product (see Chapter 10).

Netlabels

These must be distinguished from internet-only record labels in that they usually make recordings available to download for free. Some artists may also include a 'donate' button to allow fans to voluntarily 'give back' to the artist or label through money transfer services such as PayPal. These netlabels (for example, those hosted at archive.org or freemusicarchive.org) are often supportive of alternative copyright regimes such as Creative Commons (see Chapter 9).

THE IDEOLOGY OF INDEPENDENCE

A number of stereotypes may be found in discussions of the independent sector. Together these form an ideology of independence that is shared by those working in the sector, as well as by many consumers and journalists. Some of the key elements of this ideology are outlined below (see also Wall, 2003).

Fostering new talent

For many authors, the independent sector has played a disproportionate role in developing new talent, as well as in fostering new musical genres and scenes. Steve Chapple and Reebee Garofalo (1977), Dave Laing (1985), Charlie Gillett (1988), David Hesmondhalgh (1998) and Michael Azerrad (2001) have all written about the achievements of independents in promoting rock 'n' roll, punk rock, modern jazz, British post-punk and US indie-rock (see also Ogg, 2009). These authors suggest that the independents have a different business approach and ideology to the majors, and that this difference affects their business practices. Indies are often characterized as giving complete autonomy to their artists, who are then free to develop their own creativity rather than be pressurized into producing overtly chart-friendly music (Fonarow, 2001: 35). Indeed, commercial motivations are often denied by the owners and personnel working for independent companies who may see themselves as supporting the creation of innovative art, rather than of commercial product.

Diversity and homogeneity

Working in the early 1970s, Richard A. Peterson and David G. Berger (1990) argued that the recording industry between 1948 and 1973 was marked by alternating periods of corporate concentration and deconcentration that correlated with periods of homogeneity and diversity in music. Their statistics suggest that when a small number of majors dominated music sales, the diversity of music in the singles charts was reduced (in terms of fewer genres and little creative or technical innovation). In contrast, diversity (new artists and genres) was greater when the independents had a greater market share. They explained this by examining the business strategies of the majors and independents alongside the changing tastes of the public. In essence, the majors were considered to be profit-orientated and musically conservative: once a winning formula was found, they would continue to reproduce that formula rather than innovate, leading to homogeneity of product (1990: 145). In contrast, the independents were regarded as more diverse in their musical output, and more willing to take risks on creative and innovative artists. As a result, they could accommodate the 'unsated demand' that emerged amongst a public increasingly frustrated with the homogenized product sold by the majors (1990: 147). Peterson and Berger used this line of thinking to account for the sudden success of rock 'n' roll in the mid-1950s, though as noted earlier, there were other contributory factors.

Subsequent researchers have updated and critiqued the work of Peterson and Berger. For instance, Paul D. Lopes (1992) compared the singles and album charts of the late 1980s to those of the early 1970s and found that market concentration did not correlate with increasing homogeneity. His findings suggested a change in corporate strategy whereby the majors bought or entered into financial arrangements with independent companies and artists rather than allowing them to establish a significant market share (see also Ross, 2005). While this breaks Peterson and Berger's cycle of market concentration and deconcentration, it also reinforces the belief that independent labels (whether truly independent or part-owned/financed by majors) find and foster new talent.

'Closer to the street'

Independent record companies are often embedded within small, local music scenes. As they are 'close to the street', it is contended that they are better able to recognize emerging trends in public tastes (Lee, 1995: 13), and more willing to take risks on promoting new styles and artists. Where they have successfully done so, they may become iconic symbols of the particular locations and bands that they represented and promoted. For instance, in the US, Sub Pop is synonymous with early 1990s Seattle grunge, having released early albums by Tad, Mudhoney, Soundgarden, and Nirvana – bands that were all active in the local live music scene. Similarly, in the UK, Factory Records is synonymous with the city of Manchester and the late 1970s post-punk music of Joy Division, New Order and Durutti Column, as well as the acid house/rock cross-over of 1980s 'Madchester' bands such as the Happy Mondays.

The internet has also allowed non-local 'virtual scenes' to emerge around niche musical genres. Here, like-minded musicians and fans meet through online fora and may go on to create online record companies and specialist mail-order and download stores that cater to their particular musical niche. This is a particularly common practice for musicians who make electronic music, due to the relatively low costs of creating and mastering high-quality sound recordings in home recording studios.

Unconventional practices and the do-it-yourself ideology

In the late 1970s and early 1980s British punk and post-punk artists and companies absorbed the ideology of independence into their do-it-yourself aesthetic. They argued for the separation of music-making, music production, and music distribution and sale from the financial and corporate apparatus of the major record companies. The more politically minded saw themselves as anti-mainstream and anti-corporate, though many independent-signed British artists managed to reach the Top 10 singles charts during this time.

The introduction of a do-it-yourself aesthetic may be interpreted as the democratization of the recording industry, since it allowed access and participation to a far greater number of musicians and a far wider variety of music than the majors would finance at that time (see Hesmondhalgh, 1998). Many of the punk and post-punk companies adopted unconventional business practices in line with their anti-corporate beliefs. These included 'handshake deals' in lieu of properly written and witnessed legal contracts, short-term production agreements rather than long-term deals, and 50/50 agreements where net profits are split equally between artist and company. Such practices help reinforce the belief that independent record companies are primarily interested in fostering artistic innovation.

STRATEGIES FOR DEALING WITH UNCERTAINTY AND RISK

Keith Negus (1999: 31–2) argues that record companies (of all sizes) face the same basic uncertainty: the unpredictability of public tastes over time. Which existing artists and genres will continue to be successful, and which new artists and genres are worthy of future investment? Negus suggests two main responses: the 'mystical' and the 'cynical'. The 'mystical' response is that 'great music will always find a home' so A&R personnel need to be 'in the right place at the right time' (1999: 34). Such beliefs are common within the industry as they account for success in ways suggestive of special A&R knowledge or skills. The mystical response does not, of course, aid in the development of accountable corporate strategies. Instead, managers and accountants of major record companies operate in a more 'cynical' fashion by adopting approaches that appear to offer a level of control and predictability. We have already noted above the cross-media promotional opportunities presented by reality television programmes, and Chapter 6 will explore a variety of promotional approaches related to mass media, social media and sponsorship. Here, we will examine a number of broader strategies seen within the industries since the 1990s.

Overproduction

Overproduction is a long-standing strategy within the recording industry, which Negus describes as throwing 'mud against the wall' (1999: 34). In this approach, large numbers of releases are made each year, with the expectation that many will fail to find a market or prove financially viable. Those that are successful receive new investment and promotion, while those that do not will struggle to retain the attention or support of record company personnel. The in-built expectation of failure that characterizes this strategy matches the oft-cited industry belief that only one in eight or less of all released records manage to cover their costs of production (Negus, 1999: 32).

Differential promotion

Differential promotion (Hirsch, 1990: 135) is based on the idea that it is unfeasible in terms of money and other resources to give equal promotion and marketing to each and every release. Instead, the promotional resources of the company are directly targeted at the small number of artists that the company believes has the greatest chance of success. The remaining acts are assigned a minimal budget, which makes it difficult for them to compete in a crowded marketplace. In some cases, records may be made but not released because the company thinks it is not in its commercial interests to do so. Instead, the expenses that have already been incurred are written off in order to prevent further potential losses.

'Priority' artists

Prioritizing some artists over others is a risky business, as those artists given a major promotional push will need to sell enough records not only to cover their own costs but also to offset the expenses incurred by the company's many unsuccessful releases. To reduce the overall risk, the majors tend to concentrate on those artists whose music is most likely to appeal to a wide range of consumers, which further accounts for the image of majors as safe or conservative in their music choices. Priority artists should also be capable of internationalization (see below) and be marketable across a range of media, including television, film and the internet. In contrast, independents use their in-depth and/or local knowledge of niche markets to find and promote acts that may be far from safe or conservative in their musical style, but may have a loyal and profitable fan base to support them.

Co-optation of independent labels

The majors can cover the costs incurred by their less successful artists because they have extensive back catalogues and a broad portfolio of contemporary releases to rely on. This is not the case for independent labels, where a failure to promote even moderately successful releases may lead to poor cash flow and closure. For this reason, they may become co-opted by major record labels through finance, marketing or distribution deals, or by selling part or all of their business. This is a relatively low-risk strategy for the major, which gains access to the independent's back catalogue recordings and roster of acts (Negus, 1992: 40). If sold to a major, a former independent may retain its name and some personnel, while its new ownership status may be deliberately obscured in its literature and website. This practice helps maintain the appearance of indie credibility and authenticity while the retention of personnel allows the major to benefit from their niche-market knowledge and talent-spotting skills. In addition, the independent label may 'test-market' artists prior to transferring successful ones directly to major label recording contracts.

Internationalization

According to Negus (1999: 154), 'the international potential of any new artist has become an important consideration when a company is assessing a new acquisition', since internationally successful stars have high profit potential (Wall, 2003: 80). In the 1990s, approximately 40–45 per cent of all record sales made outside of the United States were 'international' artists, of which 75 per cent were American in origin (Negus, 1999: 157). By maintaining a presence in the local markets of global territories, the majors can also search for cross-over stars who might appeal to a broader international audience. For instance, the 1990s saw a number of successful Latino pop acts, including Enrique Iglesias and Ricky Martin, make top-selling English-language albums. This kind of cross-over success demonstrates an important aspect of internationalization: record companies work with expectations about what will 'travel well', such as the use of English lyrics, and aesthetic judgements about rhythms, instrumentation, tempo, and the sound of the voice (see Negus, 1999: 156). However, this practice has also led critics to condemn a system that acts against the interests of artists who want to promote their own indigenous musical styles and sounds on the world stage (see Mitchell, 1997; Taylor, 1997).

Independent record companies who sign an artist with cross-over appeal for other territories may be able to promote that artist to those territories through the internet, especially if the artist works in a niche genre. Nevertheless, it may be difficult for the company to promote and service physical sales (CDs, vinyl and so on) in those territories due to the costs associated with overseas distribution and the need for territory-specific expertise. In such cases, the independent may seek a licensing agreement (discussed above) with an overseas company.

Portfolio management and specialization

In the 1990s, the majors adopted an approach called portfolio management (Negus, 1999). In this model, investment is spread across a range of artists, genres and label brands, with operational units taking charge of specific genre styles. By doing this, the major spreads its risk profile, so that it can react relatively swiftly to changes in the market, with sales targets and budgets managed according to their level of success (1999: 47–49). Such practices give the appearance of control, but can actually lead to 'a straightforward reluctance to experiment, a reduction in risk-taking and a propensity towards a partial view of the world' (1999: 52). In other words, these portfolio units may focus on what they consider to be sure-fire hits in their specific genres, rather than seeking out new acts or pushing genre boundaries.

In contrast, independent companies may specialize solely on a niche-market genre. The market for that genre may be too small for a major label to take an interest, yet can be profitable for a smaller company to service. Such labels understand the tastes and expectations of their target markets; if managed well, fans may come to trust the label itself and feel that any artists signed to that label are worthy of their attention.

Media rights exploitation

The majors are increasingly involved in activities that move beyond the basic model of recording, marketing and distribution of music products. Instead, they are organizing their activities around the exploitation of the copyrights under their control (Negus, 1996: 56). Income from rights exploitation has grown rapidly in the 2000s as music has become 'content' for a range of media products and digital technologies. The major labels (and many independents too) now license their music catalogues to hundreds of music streaming services and download stores, and to other platforms such as internet-enabled mobile phones and computer games. Revenue is also earned when music is used in television shows, movies, computer games, internet sites and advertising campaigns, and when it is played on the radio and in public places such as shops and live venues. These activities do not replace the income derived from the sale of physical and digital products, but do suggest possible future trends. For instance, PRS for Music reports that business-to-business (B2B) revenues in the UK exceeded £1 billion per annum for the first time in 2009 and now account for more than a quarter of total UK music industry income (Page and Carey, 2009, 2010 & 2011).

Multiple rights agreements

Recording companies of all sizes will now usually ask for multiple rights agreements (or 360-degree deals) from their new signings (see also Chapter 10). These agreements allow record companies to receive a share of their artist's other revenues beyond those derived from music sales and licensing. These other revenue streams include music publishing, merchandising, sponsorship and live performance. Since record companies can no longer rely on sales and licensing income alone to recoup their investment in an artist, labels believe that multiple rights agreements are an appropriate method to minimize their financial risk. While some artists and managers are unhappy with record labels earning income from a range of different revenue streams, multiple rights deals are often the only major-label deal available to new and unproven acts.

Leveraging the fan base

The internet makes it easier for artists (whether signed to a recording contract or operating independently) to create an active and interactive relationship with their fans which can be used to both maintain and expand their fan bases. For instance, social media can be used as a direct marketing tool to advertise concert dates and downloads, and as a way to cultivate grassroots interest and involvement through digital 'street teams' that can recommend artists, recordings and concerts to others and build 'brand' loyalty (see Chapter 6 for more detail and discussion). A solid online fan base can lead, in turn, to a variety of opportunities for merchandising, interactivity and patronage. For instance, fans may produce videos, remixes and artwork or even take a financial stake in an artist's career (see Box 2.3).

Box 2.3
Crowdfunding

Crowdfunding is a form of collective financing (or micro-patronage) commonly managed through the internet and used by a wide variety of organizations including charities, political campaigns and start-up businesses. It may be used by independent musicians to fund, for example, recording, touring or marketing costs. Individual donors pledge money towards a project, such as the recording of an album, in return for a variety of incentives, ranging from a 'free' download or CD copy of the eventual product to more expensive or personalized items for those pledging larger sums. A number of online businesses (or 'platforms') have been created to facilitate crowdfunding, including Kickstarter, Rockethub, Pledge Music and ArtistShare. These platforms charge fees ranging from 4 or 5 per cent of the money raised (plus money transfer transaction fees on top) to 15 per cent all-in. They do not request ownership of any products that result from the process, so the artist retains full copyright in their work. A downside is that the platforms rarely provide marketing, so the onus lies with the artist to create a buzz around their project and to find enough donations to meet their pledge targets. This may be difficult, since the more successful projects often rely on a few relatively big donors for their success, and it may be hard to convince people to donate upfront (Kelleher, 2011).

Established artists may find crowdfunding platforms a useful way to leverage their fan base, but fan-funded projects do not necessarily require a dedicated platform to succeed. Instead, artists may use the internet to work directly with their fans. Examples include the singer-songwriter Jill Sobule, who raised nearly US$89,000 to record the album *California Years* (2009) through a tiered system of donations that included US$50 for an advanced copy of the CD and your name credited in the liner notes, and $10,000 for the opportunity to sing on the album (Roberts, 2009). In the UK, the progressive rock band Marillion has used pre-order campaigns rather than donations to fund the recording and marketing of a number of albums, with pre-ordering fans receiving special edition boxed sets and the chance to win prizes such as backstage 'meet and greets', front row concert tickets, and autographed merchandise.

CONCLUSION

This chapter has outlined the history and structure of the recorded music industry and highlighted a range of characteristics and strategies associated with the sector. The major recording companies continue to dominate the market in terms of overall sales, though the independent sector is of great importance in the discovery and development of new acts. Technological change has driven the industry since its beginnings, leading to both massive successes and near collapse. The music industry environment of the early twenty-first century continues to see technological change, and it is likely that the mix of large and small companies will change again in the future, as will the activities and strategies that those companies undertake.

FURTHER READING

For a more detailed overview of the development of the British and US recorded music industries, see Simon Frith's 'The industrialisation of popular music' (1992) and Reebee Garofalo's 'From music publishing to MP3: music and industry in the twentieth century' (1999) respectively. Insights into the working practices and strategies of the majors can be found in Keith Negus' *Producing Pop* (1992) and in *Music Genres and Corporate Cultures* (1999). The aesthetics, practices and politics of the independent sector are analysed in Wendy Fonarow's *Empire of Dirt* (2001).

3

SONGWRITING AND PUBLISHING

The craft of songwriting is often shrouded in mystery and mythology. Yet, while it is accepted as a form of creative artistic expression, it is also a learnable and teachable skill that can (and is) used as part of an industrialized process of music-making. This chapter discusses the motivations and commercial practices of songwriters, prior to exploring the field of music publishing, including traditional and new income streams and the use of sampling.

KEY FINDINGS

- Songwriting is an art form, an act of creative expression and a communicative medium.
- Songwriting is an industrialized practice with social, cultural, technological and institutional parameters that change as the wider music business changes.
- Music publishers develop and promote songwriters and songs and collect and disburse fees and royalties for the use of those songs.
- New technologies offer new tools and vocabularies for songwriters as well as 'new' sources of income, such as video games, ringtones and sample clearance fees.

SONGWRITERS, PERFORMERS AND PUBLISHERS

From the outset, it is important to clarify and define the role of a songwriter. Simply, a songwriter is someone who writes musical compositions and/or lyrics. The songwriter may also, but not necessarily, be a performer. When studying the music industries, understanding the difference between a songwriter and a performer is critical, because within traditional music industry business models each role attracts very different income streams. Performers may gain income from live performance, sales of recorded music and merchandise, plus supplementary income from product endorsements, film and television appearances and investment in entrepreneurial ventures such as clothing lines, perfumes and restaurants/clubs. In contrast, songwriters generally have one primary means of income: revenues earned from the creation and use of their songs. As individuals, few songwriters have the connections or access to record labels, pop stars or film/television production companies to make it possible for their music to be heard by a wide audience. Such connections are made through music publishers, who act on the behalf of songwriters to promote songs to major labels, acts, and various other firms and industries that require music.

The term 'music publishing' is, today, somewhat misleading. In the late nineteenth and early twentieth centuries, music publishing referred to printed sheet music and musical scores: music in published print form. In that era, the only ways to enjoy music were to play it yourself or to attend a live performance at a church, music hall or other venue. Naturally then, scores and sheet music were essential to people who wanted to hear, enjoy and learn to play popular songs of the day. While it may seem strange by today's standards, it was songwriters, not performers, who were the driving force of the newly developing music industry of the time. In America, composers like Irving Berlin wrote countless popular dance songs, Broadway show tunes and romantic ballads that went on to become timeless hits, and demand for new popular music was so strong that the concept of the professional songwriter began to emerge. A district of New York City, known as Tin Pan Alley, became synonymous with music publishing companies that employed large numbers of songwriters and lyricists to produce an endless stream of new popular music in almost assembly-line fashion. In the UK, London's Denmark Street similarly produced a cluster of music publishers, as well as recording studios and musical instrument and record shops, which collectively helped to underpin an emerging music industry infrastructure.

New technologies, such as radio, gramophone, film and then television, gradually shifted the role of the songwriter as public attention became captured by the notion of the 'pop star'. Throughout the 1950s, 1960s and 1970s most pop stars were strictly performers who relied on behind-the-scenes composers for new material. Songwriters like Hoyt Axton, Gerry Goffin and Carole King, and Bill Martin and Phil Coulter, wrote some of the most successful hits for performers including Elvis Presley, the Shirelles, and the Bay City Rollers. Alongside this, in the 1960s, bands began to develop and write their own material, rather than rely on outside songwriters: perhaps most famously and influentially, The Beatles. The 'singer-songwriter' genre also emerged at this time, influenced by the folk revival movement and stand-out artists such as Bob Dylan, who introduced introspective and socially conscious lyrics into popular music. Singer-songwriters took on the roles of performer and songwriter in one package to perform their own original works though some, such as Elton John (with Bernie Taupin in particular), found collaborative songwriting to be the route to success. Today, 'music publishing' not only refers to printed sheet music and scores, but to all the various ways in which songs – lyrics and music – are exploited: as recordings, in live performances, in films, adverts and television programmes, even in new media forms like ringtones and video games.

This chapter initially focuses on the motivations, roles and practices of professional songwriting before considering the role of the music publisher, primary revenue streams and the issue of sampling. Chapter 10 will later examine the various types of publishing agreement and the contractual terms and issues to be encountered within them.

MOTIVATIONS

Songwriting as communication

Bob Dylan is sceptical that the exact motivation behind any song can be known, arguing that the songwriting process relies upon 'the unconscious stuff that comes to you from the inner workings of your mind' (1991, cited in Zollo, 2003: 124). Yet other songwriters, including those interviewed for this chapter, claim that the primary motivation is to communicate. In this view, the songwriter is motivated by the need to engage listeners in a communicative dialogue that they may direct but not control. This is because the communicative gesture is mediated between songwriters and listeners, and subject to endless variation based on their particular frames of reference. In some instances the listener will find traces of personal experience and meaning reflected in the expression of the song, while for others the same words and music may have little impact.

Some listeners imagine that they are 'inside' a song – either in the role of the singer or as the person the singer is addressing. In such songs, the motivation for the songwriter lies in the challenge of creating a lyric the listener can enter into, perhaps through the use of personal pronouns such as 'I' and 'you'. Alternatively, the songwriter may use lyrics to vividly describe situations and/or actions and to invite the listener to sift through their bank of memories to recover and reconstruct their own thoughts, images and emotions in response to them. As Simon Frith comments, 'Pop love songs don't reflect emotions, then, but give people the romantic terms in which to articulate and so experience their emotions' (1987: 102). As the experiential backgrounds of every listener will be different, the song may be interpreted in ways that bear little resemblance to how the songwriter felt when writing the song (Brackett, 1995: 15). Perhaps this partly explains why, in a critical sense, songwriters tend to be so fiercely protective of their songs: who knows whether the listener will understand them in the way the writer had intended?

Traditions of the practice

Most songwriters, like most listeners, have heard and responded to a vast number of songs, and, as a consequence, those who write songs tend to have either
consciously or subconsciously developed a critical awareness of some of the
traditions of the practice. As Will Hodgkinson (2007: 30) states, most songwriters begin by imitating the songs they like, and the fact that most commercially successful songs fall within recognizable parameters of structure, theme
and instrumentation suggests that many are motivated by the desire to extend,
modify or add to tradition. On 'Back to Black', for example, Amy Winehouse and
Mark Ronson used a number of identifiable sounds and traditions to frame a set
of highly personal expressions (Nicholson, 2006). It may be argued that their
motivation was partly to acknowledge their influences and partly to convey individuality within established frameworks; as a result, the songs allow the listener
to hear music that is at once new and old, familiar and exploratory. We tend to
regard this in a positive manner, though Theodor Adorno and Max Horkheimer's
(2002) critique of the music industries (see Chapter 1) would instead decry the
'pseudoindividuality' that this implies (see Wall, 2003).

Self-expression and catharsis

David Brackett (1995) asserts that singer-songwriters are motivated by a need to
write in a 'confessional' style in the sense that the lyric will reflect some aspect of
the songwriter's inner experience. Writing songs is something that songwriters
do to express what they cannot say in ordinary speech. Or, as songwriter Ralph
Murphy (2007) suggests, they may also use songs to try to make sense of the
things that have happened to them in their lives. Songs may, therefore, offer a
form of catharsis rather than simply self-expression.

Certain types of British popular music lyrics have become notably more personal and detail-specific during the early years of the twenty-first century. For
instance, the finely nuanced lyrics of Alex Turner, Mike Skinner and Lily Allen
describe instances or portray perspectives that by their specificity might be
expected to be less universal, yet paradoxically strike a popular chord. It may be
the case that nowadays, with songs playing a more incidental and fleeting role in
many people's lifestyles (McLaren 2009), some lyric writers are motivated by a
desire to say more about themselves and how they view the world as individuals –
perhaps as a way to prevent their music from fading into what might be perceived
as a bland commercial background.

Social realism and politics

The degree to which songwriters are motivated to write lyrics reflecting and communicating the social conditions and realities of their time has been a matter of
great debate. What seems certain is that songs can only tell us a limited amount
about the tastes and behaviours of any society and time, with few reflecting the

social and political issues of the day. Even at its peak in the late 1960s, the political song only ever accounted for a tiny percentage of rock songs (Orman, 1980; Weinstein, 2006). In the folk genre, the protest song has been more visible, though Robbie Lieberman (1995: 160) notes that the commercial success of folk-protest and political songs in the US in the 1960s coincided with the politicization of American society. A mainstream audience existed that was more aware of and interested in what was happening in politics at the time. In recent years in the US, anti-republicans Rufus Wainwright and John Prine have gone to war with the pro-Republican sentiments of Toby Keith, effectively extending the tradition established by Pete Seeger, Woody Guthrie and others. Similarly, hip hop artists such as Public Enemy, 2Pac, KRS-One, Paris and others have used lyrics to critique social problems, racism and inequality in the US, as well as US military involvement in Kuwait, Iraq and Afghanistan.

Coincidentally, the relative absence of political song from UK popular music in the early twenty-first century has coincided with a rise in distrust and apathy towards the motivations and behaviours of political figures. Paul Morley (2009: 28, 29) argues that the protest song petered out in the 1980s when, as he puts it, 'me took over from we'. He claims that, from the listener's perspective, the protest song is now seen as worthy but quaint and a little dull. As Frith (1987: 79) asserts, '... choosing which songs and music to buy is still a means of cultural expression', and while Morley acknowledges that protest songs are still being written and recorded, he contends that it is the audience, who have grown pampered and disinterested in hearing songs that might give them troubling thoughts, that has deserted the form. For Morley, Public Enemy symbolizes the last meaningful movement in political song, a final burst of subversive agitation before the 'escapist materialist frenzy' set in.

SONGWRITING AS COMMERCIAL PRACTICE

'Signature' elements and expectations

Most of us have heard and evaluated hundreds of songs; in a critical sense we are all, as listeners, 'experts' in the field. Consequently, the professional songwriter is faced with a significant challenge: how to attract and hold the attention of listeners who have heard such a large volume of songs? According to London-based music publishers (see West, 2007) the answer is by writing and recording songs that are in some ways familiar to the listener but in other ways different (as in the case of Amy Winehouse noted earlier). It seems that the professional must, at an analytical level, be fully aware of what has gone before and possess the ability to add 'signature' elements. A song that stubbornly follows 'the rules' is likely to be unsuccessful commercially because the lack of individuality will render it indistinguishable from the many other songs the listener will have heard. In contrast, a song that lacks the features and socially agreed conventions of a 'good' song within an identifiable genre/ style may well come across as too idiosyncratic or personal to the songwriter, thus lacking in communicative reach.

Good songwriters need to think about the beginning, middle and end of a song (Lawrence cited in Hodgkinson, 2007: 24). This implies that songs are similar to many books or films in that they should carry something of what is expected from a storyline: a sequence of events that we recognize as familiar. Particularly in the editorial stages, a professional songwriter will use his or her best judgement to discern whether the song has been crafted in a way that meets the expectations of the listener, even if to some degree that expectation is to hear the unexpected.

Songwriter Andy Partridge (co-founder and principal songwriter for the band XTC) stresses the need to study the work of other songwriters, saying, 'You won't find out how a car engine works by watching it drive by. You need to pull it to pieces' (cited in Hodgkinson, 2007: 98). It follows that many professional songwriters are not only aware of the chord sequences and melodic signatures of songs that interest them, but also develop, through practice and reflection, theories about how those quantifiable elements 'work' in terms of communicating ideas to the listener. This accumulation of decisions concerning what does and does not work in other songs is referred to by Mike Jones (2006) as the development of 'embedded taste'. Acquisition of embedded taste intuitively guides the songwriter so that, while the 'new' song may be unrecognizable from the songs that helped to shape it, the interpretive critical perception of the songwriter will have been influential.

Demo recordings

Paul Statham (2009) notes how, particularly during the past decade, London-based songwriters have increasingly needed to become familiar with recording applications in order to build arrangements and performances that convey songs effectively to a producer, performer or publisher. Music publishers, he observes, are keen to work with songwriters who are self-sufficient and, with the increase in quality, affordability and usability of home recording studios, able to prepare master quality material without having to book commercial studios and hire musicians. This model, which in relative terms is economically efficient, places a number of demands upon the professional songwriter, who has to learn quickly not only how to become a competent producer and arranger but also how to find time to keep up with production trends in the commercial recording industry.

Nashville (the geographic hub for the country music genre in the US) remains the exception to this trend, as 'pencil and paper' songwriters are still in the majority. Here, a songwriter can write a song during a typical three hour writing session in the morning, have it heard by a publisher that afternoon, record it with a live band the next day and have the recording pitched later that week.

This model, particularly effective in the close-knit community culture found in Nashville, tends to generate great excitement amongst songwriters, who see the process as one that can generate quick rewards. In contrast, the wheels of industry move more slowly in London, New York, Los Angeles and Stockholm, where songwriters may be encouraged (and so more inclined) to finesse their songs and demo recordings over a longer period of time.

Pitch lists

Recording artists who do not write their own songs often use 'pitch lists' that are exclusively distributed within industry circles. These lists, which come to the songwriter via the artist's management or record producer or from the songwriter's music publisher, try to describe the type of song the artist is looking to record. In response, the songwriter is invited to interpret that request and offer the artist a song that fits the specification. Unfortunately, these specifications can be somewhat ambiguous. One pitch list circulated in Nashville called for 'songs with big lyrics', while representatives for another artist were looking for 'awesome songs'. The songwriter is not necessarily invited to write the kind of song he or she would normally write but to work within a set of clearly (or sometimes not so clearly) defined parameters. This can give the more versatile and adaptable songwriter a distinct advantage, particularly if he or she has the technical ability to make a demo that sounds a little like the artist. In theory, the provision of this added dimension will make it easier for the artist to imagine him or herself singing the song.

Library music

Songwriters with a broad perspective on how their songs can be used may be motivated to make songs and recordings available to the publisher in both vocal and instrumental formats. This doubles the possible number of opportunities for the composition to be used as 'library music' or 'production music'. This music is not available for sale to the general public, but is offered to broadcasters and other organizations that use music on a regular basis (such as advertising agencies, commercial production facilities and television production companies). A separate licence is required for each use of the music, though blanket licences can be issued (offering unlimited use for a fixed fee), and royalty-free productions are also available – where, for a one-off fee (sometimes over £100 per CD), the music can be used over and over again without additional costs or licences. It should be noted that songwriters and musicians are paid on a work-for-hire basis, which is to say that while they are paid for their time and effort, they retain no ownership of the creative works generated. Instead, the producer owns 100 per cent of the sound recording, performance and composition copyright, which means that the music can be licensed without prior agreement of the songwriter.

It is common for producers and editors working in the visual media to search a music library catalogue for a piece of music that fits a particular atmospheric context. Thus, from a songwriting perspective, the aim is to write descriptive or evocative music and lyrics, and to write songs that fall clearly within an easily identifiable theme and genre. Here, knowledge of conventional songwriting practices in specific genres is particularly useful for the songwriter. Library music compositions are frequently produced in multiple versions so that the piece can be used in different contexts and for different purposes (particularly in radio and television advertising, where durations of commercials are fixed by broadcasters). These may include a full music track of about 3 minutes, a 60-second version, a 30-second version, a 15-second version, and sometimes a short 'sting' of 3–5 seconds.

For those songwriters less motivated by public attention and perhaps less keen on performing live, this area of commercial practice can hold a particular appeal. There are large international companies who produce thousands of library tracks per year and have a permanent roster of composers, performers, studio engineers and producers on their staff (such as Universal Publishing Production Music and EMI Production Music, each of which are subsidiaries of major recording companies). There are also smaller independent companies and even one-person micro-businesses who supply music to particular clients.

Co-writing with recording artists

It is common practice for recording artists who are not necessarily skilled songwriters themselves to collaborate with professional songwriters. In this scenario, it is envisioned that the artist will convey an idea he or she wishes to express in song to the songwriter, who in turn will be able to 'shape' the idea into a composition that allows the artist a degree of ownership, both creative and financial, while hopefully preserving a balance between quirk and convention. The songwriter is under considerable pressure to perform. For example, if, despite their best efforts, the writing session produces nothing of liking to the artist, that artist may simply move on to another collaborator. If they are a successful act, those collaborators are unlikely to be in short supply. Whatever the outcome, the songwriter will need to be motivated by a diplomatic and empathetic willingness to enable the artist to convey their expression.

Perhaps unexpectedly, reality music television programmes like *X Factor* may be credited with providing additional opportunities for songwriters. This argument contends that, upon their departure from the show, most if not all of the singers have ready-made audiences but few original songs. Enter the songwriter-for-hire (see Box 3.1). The talent show act may issue a pitch list or seek professional co-writers as noted above, but for those acts needing to release music quickly there is a need for songs that are ready to record. In this instance, a songwriter may even be moved to write and pitch a song with a specific contestant in mind.

Box 3.1
Profile: Cathy Dennis

Cathy Dennis is a prolific songwriter who was 'discovered' by manager Simon Fuller in the late 1980s, who signed her to his company 19 Management. In the 1990s she had a successful solo career that saw ten consecutive Top 40 UK hit singles and the release of three albums (Brown, 2008). She then decided to focus on songwriting rather than performing, but continued working with Fuller. She wrote songs for his S Club 7 project (1998–2003), a manufactured boy and girl pop group that starred in four television series made for the BBC between 1999 and 2002. When Fuller launched *Pop Idol* (2001–2003) in the UK and then *American Idol* (since 2002) in the US, Dennis was called upon to help write songs for contestants and winners such as Will Young, Gareth Gates, Kelly Clarkson and Clay Aiken (Brown, 2008). She has also written songs for numerous other performers, including Celine Dion, Janet Jackson, Britney Spears and Katy Perry, typically contributing lyrics and melody lines to pre-existing backing tracks. An exception is the Ivor Novello Award winning song 'Can't Get You Out of My Head' that she co-wrote with Rob Davis. The song was recorded and released by Kylie Minogue in 2001 to international success, and is credited with revitalizing the Australian singer's career (Brown, 2008; M *Magazine*, 2011).

SONGWRITING METHODS AND TOOLS

There are many ways to write a song, but professional songwriters tend to write them in one of two ways: by writing a title and picking up an instrument to find music that can extend the theme suggested by the title, or by writing a musical section and then embarking upon a search for words that reflect the music (West, 2007). Once these initial steps have been taken, the task of completing the song is a problem-solving process that can vary according to the type of song and songwriter involved. Some writers, like Guy Clark (whose songs have been recorded by Johnny Cash, Ricky Skaggs and Jimmy Buffett), are happy to stockpile song ideas and build them line-by-line whenever the mood strikes, whereas others are reluctant to start a new composition before the last is finished.

For many, the establishment of a title in the early stages of the songwriting task is considered particularly important as it can be used to direct the whole mood of the composition. Using this strategy, words and music are added that are appropriate to the focal concept, and the song develops a structure, tone and mode of delivery, all of which convey the initial expression as embodied by the title. This developmental process is an exploratory one and may well lead the songwriter away from his or her initial concept. However, songwriters should ensure that they take the time to explore other avenues, and leave critical decisions about the final shape and content of the song until after this is done (Braheny, 2006).

Songwriters often consider the genre in which they intend to work before embarking upon the song and, in so doing, they acknowledge certain conventions of the genre that may guide the construction of the song. In this way, the music of the past reappears in different shapes and disguises. This filtering process inevitably opens up the possibility for the parameters of the genre to be expanded. How the new song will be received by the listener often depends upon the ability of the songwriter to balance the signifiers of the genre with the elements of individual personality that constitute signature.

Collaborative writing

Writing face-to-face with another songwriter is a markedly different experience to writing alone. For instance, the presence of the other person will usually require that problem-solving decisions are made at conversational speed, when they might otherwise have been pondered over in greater evaluative depth. Instead, the collaborators must respond instinctively rather than analytically to each other's ideas. Ideas that initially make their way into a song are therefore just as likely to make their way back out again at a later stage. If and when it is necessary to persuade the other writer that an idea he or she has had does not contribute to the development of the song, the ability to be tactful and to offer rationale is required. Good collaborators will bring and provoke ideas that may have never emerged from a solo situation: this potential for the generation of songs with 'something extra' is one reason why publishers tend to be keen for songwriters to collaborate.

Ownership of co-written songs

Unless a prior agreement has been made, the rights to co-written songs are traditionally split evenly in terms of ownership, regardless of the degree to which each writer has contributed. It should be noted that concepts, titles, chord progressions and rhythm patterns are in general not copyrightable (Braheny, 2006: 156) and that studio musicians, producers and singers who make small amendments to melodies and lyrics are not entitled to a share of ownership without the permission of the original composer (Klavens, 1989). In addition, contributions to a joint work cannot be separated, which means that collaborators cannot simply remove an existing contribution and replace it with another. In short, collaborators are encouraged – either in person or through the relevant publisher – to register works, reach agreement on how the rights to the work are split and to respect the integrity of contributions made by co-authors. For instance, different individuals or combinations of individuals may be responsible for writing the lyrics, composing the topline melody (the melody of the lyric

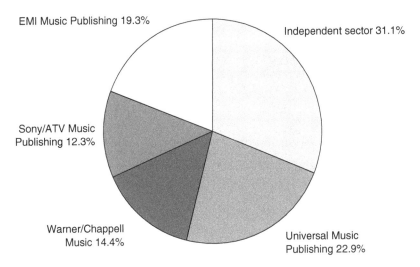

Figure 3.1 Global music publishing market shares 2010 (Data source: Informa Telecoms and Media, 2011)

or other main melodic line), and arranging the song. The complexities and potential for litigation that co-written songs present mean that many publishing contracts now use language that assumes songs are 'written in equal shares by all co-writers' (Harrison, 2011: 113).

MUSIC PUBLISHING

Music publishing companies vary from the very large (see Figure 3.1) to the very small, though all work with songwriters to develop and promote songs for commercial benefit.

Each major recording company has its own publishing arm, and these multinational publishing companies own vast catalogues of songs ranging from Broadway show tunes to contemporary compositions (see Box 3.2). They offer a comprehensive range of services including the development of songwriters, the printing and sale of sheet music, song 'plugging' (where songs are promoted and sold to artists, record companies, film producers, and others), and the administration of copyrights and licences (see also Chapters 9 and 10). These publishing arms usually operate in separation from the record company to which they are affiliated, though in effect they are part of the same business conglomerate. In this model, songwriter-performers are encouraged to sign publishing deals with the publisher affiliated with their record company – an arrangement that, in the US, strongly favours the record company through the use of 'controlled composition' clauses (see Chapters 9 and 10).

Box 3.2
The major transnational music publishers

Music publishing has, like music recording, been subject to considerable consolidation, and the market is now largely controlled by four major transnational companies.

EMI Music Publishing

EMI Music Publishing has a catalogue of over one million songs, with over a thousand having reached number one in the UK and US. EMI boasts the signatures of some of the world's top songwriters including Alicia Keys, Taio Cruz, James Blunt, Salif Keita and Norah Jones. In 2011, it was agreed that EMI Music Publishing would be sold to Sony/ATV Music Publishing.

Sony/ATV Music Publishing

Sony/ATV Music Publishing was formed in 1994 as a 50/50 joint venture between Sony and Michael Jackson (who owned ATV Music Publishing). Jackson's share is now owned by the Estate of Michael Jackson. It owns or administers over 750,000 copyrights by artists such as The Beatles, Bob Dylan, Diane Warren and Wyclef Jean.

Warner/Chappell Music

Warner/Chappell Music has a 200-year-old catalogue that features writers as diverse as George and Ira Gershwin, Burt Bacharach and Led Zeppelin. It considers itself to be the first port of call for A&R executives, record producers and film and television production companies worldwide, and counts Bruno Mars, Katy Perry, Radiohead and Kelly Clarkson within its twenty-first century roster.

Universal Music Publishing

Universal Music Publishing is the world's biggest music publisher. Like the other major music publishers, it offers services in development, marketing, global administration and collection, registration, income tracking, sample clearance and subpublishing. It includes Adele, Jill Scott, Paul Simon and Coldplay amongst its affiliated songwriters.

   Independent music publishers are also common, and may be operated by smaller independent record labels, production companies, or even individual artists. These indie publishers may control anything from one or two songs to hundreds of thousands, and many service niche music markets such as religious music, music for education, and scores for orchestras and choirs.

What do music publishers do?

The larger music publishers are organized in terms of creative and administrative tasks. Within the creative division, 'professional managers' sign, promote, and sometimes develop songs and songwriters in much the same way that a record company A&R department works with performing artists (see Chapter 2). The administrative division deals with licensing, accounting, legal issues and other forms of back-room administration. Between them, these divisions undertake three main roles: registration, exploitation and collection (Howard, 2005: 18).

Registration means ensuring that all new songs written by a composer are properly copyrighted in accordance with local, national and sometimes international laws: proof of ownership is an essential and mandatory first step in gaining income from new music.

Exploitation, despite its sometimes negative connotations, simply means that publishing companies seek to place a song in as many different contexts as possible. This exploitation necessarily involves liaison between the music publisher and record labels, management, lawyers and other persons concerned with the mechanism of music sales/use, and as a consequence an effective publisher has a range of industry 'contacts'. As Sean Devine (2009) points out, since many in the music industry will not deal directly with songwriters, publishers are often tactful mediators who must represent and translate a variety of viewpoints.

Collection could be seen as perhaps the most critical role for any publishing company to undertake, since each time a song is used, a fee is charged and methods must be in place to ensure that this fee is received. Fees can vary dramatically, depending on a number of issues such as: how much of the song is used, and where and how frequently the song is played. In some cases it may be feasible for individual songwriters to manage the roles of exploitation and collection themselves, but for the vast and overwhelming majority of songwriters, this process would be a practical impossibility. Imagine, for instance, attempting to monitor every radio station in the world to determine whether one of your songs was played, or checking every restaurant, hair salon, cinema and hotel to see if one of your songs was played on the radio, performed by a house band, used in a film, or appeared on the track listing of an artist's album. Publishing companies are allied with royalty collection agencies and performing rights organizations (PROs) (see Chapter 9), who have sophisticated formulae and rules in place to collect monies from the exploitation of songs both nationally and internationally and to then redistribute those monies to publishing companies and songwriters.

Searching for a publishing deal

Non-published songwriters often tell of difficulties they have had in gaining access to music publishers. In fairness to publishers, it is easy to see that there are not enough hours in the day to listen to every song that they receive. Publishers have to be selective in the listening process, and this means that a listening opportunity will often be 'solicited', perhaps in the form of a recommendation from a trusted friend. Word of mouth is tremendously influential in the music capitals, and publishers are constantly drawn towards songwriters whose work is drawing attention 'beneath the radar'. The imperative for the songwriter is clearly to do all that is possible to become 'visible' within a music community through, for example, live appearances and engaging in social networking of various forms.

TRADITIONAL INCOME STREAMS

Publishing royalties

Publishing royalties are the monies earned when an individual or firm uses a song (music or lyric). In economic terms, a royalty payment is very much like a payment of rent on a property. A landlord might let a house to a tenant in exchange for a fee for the use of that property. The same holds true with publishing royalties: the songwriter/publisher owns the intellectual property (the song) and if someone wishes to use it then the songwriter/publisher is entitled to be compensated for this use. Income from these streams can range from 50 to 80 per cent. Three main types of royalty payment may be recognized in relation to music publishing: performance/broadcast royalties, mechanical royalties and royalties from printed music.

Performance royalties. Also known as broadcast royalties, performance royalties are earned by the songwriter and publisher every time a song is played in public. Radio and television programmes generate the highest levels of performance royalties, but monies are also collected in other kinds of public performance: music played in places like pubs, clubs, restaurants, hotels, and cinemas. Even school musical productions and buskers are (legally) obliged to pay royalties to the songwriter and publisher.

Mechanical royalties. When a song is recorded as a sound recording, mechanical royalties are due when copies of that sound recording (which incorporates the intellectual property of the songwriter) are made. This is the case whether copying onto physical formats such as CD and LP or onto digital formats such as MP3.

Sheet music royalties. Published sheet music, scores and folios are still an important source of revenue for songwriters and publishers, as there will likely always be a demand for musicians to learn, study and practice classic hits as well as new chart music.

Sync fees

A sync fee is a highly variable one-off payment made to a songwriter and publisher when a company wishes to use a song in a television programme, film or advert for a specified period of time. The non-exclusive sync licence allows the company to record the song in question, but if it wishes to use a pre-existing recording, it must also obtain a master licence from the record company (or other party) that owns that particular master recording.

In the past, the use of popular music in commercial ventures like television shows and adverts was perceived by many idealistic musicians and songwriters as an act of 'selling out' – of trading artistic integrity for money. This idea changed in the 1980s when both artists and audiences, partly due to the popularity of MTV, became much more comfortable with seeing music and images together, whether in television, video, film, advertising or merchandising tie-ins. Today, placement in these media is now highly sought after by many musicians, songwriters, record companies and publishers as it offers the chance for their work to reach large numbers of new listeners and potentially create new fans.

'NEW' INCOME STREAMS

The so-called 'new media' discussed below are becoming increasingly important to songwriters and music publishers, as are other opportunities that have emerged in recent years, such as video games and ringtones.

Video games

Video games are an important new medium for the exploitation of popular music and songs. Some video game titles, like the *Grand Theft Auto* series, utilize popular music and songs in an atmospheric way – to help set the scene and context for gameplay. Other titles, like *SingStar*, *Rock Band* and *Guitar Hero*, allow players to actually perform a song through karaoke and other musical controllers/ interfaces. Video games have proven to be a boon for songwriters, publishers and record companies through its seemingly insatiable demand for popular music titles. It is reasonable to believe that many young gamers now hear classic rock and pop tracks for the first time not through radio or music television, but rather through video games. Indeed, some platforms, systems and games now provide for digital downloading of new tracks directly to a games console, bypassing the need for a standalone music player.

Mobile phones

Advances in mobile phone technologies have created additional new forms of popular music use and consumption. Over the past decade, manufacturers have produced successive generations of 'smartphones' – mobile phones with capacities far beyond basic voice calls. This important new relationship between mobile phones and music began in the early 2000s with the development of customizable and programmable ringtones (that play when someone calls you) and, more recently, ringback tones (that are played while you wait for someone to answer your call). Over the past ten years, these ringtones have become increasingly sophisticated: from the selection or composition of monophonic ringtones (where only one note could be played at a time) to customizable polyphonic ringtones (where multiple tones, for example chords, could be played), to MIDI-generated sounds and music. Inevitably, technology has progressed to the point that today most new mobile phones are capable of using any tone, sound, or song in high-quality digital formats.

These developments have led to a number of implications for songwriters and the music industry more generally. First, a great number of songwriters have been employed by hardware and software firms around the world to transcribe and adapt classical and popular songs into ringtone formats. Second, more entrepreneurially minded songwriters were composing tracks specifically intended to be used as ringtones – not as traditional songs. For instance, in 2003, the so-called 'Crazy Frog' ringtone began circulating across peer-to-peer websites. By 2004 it was picked up by European marketers of ringtones and by 2005 was the most popular ringtone of all time. Later that year, musicians calling themselves 'Crazy Frog' released a new version of the ringtone remixed/sampled with Harold Faltermeyer's 1985 instrumental hit 'Axel F'. The song debuted at number one in the UK, with subsequent album sales of over 100,000 units, emphatically demonstrating to the traditional music industry that mobile phones are now a vital market to be considered in the exploitation of new music.

Other opportunities

The introduction of digital television, the rapid expansion of the internet, and growth in music-related merchandising and product tie-ins have made sync rights a central component of the contemporary music industry. Even the greetings card industry, which has increasingly made use of famous lyrics and even melodies, is required to pay a sync fee. Unsurprisingly, the sync world is incredibly competitive. Yet it is interesting to note that artists who generate significant income from sync rights are often relatively unsuccessful in terms of mechanical sales. As technologies continue to develop, songwriters and publishers will need to maintain an awareness of the importance of new media and other opportunities alongside traditional music industry business models. They will need to be more proactive in the ways they seek to license their copyrights and most publishers are now actively seeking sync and merchandising deals for the music and lyrics they represent. As a consequence, song catalogues that may have fallen by the wayside are now being re-evaluated within the context of the new media landscape.

SAMPLING

Sampling (the use and manipulation of short clips of previously recorded audio) began with analogue tape-splicing in the 1940s (principally within the electro-acoustic music known as Musique Concrète), and was used to great effect within pop and rock music by The Beatles, Jimi Hendrix, Miles Davis, Frank Zappa and others from the mid-1960s onwards. The development of digital sampling equipment in the late-1970s and 1980s transformed the creative process further by making it easier and more affordable to sample and manipulate sounds. Indeed, as Andrew Blake (2007) notes, sampled sounds have now become commonplace in almost all commercial pop music, both live and on record.

For songwriters, sampling and the more recent (and related) practices of interpolation (re-recording and using a melody or other element) and mash-up (overlaying two or more recordings on top of each other) (see Chapter 9) have become significant and new creative and economic markets for lyrics and music. In sampling, the use of just a small excerpt from a song (or a particular recording of a song) may sometimes form the 'hook' or most memorable part of a new track. Legal definitions vary from country to country, but where the sample is recognizable and identifiable, the permission of all relevant copyright owners is required – regardless of how much or how little of the recording was used.

Juxtaposition

In some cases, artists will deliberately juxtapose starkly different sounds and genres in order to make creative and political statements. For instance, Public Enemy's 'He Got Game' (1998) utilizes a sample of Stephen Stills' 1967 song 'For What It's Worth' as made popular by his group Buffalo Springfield. The lyrics of the original song were composed by Stills in response to clashes between hippies and the police in southern California in the late 1960s. The song went on to become a generational anti-war anthem, broadly symbolizing the American counterculture's disapproval of the Vietnam War. By using the immediately recognizable guitar riff from the original track, Public Enemy created an entirely new political statement about the status of race relations in contemporary America through musical allusion. More practically, the success of the Public Enemy track introduced Stills' song to an entirely new audience of music listeners, and generated substantial income for him as both songwriter and performer from a song that was nearly 20 years old. In another instance, the singer Mpho lifted the 'signature' introductory section of 'Echo Beach' by Martha and the Muffins and used it, in an identical state, as the introduction to a 'new' song, 'Box n Locks' in 2009. Here, the sample was used to disorientate the listener, who will have been unsure which song he or she was actually listening to. As most of the royalties collected for this song will have gone to the original composer, it seems likely that the purpose of using the sample might not have been financial gain, but to increase publicity for the act by using a recognizable hook.

Decontextualization

In other cases, songwriters have refused to allow their songs to be sampled or used outside of their original context. Drawing on Jean Baudrillard's (1994) discussion of simulacra and simulacrum, it can be argued that when sounds are removed from their original context, the listener is manipulated in the sense that he or she can no longer place those sounds within that original context. The new presentation thus becomes as 'real' or 'authentic' as the original, with the subsequent loss of the original artist's intentions. Nevertheless, in their discussion of Moby's *Play* – a hugely successful album that took a number of samples from the field recordings of John and Alan Lomax – Hugh Barker and Yuval Taylor (2007: 320–1) argue that the emotions of the original recordings survived the transition to be presented 'without irony'. In this instance, it seems the question of authenticity is two-fold: is the songwriter ethically entitled to re-contextualize the works of those who are unable to deny him the right, and to what degree is the listener being deceived by the process of decontextualization?

As Barker and Taylor (2007: 331) acknowledge, this blurring of contextual definition in popular music has made it increasingly difficult to make judgements about what is or is not authentic. Malcolm McLaren (2009: 41) extends the argument, inferring that the creation of a 'karaoke culture' has made the creation of authentic works a near impossibility, with future generations regarding only the works generated prior to the age of decontextualization as authentic.

Sample clearance

Those who seek to sample a pre-existing piece of music need to obtain the permission (known as sample clearance) of all relevant copyright owners in order for that sample to be used legally within a new sound recording. Permission and usage fees are subject to negotiated licences arranged with the owner of the sound recording copyright (usually another record company) and the publisher (where the sample includes lyrics or a recognizable melody).

Sample clearance deals for the sound recording include simple buyouts (a lump-sum payment ranging from US$500 to US$50,000 or more) and royalty deals (from US$0.01 to US$0.15 per track). Buyouts are most common as they do not require an ongoing administrative burden (McLeod and DiCola, 2011: 153). Music publishers often demand a percentage ownership of the new composition, plus royalties and possibly even co-administration to ensure how the new track is used (Passman, 2009: 320). Contract negotiations can be highly lucrative, which has led to the creation of a separate industry of sample clearance firms (though some record companies and publishers may deal with it in-house) to ensure that permissions and payments are correctly in place. Should a sample be used without permission and a licence negotiated retrospectively, it is likely that the fees and demands of the copyright owner will be much greater. Alternatively, if a songwriter/artist controls his or her own publishing and sound recording copyrights, permission for use can be granted using a Creative Commons licence (see Chapter 9).

Sample clearance is also needed where a sample has been manipulated or altered to sound different, and there are no hard and fast rules regarding how much of a sample can be used, how often, in what context and so on, or indeed how much should be paid for its use: it is all subject to negotiation. The law on sample clearance is largely determined through a string of judgements in specific legal cases (see McLeod and DiCola, 2011), and there are artists who deliberately, as part of a creative and sometimes political aesthetic and practice, use samples without obtaining permission. Such artists will be discussed later in Chapter 9, when we look at how some artists have responded creatively to the issue of internet piracy.

CONCLUSION

The contemporary music industry is undergoing a period of tremendous change and upheaval, yet songwriting and publishing remain central to it. Today, the entertainment industries, inclusive of the music industries, are converging to create an entirely new range of opportunities for the exploitation of songs. New media like video games, ringtones and sampling sit comfortably beside more traditional outlets like radio, television and film. Moreover, socio-cultural and political changes have altered the way musicians and audiences understand the relationship between music and other media. Where once songwriters who lent their compositions to advertisements or film soundtracks were seen as 'selling out', today synching music to film, adverts and television programmes is a strongly competitive and desired career benchmark, as each broadcast is likely to reach millions of people.

FURTHER READING

Paul Zollo's *Songwriters on Songwriting* (2003) offers numerous interviews (from Pete Seeger and Bob Dylan to Todd Rundgren, Frank Zappa, and Madonna) that delve into the creative process of songwriting. For those interested in the issues raised by the practice of sampling, *Creative License: the law and culture of digital sampling* (2011) by Kembrew McLeod and Peter DiCola is highly recommended. Further discussion of music publishing can be found in Ron Sobel and Dick Weissman's *Music Publishing: the Roadmap to Royalties* (2008).

4

MUSIC PRODUCTION

The recording studio is where most of the music we hear on the radio, buy in the shops or download from the internet is made. In the past, professional studio recordings required expensive studios, but developments in technology have increasingly shifted the recording process to other places. This chapter explores the impacts of technological change upon the recording studio, and how this affects the business of recorded music. It also discusses the professional practices of recording engineers and record producers, and highlights the importance of the project studio, MIDI technology and mobile music applications.

KEY FINDINGS

- The music production process involves a series of established professional practices, roles and technologies, and is both an industrialized and a creative one.
- Technological and cultural shifts have contributed to changes in the ways that recordings are created, manufactured and distributed.
- Contemporary recording practices alter and enhance rather than replace the professional approaches that have been developed over the life of the record industry.

CHANGING MODELS AND THE MYTHOLOGY OF THE RECORDING STUDIO

In the early days of recorded music the places where sounds were recorded were not known as studios but as 'labs' (Hull et al., 2011: 220), and recording engineers required a high level of abstract and specialist technical knowledge in order to capture audio. While professional studio engineers and producers today may still possess a high degree of abstract and technical knowledge, developments in digital home recording technology have presented non-specialists and amateurs with the opportunity to record their own music without the aid of professionals. Consequently, the traditional recording studio model faces significant challenges and it has become increasingly difficult for recording studios to operate and sustain their businesses in the same ways as in the past. Andrew Leyshon (2009) describes the outcome of these changes as the 'vertical disintegration' of production and argues that this is having profound economic impacts throughout the recorded music industries. For example, record companies are increasingly devolving the responsibility and cost of making albums to external management and production companies.

Media narratives and creative alchemy

Stories and anecdotes about the conditions of an album's recording often have iconic and historic status, and are disseminated and mythologized through the music press, television and radio, and through biographical and fan-orientated books about artists and records. These stories evoke scenes of creative alchemy, of flashes of genius behind closed doors, and of a rarefied atmosphere of musical magic-making leading to a career-defining, groundbreaking or milestone creative work. Television documentaries regularly portray recording studios as 'the place where the magic happens', where studio 'wizards' and impresario-producers invest projects with something far more than their professional expertise. Some studios have even attained a degree of importance in popular music history that is separate to, and to an extent even independent of, the recordings that have been made there. Examples include EMI's Abbey Road Studios in London, Peter Gabriel's Real World Studios in Wiltshire, and Avatar Studios (formerly The Power Station) in New York.

Record company publicists, and to an extent music fans, perpetuate this myth-making exercise, which contributes to a 'great artist/great recording' narrative of music history. In such narratives, popular music is described in terms of individual visionaries creating works that drive the development of popular music culture. This not only contributes to a particular album's place in the canon of popular music history but can also have a profound impact on its commercial success, both as a contemporary product and as a 'catalogue' item.

Such narratives are problematic, in the sense that they select and represent only the facts and recordings that are consistent with their story. The 'groundbreaking' albums chosen are generally those that sold (and continue to sell) in very large numbers, and are familiar to large groups of people in no small part because of the large marketing budgets, promotional activities and mythologizing that surround them. The narratives overlook the thousands of other contemporaneous music recordings that occupy similar territory or explore similar (or opposing) musical directions. It is important, therefore, to be cautious of such metanarratives (see Chapter 1), and to both study and demystify the production processes through which recordings are made.

THE PRODUCTION PROCESS

The recording studio is the place where most of the professional recordings we buy in shops, hear on the radio, download online and hear across a range of other media and contexts are created. In fact, it may be more appropriate to say that the vast majority of the recordings we consume on a day-to-day basis are actually studio creations, rather than simply recordings. That is to say, the music that we hear does not exist in any real sense other than as a product of the technologies and practices of the recording studio.

Credit is often given to The Beach Boys' *Pet Sounds* (1966) and The Beatles' *Sergeant Pepper's Lonely Hearts Club Band* (1967) for pioneering the art of using the studio and multi-track recording as tools for the creation of music, rather than simply for the capture and reproduction of musical performances. By layering, manipulating, looping and altering sounds using reel-to-reel tape and other studio tools, these pioneers (and other, less famous ones) were able to create sounds that could not have been made by simply pointing microphones at musicians playing instruments and hitting the 'Record' button. Yet studio manipulation of sound had long been a part of the artifice of popular music. For instance, in the late 1920s, when discs were recorded through a single sound horn, the musicians would be lined up – quietest instruments at the front, loudest at the back – so that home listeners could hear an idealized blend of sounds.

Recordings are creative works in themselves, and while studio and techno-logical sounds, effects and manipulations may be commonplace today, their emergence is generally understood as a 'coming of age' for the recorded music business. In effect, the recording studio is the place where the 'electric' era of the music business (after the 'print' era) found its own means of expression, mediation, and state of the art. It is possible, for instance, to write out every single note of Radiohead's *OK Computer* (1997) album, and to faithfully capture the melodies, harmonies, lyrics and rhythms of each tune in accurate detail, but *OK Computer* is clearly something far more than the sum of these musicological features. That 'something more' exists as part of the craft of assembling a 'record' – a term used throughout this chapter to refer to any recorded music artefact, irrespective of its particular media: vinyl, cassette, CD, download etc. – and is something that will be examined and addressed below.

Phases in the production process

While there is perhaps no 'typical' recording session, certain phases of the pro-duction process are common to the creation of many, if not most records avail-able today (see Figure 4.1). First, there is a pre-production phase of preparation and administration. This includes, but is not limited to, listening, dissecting and analysing demo recordings, making changes to song structures, lyrics and arrangements, creating and approving the recording budget, and sourcing, hir-ing and negotiating rates for studios, engineers and any additional musicians or equipment that might be required (on an hourly, daily or sometimes longer

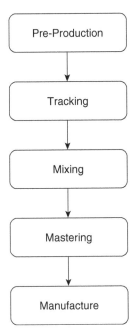

Figure 4.1   Phases in the production process

basis). Many of these things can and should be done before entering the record-ing studio. This is particularly important since studio costs are often charged to an artist's recording budget, and so are repayable from the monies advanced to an artist under their recording contract (see Chapter 10).

Once in the studio and fully set up, the recording process proceeds from tracking (capturing performances on separate 'tracks' of multi-track recording equipment where they can be individually manipulated) to mixing (usually to a two-channel stereo version of the completed song), to mastering (ensuring con-sistency in the overall sound of the recordings) and finally to manufacture. This whole process is, very loosely, the production process from start to finish.

There are endless variations within these phases, with tracking sometimes occurring in more than one studio, while the mixing and mastering phases can happen in other, specialist studios. Some recording projects take place over a number of years in fits and starts, while others take place entirely using home studio equipment. More often there is a combination of home and professional studio. For instance, electronics, sampling and sequencing may be tracked on a computer-based set-up in a small project studio. If no external audio is being recorded, this is known as working 'in the box' and is common for MIDI-based set-ups (discussed later). External audio sources such as drums, guitars and other instruments may then be added later in a professional studio. Likewise, the term 'professional studio' describes an enormous range of facilities, from a small one-person operation with some equipment in a converted garage, to a facility with dozens of employees, a variety of acoustic spaces, and a broad range of state of the art (or indeed antique) equipment. Consequently, the following sections provide indicative overviews of the production process.

TRACKING

The recording studio is, generally speaking, a room with recording equipment in it, though it can, of course, be far more complex than that. Often there is a second, sound-proofed room attached to the first, sometimes known as an 'isolation booth', in which musicians can perform without interfering noises from internal or external sources. Microphones capture the sound, which is relayed via cables to multi-track recording equipment.

From the days of magnetic tape, to our present computerized recording tools, such as Apple's Logic and DigiDesign's ProTools software suites, the practice of multi-track recording has had a major influence on the way that music is crafted in the studio. For example, it is possible (though not necessarily desirable) for a drummer to lay down all of the drum tracks for each song of an album before the band's bass guitarist even arrives at the studio. Yet the practice of tracking (capturing the individual parts of the recording) is often a much more complex and considered process than simply recording the drum parts, then the bass, then the guitar and finally the vocals – although that very simplistic approach does still, occasionally, take place within rock music.

The easiest way to understand what is meant by 'tracks' is to think of individual recordings stacked on top of each other, which, when played simultaneously, produce a completed song. It is possible to turn each of the individually tracked recordings on or off, to make them louder or softer, and to sonically manipulate them in almost any other way, without affecting the sound of all the other component tracks. The process of tracking is, therefore, not simply in the interests of manageability and convenience, but primarily for the flexibility it offers for manipulating, arranging, editing and adding elements and effects to each individual part.

The tracking sequence

The tracking sequence is highly flexible and depends on both the needs of a song, and the particular requirements of the producer, engineer or artist working on it. The entire band may be recorded live and at one time if the immediacy and interaction of that band is part of the recording aesthetic required. However, it is more common for rock and pop music recording sessions to follow some version of the following sequence.

First, a tempo will be agreed and a 'click-track' established to enable the musicians to lock in to a solid and unchanging rhythm. The metronomic click-track is a guide to ensure that the tempo of the song does not drift from one part to another, and will not appear on the final recording. Next, the drums may be recorded. Microphones are selected and set up to capture the individual sounds of the various drums and cymbals, with an overhead microphone capturing the overall sound of the kit. The result is a 'clean' recording of the drums (without any effects applied) across multiple tracks, with each track allocated a different part of the drum recording (such as the snare, hi-hat cymbal, kick drum, overhead microphone and so on). Rather than simply have the drummer listen to the click-track and perform all the parts of the song from one end to the other, it is more common (depending on the complexity and 'feel' of the song) to have the vocalist, bass player, or even the whole band playing along too, while the drummer is recorded separately in an isolation booth. The band may also be recorded at this time to create a 'guide track' that can be used repeatedly by the drummer and others when recording individual parts. For instance, the bass player might hear the drums and guide vocals in his or her headphones while performing and recording the bass part. Other instruments are then layered in a similar way until the recording is complete. The guide track is rarely used in the final product, but it gives individual musicians something to respond to and play against while recording their parts.

An alternative approach to tracking has its origins in electronic, and particularly dance, music forms. Rather than recording musicians playing different instruments one at a time, the component parts of a piece of music are created within recording and multi-track software using software synthesizers, samples and MIDI instruments. This approach will be explained in more detail below, but it is important here to note that the tracking process and the composition process may be combined. This is true especially for electronic music, but also for many improvised music forms.

The tracking sequence outlined above is, of course, an over-simplification of highly varied process. It is entirely possible to write whole books about the process of recording drum kits alone. It requires, for instance, an understanding of the characteristics of microphones and microphone placement, principles of sound such as phase and frequency, and a grasp of recording techniques and tools such as 'noise gates' (that keep out unwanted audible 'spill' from one drum into another's microphone). The same is true of the other instruments in the process, so knowledge of these characteristics, principles and tools is important when creating music in the studio environment.

Overdubs and effects

Multi-track recording makes it possible to re-record parts, to 'drop in' to a recording part-way through in order to overdub additional parts, and to record multiple takes of vocals that may be overlaid to provide a 'fuller' sound to the voice. Likewise, during the tracking process, the studio team of engineer, producer and artist (though these can sometimes be one and the same) will make decisions about how to treat the different parts. For instance, microphone placement, the choice of guitar amplifier, the way the drums are tuned, the acoustic environment in which the parts are recorded, the EQ (equalization) settings that are applied when recording the different instruments, and the selection of effects that may be applied. Each decision can have a profound influence on the finished sound of the record, and can significantly affect the range of possible choices and aesthetic decisions that can be made in subsequent parts of the production process.

Non-destructive editing

'Non-destructive' is a term used in audio recording to denote any process that can alter recorded sounds without changing or destroying the original sound recording. That is, anything that can be applied can be un-applied. For example, reverb effects may be added to a voice without changing the original recording of that voice (whether on tape or as a digital file on a computer). The reverb is something that exists independently, and can be changed or removed at a later stage. Effects such as compression, reverb and delay almost always play a role in shaping the sound of individual tracks and recordings, as does the multi-tracking process as a whole.

The shift to digital recording expands the possibilities of non-destructive editing further. For instance, Mark Katz (2010: 50–2) notes the prevalence of rhythm quantization and pitch correction in modern recordings. These allow imperfect musical and vocal performances to be amended without requiring the musician or singer to make repeated takes. This is a widespread practice within the recording industry and saves both time and money in the studio, yet it is controversial since it 'seems to avoid the craft and hard work that we expect from the musicians we most revere' (Katz, 2010: 52).

With digital technologies of recording becoming more sophisticated and more affordable, there are significant savings to be made in music production. This does not make professional recording studios obsolete, nor does it threaten their obsolescence; rather, it reconfigures their relationship with and involvement in the process of recording music (see Box 4.1).

Box 4.1
Mark Tavern on contemporary studio practice

Mark Tavern is an A&R Administrator at The Island Def Jam Music Group. Here, he explains some of the impacts of the developments in recording technology on contemporary studio practice (Tavern, 2011):

The trend I've seen recently (at least in pop/hip hop recording done by the majors) is that the songwriting takes place in a home studio or production room/writing room that is just a small control room with vocal booth and a small console or maybe just a ProTools rig. A larger, better-equipped studio is then used only when (and if) additional musicians need to be tracked, specifically a drum kit or live band that can't be accommodated in a smaller space. (Much of the 'writing' is actually tracking out synth parts or beats that don't require a live room.)

Rock records are a bit different as the writing is [often] taking place with the entire band in a larger studio that can accommodate everyone and, once writing is done, allows for individual overdubs to take place in the same setting. Indeed, it is vitally important that the writing and pre-production be done before the clock starts at the studio. Tremendous amounts of money are wasted if no tracking is taking place while you're paying!

Interestingly, this has become a big issue, as the act of writing a song has now become intimately entwined with, and almost the same as, the actual tracking of it. As a result, there can be costly confusion (both financial and creative) about when the material is technically ready for mixing. I have tons of stories of setting up mixing dates only to find out that the ProTools files sent to the mix engineer are just a two-track beat and an uncomped vocal* that's not tracked and definitely not ready to mix, even though when you listen to the files it sounds complete. Computer recording is so accessible that it's easy to be sloppy and not plan ahead. It's that planning that helps the process go smoothly and keeps the overall cost down.

* A 'comped' vocal is a composite of all of the multiple recorded tracks in a digital multi-track session: the final edited version. An 'uncomped' vocal is a collection of different versions with no distinction made as to which is the desired take or combination of takes for the mix.

MIXING

Once all of the basic audio components are in place and the tracking process complete, the music can then be mixed. At its simplest, this is the process of finding a pleasing balance between each of the component parts in terms of their respective volumes, placement in the stereo field, and acoustic properties. The mix is also where a lot of the processing and addition of effects often takes place, and can frequently be as much a creative part of the recording process as the act of songwriting itself. It treads a fine line between exact science, delicate art, and a very subjective (though usually well-informed) sense of what 'sounds good'.

Critical listening

Mixing tends to take place in a room that has been sonically treated using acoustic tiles and designed with the acoustic properties of that room in mind. Precise critical listening is required to enable the music to be accurately mixed, and for sonic treatments to be applied appropriately. High-end studio monitoring speakers are used in this process, but the mix will also frequently be listened to on different kinds and qualities of speakers and home stereo equipment, in order to emulate 'real world' listening environments. Many studios use bookshelf-sized 'near-field' monitors (such as the near-ubiquitous Yamaha NS-10 speakers), rather than large speakers placed at a greater distance, in order to emulate 'typical' listening, and a 'good mix' is frequently considered to be one that sounds good across a range of situations. Relatively poor quality speakers or car stereos may also be employed for reference listening on the logic that 'If we can make it sound good on that, it'll sound good on anything ...'

The mixing process

If a separate mix engineer is employed, that engineer will usually be supplied with a rough mix by the tracking engineer, and perhaps a description of what the artist would like the recording to sound like (occasionally with references to other recordings that the artist feels have a sound worth emulating or approximating). The mix engineer will then start 'from the ground up', by building a mix from the component parts. The drum tracks will be listened to and processed first, before working on the bass part in the context of the processed drums, and then each of the other instruments in turn. Consideration must be given to how different sounds relate to or complement each other. For instance, trumpets and human voices occupy very similar parts of the audio frequency spectrum so will often clash when heard together. While these clashes are more usually dealt with at the level of song arrangement and structure, a mix engineer may find it necessary to treat the sounds differently in order to separate and define them. A mix engineer may also treat and 'tidy up' any extraneous sounds in a recording, add new elements that were not included in the tracking process, or remove entirely or in part some previously recorded elements.

The artist and/or producer will normally listen to the completed mix and give feedback to the engineer such as 'the vocals need to be louder', 'the bass could be warmer', or 'can we have echo on that drum hit?' When working with more than one song or on an album, the mix of each song is usually considered in relation to the mix of the others. For instance, the same effects and treatments may be added to each song so that they maintain a uniform consistency of sound.

Stereo-imaging and the 'sound-box'

Since the late 1960s most music formats (cassette, LP, CD and MP3 for instance) have been mixed and released as two-track stereo recordings. Stereo recording creates a virtual space within which the various instruments, vocals and other sounds are heard and experienced by listeners – a space conceptualized by Allan Moore (2001) as the 'sound-box'. When listening to a stereo recording through headphones or stereo speakers, sounds may be perceived as placed towards the left or right of the stereo image. This lateral placement of sounds is controlled during the mixing process, and the typical set-up is for the vocals, bass, snare and kick drum to be situated more or less centrally, with other instruments 'panned' to either side. This arrangement became established in the early 1970s and is now considered to be a 'production norm' (Dockwray and Moore 2010: 181). The sound-box can also be used for thinking about how other elements of the mix are situated in the virtual listening space. For instance, some sounds may be perceived as 'in the foreground' or 'in the background', depending on their comparative volume in relation to the rest of the mix or through the use of reverb effects.

The late 1990s saw the introduction of new consumer audio formats based around 5.1 surround sound mixes: DVD-A and SACD. These employ a technology that was developed for use in cinemas, and makes use of five audio speakers arranged around a central listener. Individual sonic elements of a mix may be panned around any combination of them, thus widening the potential for experiencing the 'sound-box'. Surround sound recordings have not become industry standard, which may in part be due to the shift in consumer preferences towards portable media and downloadable MP3 files (Holman, 2008).

The mixdown

The mixdown process will usually transform the multi-track recording into a two-track stereo master stored on a hard disk, CD-R, DVD-Audio or magnetic tape. With the development of more complex recording systems (from 24- to 96-track studios in some cases), the mix process has become increasingly sophisticated. The mixdown used to be a rehearsed and choreographed 'performance', often involving more than one person to make sure all of the different elements happened correctly and at the right times. For instance: applying reverb and other effects, or adjusting equalization and volume on one or more tracks simultaneously, while the song is played in real time. Studio technology has been developed to address this problem, and most mixes are now predominantly (if not entirely) automated within a software environment. Nevertheless, the precursors to that technology are not entirely obsolete, and many mixing consoles use technologies such as 'Flying Faders': automated and programmable controls that can help to coordinate a multi-track mix within only limited personnel.

MASTERING

Mastering is a little-understood process (certainly by most consumers, but also by many music industry personnel, who regard it as a 'dark art') in which the stereo mix created in the mixing phase is processed further. Mastering engineers fine-tune completed stereo mixes at the level of the overall song, rather than on a track-by-track basis, using equalization, limiting, compression, and other audio processing techniques. They ensure sonic consistency across an entire album or EP, and make allowances for the technical and aesthetic parameters of the various contexts within which the music might be played or reproduced (such as radio broadcasting, nightclubs, CD or vinyl). Editorial decisions are also made at the mastering stage, such as the gaps between songs, the order of the songs, and where to place track ID points when creating CDs.

Specialist mastering studios

As the mastering process requires careful, close listening and detailed analysis of the recording, mastering studios are often equipped with expensive, high-end equipment and specially designed rooms in which to work. Consequently, not all recording studios offer mastering as a service, and it is a job frequently handled by specialist facilities or personnel. Indeed it is not uncommon for a record made in London to be mastered at a facility in New York or Los Angeles. In the past, master recordings on magnetic tape were sent physically to mastering studios, but the development of digital master recordings means that they are now increasingly delivered through the internet using FTP (File Transfer Protocol), 'large file' transfer services such as Sendspace or YouSendIt, and specialist online services such as SoundCloud. The mastering process can give a 'finished' sound to a record, and have a significant impact on the overall impression of the final product (see Box 4.2). Yet, it is still important to ensure that the tracking and mixing stages are completed to the highest quality, as it is difficult to make a 'bad' recording sound good.

Box 4.2
Ian Wallman on mastering and the Loudness Wars

Ian Wallman is a freelance record producer, remixer and engineer. Here, Ian discusses mastering from the perspective of one who has taken on mastering work, as well as someone who has sent work away to be mastered by specialists (Wallman, 2011):

Perhaps the key factor in choosing to use a mastering engineer is the fact that by the time a producer has finished recording and mixing an album any perspective is often lost; you are simply too close to it (you could use the 'wood for the trees' analogy). With a 'fresh set of ears', the mastering engineer can make impartial judgements on the final balance of EQ and compression. [However,] with basic mastering software now available to everyone (even in Apple's free Garage Band software) the default position of using a professional mastering engineer for low budget projects is now often a thing of the past. I'm very fortunate to work across many different genres and (thankfully) budgets, and each project requires a different approach. Obviously self-funded bands have limited budgets so in many cases they are reluctant to pay for a professional mastering engineer, so in these cases I will often take on this role.

Each genre requires a different approach. For pop music the final master has to be loud, energetic and bright, requiring a rather heavy amount of processing. This approach would not be appropriate for jazz or classical recording where the desired result would be transparent and dynamic. An excellent example of appropriate mastering is the Damien Rice album O (2002), which has an incredible 'dynamic range', meaning that there is a big contrast between the very quiet/intimate [sections] and the loud sections. The first occasion I played this album was on a long motorway journey. I found myself constantly turning up and then down to hear the content; though initially frustrated I later played the album at home/late at night – suddenly the mastering approach made sense; had the mastering engineer squashed the dynamics out of the record it would have sounded great in the car but have completely lost the emotional energy brought about through the dynamic range. This is a common criticism of many modern albums: if you listen to pre-1980s recordings (not remastered) they can initially seem quiet, but what they do have is a much greater dynamic range (early Back Sabbath albums are fantastic examples).

A significant area of production work I do is remixing, I have been fortunate to have had mixes accepted by Beyoncé, Lady Gaga and Michael Bublé. When I submit mixes for approval I always do a fairly heavy amount of mastering. This is because you are usually pitching against a large number of producers, and so your track has to be of comparable volume/loudness – it's a simple fact of life that 'LOUD = BETTER' is the perception of most A&R departments. Once mixes are accepted I will always send a 'pre-mastered' version because large record companies can afford the best mastering engineers in the business.

The Loudness Wars

As new formats and technologies evolve, and as fashions and expectations change in terms of the sonic properties of recordings, so mastering (and remastering) develops over time. In recent years, there has been much discussion about the mastering of albums for release on compact disc (CD). The mastering process for CD differs from that required for vinyl records, so when older releases intended for vinyl were later reissued on CD, the audio recordings needed to be re-processed. To make these CDs 'sound good' or at least 'sound impressive', pressure mounted to make them louder and 'punchier'. Over time this has become competitive, with rock and pop albums in particular being mastered in an attempt to 'sound louder' than their competitors in the marketplace. This is known as the Loudness Wars (see Milner, 2009). Yet each recorded media, including CD, has a fixed value for maximum absolute loudness, following which distortion occurs. This has led mastering engineers to use audio compression to reduce the dynamic range of the recording and thus increase the perceived loudness of the track.

Dynamic range

Dynamic range expresses the difference between the loud and the quiet sounds on the recording. A track with a large dynamic range contains a significant difference in volume between the quiet and loud parts of the music. Audio compression reduces the dynamic range by making the quiet parts louder, hence the difference between them becomes less pronounced and the overall impression is that the track sounds louder. You may have experienced this while watching a film on television that is interrupted by commercials. The advertisements will always seem louder than the film because the makers of the commercials want their ads to stand out. The loudest sound on an advertisement is, though, no louder in absolute terms than the loudest sound (say, a gunshot or explosion) in the film; the overall perception is different because the other sounds in the movie are quiet in comparison.

Over-compression

Detractors claim that the Loudness Wars have led to over-compression resulting in audio distortion and to some re-released albums that sound worse on CD than on vinyl (Levine, 2007; Lamere, 2009). Tracks that have a greater dynamic range have a sense of space, so when loud events do occur, they have a greater dramatic impact – an impact that is lost due to compression. In addition, compressed audio has a denser sound, and can contribute to a sense of 'ear-fatigue' when listening. This denser sound can be very desirable to a point in many forms of rock and pop music, but less so in classical or jazz recordings.

New albums continue to be released that are deliberately mastered to sound ever louder and more sonically dense. For instance, Metallica's *Death Magnetic* (2008) CD, produced by Rick Rubin, was so highly compressed that some consumers complained it was significantly distorted, particularly in comparison with a less-compressed mix available as downloadable content from the computer game *Guitar Hero* (Shepherd, 2008). Nevertheless, most professional recordings use compression to good effect, and the one thing that is often overlooked in mastering for 'loudness' is the simple fact that listeners will adjust their own volume to a listening level that's comfortable for them: if they want something to sound louder, they'll turn their home stereo up.

MANUFACTURING

While digital downloads are increasingly popular, the final product of a recording is still, frequently, a physical CD that is mass produced by a pressing plant. Due to the economics of mass production, the larger the number of discs produced, the lower the per-unit price that can be charged by the pressing plant, thereby affecting the potential profit margin for the record company. It is worth reiterating that record labels work on a high fixed cost, low marginal cost basis: once the high initial recording costs of an album are paid, it becomes important to keep the per-unit replication costs as low as possible. Conversely, if the record company believes that additional sales can be generated or that a higher retail price will warrant it, they will sometimes release products in more complex and expensive packaging or with additional content such as postcards, posters and so on. They may seek to reduce their costs by manufacturing in larger quantities, but they must be careful not to over-order stock that they might not be able to sell.

Artwork

Artwork and packaging are usually necessary for the release of music in physical formats such as CD, and artwork is also recommended for digital formats, as eye-catching art can attract potential consumers. It may give the consumer indications as to the genre and style of the music it is associated with, and attractive packaging can be an important marketing tool. For example, LP album covers were important to the genre of progressive rock in the 1970s, as the genre rarely gained mainstream broadcast radio airplay, and albums needed to stand out in the racks of a music store. Similarly, 4AD Records commissioned specific design teams (23 Envelope and later v23) to create sleeve art for nearly all of its 1980s releases. The artwork gave the label a recognizable visual aesthetic that complemented the musical style of label acts such as Cocteau Twins and Dead Can Dance, and would attract potential consumers to the other acts released by the label.

Pressing plants frequently operate their own printing presses so that artwork and booklets for finished CDs can be made on-site. They will even assemble CDs into their plastic jewel cases or cardboard 'digipak' cases prior to shipping them to a record label warehouse. Nonetheless, many independent labels and self-releasing artists choose to assemble the discs and packaging themselves in order to save money. Once delivered by the pressing plant, the production process is complete. It is then followed by distribution, marketing and sales of CDs to the public, which are discussed in Chapters 5 and 6.

PRODUCTION CAREERS AND ROLES

Traditional careers (see Box 4.3) in the production studio have changed over time. While many of the work roles still exist, the hierarchy, from studio tea boy to runner, tape operator, junior engineer, senior engineer, record producer and then executive producer, is much less rigidly defined. This is especially true for studios that can no longer afford the luxury of full-time junior engineers, or no longer use magnetic tape. The following sections examine the roles of recording engineers and producers.

Box 4.3
Profile: Nigel Godrich

An archetypal example of rising through the ranks can be seen in the career of record producer Nigel Godrich. Godrich was a graduate of the School of Audio Engineering (SAE) and began his career at a studio called Audio One. As he puts it, 'I was literally a tea boy. It was a five-floor building, and I had a pager. All day it would be like, "three teas and two coffees in studio one please."' Godrich eventually rose to the position of sound engineer, and worked on Radiohead's 1995 album *The Bends*. The band enjoyed working with him, which led to his being co-producer or producer of the bands' later albums, and to work with Beck, Air, Paul McCartney and many others. Godrich's career trajectory, while hardly typical today, is still considered to be the traditional route through the studio production hierarchy (Godrich, n.d.).

Recording engineers

The people who record audio are known as 'engineers' for the simple historical reason that the job was traditionally an engineering trade, and a good practical knowledge of electronics was required. For the most part, perhaps until the 1960s and 1970s, the engineers who operated recording consoles were generally the same people who could build them. Over time, the increasing complexity of studio equipment and availability of specialist studio electronics have led to a different kind of specialism. Today, recording engineers combine an understanding of the properties of sound, a familiarity with a range of different recording techniques, and an appreciation of the aesthetics of different types of recordings from different genres. Nevertheless, there are also genre specialists. For instance, an engineer with expertise in recording rock music may also have a good idea about how to record an orchestra, but in practice a skilled specialist is more likely to be employed, and may well make a significant difference to the end product. Likewise, a classical music engineer may be capable of producing a technically competent rock recording, but lack in-depth knowledge regarding the canon of pop and rock recordings. This will make it more difficult to make the aesthetic and technical choices that artists and producers require to achieve a particular sound or to meet record company desires regarding the 'sound' of generic marketing categories (such as indie, emo, pop-punk, and so on).

A recording engineer may be a salaried employee of a large recording studio company, but anecdotal evidence suggests that in recent years there has been a tendency towards freelancing: working across a range of recording studios, including those that are artist-owned (Ashworth, 2009). Ostensibly this is because recording studios are finding it more and more difficult to economically justify the employment of full-time staff. Two possible causes for this are the proliferation of cheaper recording alternatives, and the trickle-down effect of falling CD sales.

Record producers

Record producers, like recording engineers, may have complex working relationships with recording companies and recording studios. Some are 'in-house' producers tied to particular studios, while others may be employed by a particular record label and work exclusively with that label's roster of artists. In the latter case, the producer may be required to use studios in which the label has a financial interest, though Leyshon (2009) notes that this has become less common in the 2000s. There are also self-employed freelance producers who negotiate with the record company, artist and artist manager to book an appropriate studio for a specific project. There are also different kinds of record producer in terms of their approach to their work, and the choice of producer can have a significant influence over the sound, commercial viability, and cultural and popular meanings of a piece of recorded music.

The producer will often begin work with the artist in the pre-production phase, discussing such things as song selection and arrangements, melodic hooks and the choice of musical key. The producer usually also has the responsibility of ensuring that the project is managed well, and is delivered both on time and within budget. The artist/producer relationship is often subject to numerous tensions, especially when there are differing expectations, or when the record company has commercial priorities that differ from an artist's creative ones. It is crucial that the right producer is found to work on a project, and that the producer develops effective working relationships with the artist, songwriters, musicians and engineers involved. The producer must get the best performance out of an artist, work with issues of ego and self-consciousness, and mediate musical disputes diplomatically. For instance, where there is more than one songwriter in a band, whose songs should be recorded? And if there are several potential lead singers, who will be chosen to sing which parts? Personality management and diplomacy may be the most important talents for a producer to possess or develop, as there may also be a need to deal with other issues between band members, or personal situations between band members and their partners or entourage.

The combination of artist and producer is often an important component in the creation and subsequent business of recorded music, since the involvement of a well-known producer can be a significant component in the marketing of a product. An album produced by Brian Eno, for instance, can generate demand for a product among certain types of music fans, even if the artist in question is not perhaps someone that the individual consumer might typically be interested in (such as Coldplay or Paul Simon). While the artists Eno works with are often already very popular in their own right, their desire to work with him as a producer for what are presumably artistic and creative reasons also has the knock-on commercial effect of developing a secondary audience among fans of Eno's music production work.

Production styles

Some producers may be defined as 'auteurs' who apply their unique and personal vision and style to each project they work on. They are identifiable by their 'signature sound' regardless of the artist whose name adorns the record sleeve. A classic example is Phil Spector, whose 'Wall of Sound' approach to music production characterized the hit records of many recording artists in the 1960s. Another is Manfred Eicher, producer and owner of the ECM record label, who has developed a consistent and identifiable sound within European jazz. This is often described as a 'melancholic' or 'Nordic' tone, interpreted as an isolated, lonely, cold and introspective approach to music performance.

Some record producers come from a strongly musical background themselves and may become deeply involved in the arrangement and composition of songs. For instance, Grace Jones's 1985 album *Slave to the Rhythm* is widely considered to be as much, if not more, the creative work of producer Trevor Horn. In contrast, those from a sound engineering background may be more interested in the technological aspects of recording, while others tend towards a more experimental approach or are known for their skill in crafting overtly commercial 'chart hits'.

Artists may also self-produce their own projects. This is common in do-it-yourself home recording set-ups, but less common for the larger ventures of major and independent recording companies. The worry for the record company is that this level of control may lead to a loss of perspective regarding the quality of the songs or to financial and/or artistic over-indulgence. Nevertheless, if an artist has a proven track record of making successful records and was seen to be heavily involved in the creative decisions that led to that success, they are more likely to be allowed to produce themselves, though an associate or co-producer may also be employed to deal with the business aspects of the production (Hull et al., 2011: 216).

PROJECT STUDIOS, MIDI AND OTHER DEVELOPMENTS

Project studios

Increasingly, a great number of commercially released recordings are created and crafted in more humble settings than a professional recording studio. These are known as project studios, home studios or bedroom studios. It has, of course, been possible to record outside of a professional studio environment for many years. For instance, Bruce Springsteen's highly regarded 1982 album *Nebraska* was recorded on a TASCAM Portastudio 4-track cassette recorder in his bedroom. Yet, the availability of increasingly sophisticated and affordable home recording technology means that professional sounding recordings are now within the grasp of many if not most musicians who wish to record and release music. Free downloadable software is available for the modern home computer that incorporates multi-track recording, editing and processing capabilities that would have been enviable in high-end recording studios barely 20 years ago.

As a result, there is now a growing overlap between what is possible to produce at home, and what can be achieved in a high-end production studio. Moreover, there are potential advantages other than the creative freedom to record in one's own time without having to consider a studio's hourly rate. Many artists who use contemporary DIY techniques speak of an ability to create works that are the result of experimentation and a willingness to make 'mistakes' that add to the overall uniqueness of the finished product. But the budgetary consideration is an important one when it comes to the overall profitability or sustainability of a recording project. For instance, Bon Iver's 2008 album *For Emma Forever Ago* sold over 200,000 copies (including digital sales) but incurred almost no recording costs because of its self-produced 'DIY' approach (Ashworth, 2009). Critics have praised the album for its aesthetics and sense of place, and suggest that these result directly from the conditions of the recording process: months spent writing and recording in a remote cabin in northern Wisconsin, free from commercial expectations or motivations.

Home recording might be seen as bad news for those working in the professional recording industry, but some engineers and producers see it as an opportunity to be flexible (Ashworth, 2009). They can offer specialist skills to develop and enhance DIY recording projects by adding elements such as orchestral string sections that are difficult to capture with budget equipment in a home environment. They might also move into production deals where they find and develop artists, or work on a freelance basis in artist-owned studios.

MIDI

One of the key technologies driving the rise of project studios was the development of the Musical Instrument Digital Interface (MIDI). MIDI is a machine language that allows different electronic instruments (such as synthesizers) to control or be controlled by a set of instructions recorded using a very small amount of digital data. It allows complex musical information to be captured, stored and processed on computers and storage devices, even those of relatively limited capacity. The protocol was devised as early as 1982 and includes information such as which note to play, how loud to play it, how long to play it for, what effects such as pitch bend or vibrato to apply, and so on. These variables can be expressed simply and numerically in a much more concise way than the digital information needed to capture the complexity of actual audio sound recordings.

A MIDI file is not generally used as a consumer format, as it requires hardware or software synthesizers to be present for the musical sounds to be generated. Its utility is that the creator of the music may control a range of instruments and sounds simultaneously across a range of different tracks that can be edited and manipulated in a manner analogous to the multi-track recording equipment of a professional studio. Electronic and other musicians who use synthesizers, samplers, sequencers and so on in their musical palette are able to use MIDI to layer multiple instruments together, mix between them, and add effects independently to each, prior to committing a mix of that music to tape.

Moreover, MIDI sequencing software has been integrated into digital audio editing software packages, creating a powerful combination of tools within a single Digital Audio Workstation (DAW). Of course, the machines on which the audio is captured and manipulated are only a part of the story, and professional engineers and producers would be quick to point out that far more important considerations such as high-end microphones, good acoustic spaces, professional grade analogue-digital converters, pre-amplifiers, monitoring equipment – and above all, the expertise and judgement of a trained professional – can never truly be replaced by cheaply available home technology. There is certainly some weight to this argument. However, the sheer availability and power of home recording technology, semi-professional equipment and software packages incorporating both MIDI and digital audio has contributed to a phenomenal increase of commercially released music since the 1990s.

Mash-ups

Digital technologies have been instrumental in radically changing not only how music can be recorded and by whom, but also, to some extent, what that music can now sound like. Experimentation in response to newly available technologies has resulted in some interesting new sounds and genres of music (such as Grime and Dubstep), as well as some new kinds of recording practices, including some that the mainstream recording industries are less than comfortable with or, in some cases, strongly oppose.

The phenomenon of the 'mash-up' provides many interesting case studies in this respect. For instance, DJ Danger Mouse blended samples from rapper Jay-Z's *Black Album* (2003) and The Beatles' *The White Album* (1968) to produce the *Grey Album* (2004), which caused a legal and popular storm when released on the internet. EMI, who owned the rights to *The White Album* master recordings, attempted to stop the release of the *Grey Album*, and commenced legal proceedings to stop its distribution. The album itself was favourably reviewed, and became something of a cause célèbre among copyright reform campaigners who argued that this kind of musical production was characteristic of a new technologically enabled approach to music-making that existing copyright law could not address, and should not suppress.

Music for mobile phones and other mobile devices

Contemporary mobile phones have the processing power and storage to handle actual recorded audio in addition to MIDI-based monophonic and polyphonic ringtones. These 'realtones' (or 'mastertones') are usually lifted directly from the finished, mastered audio of a commercially released recording, but in some cases the music will be remastered or remixed. This is because the small speakers of mobile phones can only reproduce a limited set of frequencies, and failure to take this into account can lead to poor-quality results. On a related point, the distance between home recording and professional recording in terms of audio fidelity may be reducing as audiences increasingly listen to music as compressed MP3 files on mobile devices or computer speakers. The poor audio quality of the playback speakers and the 'lossy' sound of the MP3 (which discards audio information in order to reduce the digital file size) mean that it can be hard to tell the difference between a high-quality recording made with expensive equipment, and one made in a relatively inexpensive project studio (Ashworth, 2009). A listener's perception of audio fidelity is, therefore, affected by the equipment and format that they habitually use.

For some genres, such as Grime, there are audiences who listen primarily on mobile devices. Consequently, producers mix their tracks with the mobile phone in mind as an end-user listening device. This is not a new phenomenon, in the sense that music producers have long considered the limitations of the transistor radio or gramophone record when making aesthetic decisions in the studio, and there are many popular tracks from the 1950s and 1960s that sound the way they do specifically because of the sonic limitations of AM radio broadcasts. Yet it is fair to say that listening to low-quality MP3 recordings of cheaply produced Grime tracks underpins the cultural origins of the genre in the bedrooms of young London producers. Indeed it has even been celebrated in the music, such as in the track 'No Bass' by Chronik and Slix.

CONCLUSION

In part, music production has developed as the result of 'important' records influencing and being emulated by a large number of people; but it is also true to say that some of the sounds and approaches that have been emblematic of their time have come about due to the possibilities opened up by developments in studio technology. Classic albums such as *Pet Sounds*, *Sergeant Pepper's Lonely Hearts Club Band*, and *OK Computer* have pushed at the boundaries of what is possible in the recording studio, and their multi-million selling success has brought the results of those experiments to wider public attention. In so doing, they have expanded the palette of sounds and techniques available to recording artists today. At the same time, home recording and DIY techniques enabled by digital technologies and the declining costs of recording equipment have opened up new possibilities. Artists and home recording enthusiasts can make recordings that not only are cheap to make, but also perhaps encourage a more relaxed and creatively fulfilling approach to recording music. At the same time, these techniques may lead to experimentation and the creation of new subgenres and musical phenomena. These developments do not render the professional skills of recording, mixing and mastering redundant. Instead, new cultural practices and professional, semi-professional and amateur activities cast these skills in a new light and transform the relationships between artists, studios, engineers and producers.

FURTHER READING

Mark Katz's *Capturing Sound* (2010) offers a highly readable history of record production from its origins in the nineteenth century to recent developments including autotuning and the impacts of the internet, while Tomlinson Holman's *Surround Sound* (2008) gives an in-depth account and discussion of the development of surround sound technology, and Greg Milner's *Perfecting Sound Forever* (2009) includes background and analysis of the Loudness Wars. The *Art of Record Production* website and journal (see www.artofrecordproduction.com) contains useful resources for the academic study of music production, while practical advice is available in numerous magazines such as *Sound on Sound* and *Future Music*.

5

MUSIC DISTRIBUTION

Once music has been recorded and manufactured, it needs to be delivered to consumers and other music users efficiently and profitably. This chapter explains and explores the practices of both physical and digital distributors and unpicks the role of digital aggregators. It also considers mass-market, independent, online and second-hand retailers, and examines developments in online streaming, direct-to-fan distribution, and music media distribution.

KEY FINDINGS

- Mass-market retailers, such as major supermarket chains, have considerable bargaining power.
- The number of independent music stores is in decline, yet the internet also opens up new opportunities for the sector.
- Online digital distribution promises unlimited inventory and the potential of 'the long tail'.
- The internet allows artists to take control of their own distribution.
- Online streaming may offer a legitimate alternative to music piracy.

INTRODUCING MUSIC DISTRIBUTION

Patrik Wikström (2009) argues that music is primarily (and importantly) a copyright business. While it is true that the control of intellectual property is a key way to derive revenue from music, until very recently the majority of the recorded music industry's revenues came from processes of manufacture and distribution. Indeed, the record industry may appear to more closely resemble a manufacturing industry than a cultural industry. Of course, to classify it as a purely manufacturing business overlooks how music recordings on vinyl, cassette and CD constitute cultural artefacts with considerable symbolic meaning and value: they do not simply offer utilitarian value as 'products' in the manner of, say, electric toasters, light bulbs and many other consumer goods. Yet it is still important to understand the process of music distribution as one that involves warehouses, trucks, ordering and stock-taking systems, returns systems, sales reps who need to convince retailers to carry certain items of stock, and retailers who need to sell to the public.

What is being distributed?

Music distribution companies do not distribute music or even distribute copies of music recordings: they distribute physical copies of recorded music products. This distinction is important because it clarifies the difference between digital distribution (the online dissemination of digital files) and the physical distribution of products that can be held in one's hand. While it might seem a largely inconsequential difference at first, since both are ways of getting recorded music from producer to consumer, it is in fact profoundly significant. Physical items and digital files, or 'stuff made out of atoms' and 'stuff made out of bits' (binary digits) as Nicholas Negroponte (1995) describes them, have fundamentally different properties and characteristics, with each having its own parameters, procedures and economic frameworks. Physical distribution will be considered in the first part of the chapter, while digital distribution is discussed in the second. The latter half of the chapter also examines media integration, which refers to the various ways that media forms have become centred on music not simply as a promotional platform, but as an integral part of how the music industries communicate their products and services to consumers.

Interdependence

Physical products and distribution continue to be important aspects of the ecology and health of the recorded music industries, yet they have come under serious pressure in recent years. Several significant music distribution companies have declared bankruptcy and closed their doors, causing significant problems for the retail sector in particular. For instance, Entertainment UK (owned by the Woolworths Group) went into administration in 2008, and led to the closure of music retailer Zavvi (formerly Virgin Megastores), and subsequently the Woolworths chain of high street stores (which also sold music). In addition, physical products are subject to natural and man-made catastrophes. In 2011 a large warehouse just outside London, containing the stock of one of the largest independent music distributors in the world, was the victim of arson attacks during a series of riots taking place across the UK. Large quantities of CDs and records were destroyed, affecting the ongoing viability of the many record labels and artists who had produced them. The financial fortunes of distribution networks have a significant impact upon the overall fortunes of the record labels that use them and many record labels have been forced to close when their distribution company has failed. The interconnectivity and interdependence of this ecology is worth highlighting right from the outset as we begin to explore the nature of the relationship between producer, distributor, retailer and consumer, and the ways that music products and music media experiences travel from musician to audience.

PHYSICAL DISTRIBUTION

Once physical products such as CDs have been manufactured the record label will usually pass them on to a distributor. The distributor's role is to convince retailers that they should stock their products, and to ensure that those products are supplied and replenished in a timely fashion. The major recording companies each own their own international distribution networks that also distribute records on behalf of other companies. The economic realities of their global operations mean that the records they distribute need to be ones likely to attract large-scale sales so that their high fixed costs can be covered. The products of smaller record companies and niche musical genres are unlikely to be taken on by the major international distribution companies, but may instead work with the independent sector or with major-label-owned or part-owned 'pseudo-independents'. The latter sector includes Fontana Distribution (Universal), RED Music (Sony), Alternative Distribution Alliance (Warner) and EMI Label Services/Caroline Distribution (EMI). Pseudo-independent distribution allows the major transnational companies to gain additional revenue from the local and regional independent recording sector and to promote their own 'niche artists' – those for whom a global campaign and mass sales are unlikely to be forthcoming, yet who have a significant subcultural, genre or fan following.

'True' independent distribution companies are ones that are not financially controlled or part-owned by a major recording company. They include national-level companies such as eOne Distribution (formerly Koch Entertainment) in the US and Proper Music Distribution in the UK, and smaller more regional organizations. Like the pseudo-independents, these companies work with smaller recording companies, and have a sales force and marketing drive that is geared towards niche music markets and lower levels of sales. Individual records may sell considerably fewer copies than those of the majors, yet taken together they can still yield an overall profit. Marketing and distribution can also be achieved by artists grouping together to do it themselves, though the Brazilian model of Fora do Eixo discussed in Box 5.1 has yet to be adopted more broadly.

Box 5.1
Fora do Eixo (Off-Axis)

Access to distribution can often be problematic for smaller, independent artists and labels. Many such artists sell their CDs at their live concerts, but access to a wider retail market can be difficult to attain. In order to address this issue, a network of independent music collectives in Brazil known as Fora do Eixo organize 'nomadic' CD and merchandise stores that are established at venues where bands within the network are performing. Rather than distributing their products into traditional stores, artists from around the country send their CDs, t-shirts, and other merchandise to a central hub, from which they are taken to various live events staged in different cities all over the country. A representative from the local Fora do Eixo collective will operate a stall at the gig of a live band. So for instance, one band might be playing in a small venue in Rio de Janeiro and that band's CDs and t-shirts are available for sale in the foyer, alongside the CDs of dozens of other bands from around the country. The collective takes a small percentage of the sales, as do the artists who are performing and have brought the crowd, but a large proportion of the revenue will return to the recording artist. While the sales figures for individual items at each gig may very often be small, the cumulative effect of sales across the many hundreds of gigs held across Brazil can be significant.

Territories and reciprocal agreements

In any given territory, music products are generally distributed via a single distribution company, so that retailers will not experience confusion regarding the sourcing of, and payment for, a particular release. Distributors will often cover more than one territory; with some having a worldwide reach. Independent distributors may have reciprocal agreements with distributors in other territories, whereby they will each distribute releases by the same record labels; nevertheless, it is more common for labels to negotiate distribution deals on a territory by territory basis. Geography and distance play a significant role in physical distribution, because for many labels, the cost of shipping to another country outweighs the potential benefits of any additional sales likely to result from distribution in that country. This is why licensing deals are more common (as discussed in Chapter 2).

Product tracking and counting

In order for distributors, retailers and record labels to keep track of the enormous numbers of products that move through their distribution systems, a sophisticated identification and record-keeping methodology has evolved over the years. This methodology relies upon a universal and standardized method of numbering and labelling each individual product as well as each individual song. This permits automated counting, tracking and reporting on sales, distribution and returns for retailers, labels and distributors. The main methods are bar codes, record label catalogue numbers, and International Standard Recording Codes (ISRCs).

Bar codes. Bar codes are usually printed on the album artwork of CDs and other products so that sales data can be scanned and tracked electronically at the point of sale. In order to have a standardized bar code on their products, a record company needs to be a member of a national bar code association, such as GS1UK and GS1US™ in the UK and US respectively, which each charge annual membership fees. There are several standards for bar codes, though the most widely used are the 12-digit UPC-A code (in the USA) and the 13-digit EAN-13 code (in the UK). According to the BPI *Guidelines on Barcoding* (2006a) EAN-13 identifies the country and company of origin, the product number for a particular recording, and the specific media format (CD, cassette, vinyl and so on). Bar codes are necessary to track sales through stores, and are assigned by the record label at the point of manufacture so that they can be integrated into the printing process. They are not, however, necessary for all types of release. Artists who sell their music directly to the public through their own websites (or as merchandise at their concerts) will not need a bar code on their products unless they are also distributing those products to retail stores.

Catalogue numbers. Record labels will usually also assign unique catalogue numbers for their own releases. Unlike bar codes, these are neither standardized nor centrally administered, and are allocated according to conventions established within a particular company. Commonly they consist of a series of characters followed by a series of numbers. For instance, the first Virgin Records vinyl album, Mike Oldfield's *Tubular Bells* (1973) was assigned the catalogue number V2001, with subsequent Virgin Records releases assigned V2002, V2003 and so on. Factory Records went a step further in the late 1970s by applying its FAC catalogue numbers to all of its albums, singles, films, posters, merchandise items, and so on. Catalogue numbers are used for convenience in a label's own record-keeping system, and as shorthand for referring to a particular release with complete clarity when dealing with a distributor. The catalogue number is traditionally printed on both the disc itself and the cover artwork (usually on the spine). This is helpful for those who manufacture the disc and assemble the packaging, and to distributors and labels for archiving and ease of identification.

International Standard Recording Codes (ISRCs). In addition to a bar code and a catalogue number for the physical release, each individual recorded track requires an ISRC: a unique and permanent 12-digit code that will not change no matter what physical product may contain the track. As the code relates solely to the sound recording it also remains unchanged should the recording change ownership or be re-released in other forms (for example, as part of a compilation album) (BPI, 2006b). As it identifies individual tracks rather than products, there is no conflict with the bar code and catalogue numbers that those products may also carry. ISRCs are not randomly allocated, but are obtained from a National ISRC agency such as Phonographic Performances Ltd in the UK and the Recording Industry Association of America (RIAA) in the USA. One of the main benefits of ISRC is that it allows automatic identification of recorded music tracks for the payment of royalties.

Pricing and promotion

Record distributors earn money by charging more as a wholesale price to retailers than they themselves pay for the same products from the record labels.

In other words, there is a mark-up added to the wholesale price before it reaches the record store, and this mark-up (or margin) is the revenue earned by the distributor. The margin is set by each individual distributor and negotiated with the record label, but it is usually in the region of 30 per cent (Singerman and Lockshin, 2007). Typically, a new album release is available to the retailer for around (if not exactly) 50 per cent of its retail list price, but pricing structures, mark-ups and margins can vary wildly, and there are some major exceptions that will be discussed below.

Distributors will actively promote certain releases to retailers, encouraging them to devote scarce shelf space to the products they are distributing and, where possible, giving them privileged placement within the store. The convention of labels paying distributors a margin on products sold emerged to encourage such promotional practices: the more products sold, the more revenue generated for the label, the retailer and the distributor. Incentivizing active promotion is therefore a strong reason for the use of commission-based remuneration rather than paying a flat service fee. Needless to say, those products given priority by the record labels are those given the greatest promotional push by the distributor. This is particularly evident in major-label owned distribution companies, so artist managers must work hard to ensure that the products of their particular acts are given priority. Similarly, independent record labels that distribute through a major-owned distribution company need to work hard to ensure that the distributor's sales teams actively promote their products, as they will be competing directly with the products of the major labels that own those distribution companies.

MASS-MARKET RETAILERS

The vast majority of physical music purchases take place within supermarkets and large department stores (super-retailers) such as Walmart in the United States and Tesco in the UK, which are two of the largest retailers of CDs in the world. Getting product into their stores is a key priority for most record labels seeking a mass-market for their products, but these stores handle distribution very differently to the rest of the music retail sector, and their sheer economic power can have significant effects on pricing.

Retailers' bargaining power

Simply put, mass-market super-retailers have size on their side. Mass purchasing and distribution through a nationwide chain of stores means that they can negotiate strongly to reduce their purchase price on CDs. At the same time, because CD sales are not their core business, they are able to use them as loss leaders. That is to say, Walmart and Tesco will often retail compact discs (and other entertainment products such as DVDs) at prices near to, or even lower than the wholesale prices they pay to the record companies. By undercutting their competitors they hope to attract consumers into their stores to buy other products too.

Furthermore, record companies are keen to get their products into the hands of as many consumers as possible, and so these super-retailers are able to bargain with the labels for lower wholesale prices than those offered to other retailers. This puts tension on the relationship between the major record companies and the supermarket chains, with the power balance favouring the retailers. This is because music retail has never been a core business for the retail giants, so the threat of them no longer stocking music, or of reducing the amount of retail space given over to music products, is a serious risk. Ever-reducing wholesale prices are a fundamentally unsustainable business model for the record companies, yet they need the supermarkets in order to reach the huge sales figures required to make profits on their recordings. In some cases, exclusivity deals have been brokered that give a retail chain the sole right to sell a particular album, or the sole right to sell it for a limited time period (following which the album can be distributed more widely). In some respects this may favour the record companies since these deals are often made on a 'no returns' or 'limited returns' basis, rather than on the usual terms of 'sale or return' (Baskerville and Baskerville, 2010: 296–7). Consequently, the retailer may be left with unsold stock that cannot be returned to the record company, yet the label will still have been paid for it.

The strategies of the major retailers can have a dramatic effect on the overall profitability and break-even sales point of major record releases, as well as on the ability of other retailers to compete and survive. For this reason, the large supermarket chains may actually pose a greater threat to traditional high street and independent record stores than the internet.

Centralization

From the point of view of distribution, it is important to note two key differences (other than size) between the super-retailers and the independent and smaller retailers. First, it is possible for the major record labels to distribute product to all Tesco stores (or all Walmart stores and so on) by supplying one central depot. The retailer handles their own distribution to their own stores with their own warehousing and supply assets and methodologies. In contrast, selling through independent stores requires distributors that can individually visit each store or consign goods via post or courier to each outlet. Second, the major retailers deal almost exclusively with the larger record companies. This is because, in part, it is simply not cost-effective for them to deal with the smaller labels, and in part because some independent record company products are released in such small quantities that they cannot provide stock to all stores within a chain. Primarily, however, it is because the major retailers are only interested in selling music that will attract large numbers of purchasers. In short, they are (like the major record labels) in the business of profit-maximization; they are not in the business of ensuring that popular music culture is equitably represented in the marketplace. As shelf space is a scarcity, 'hits' take priority.

Large chain stores

Large chain stores, such as HMV in the UK and F.Y.E. in the US, also enjoy some of the bulk purchasing power of the super-retailers. As specialists they can dedicate a far greater amount of shelf space to CDs than a generalist such as Walmart or Tesco, and as a result their stock is far more diverse. They are also much more likely to receive product from independent labels and distributors. It is significant, though, that as profits from CD sales have declined over time (in part due to reduced sales, and in part due to decreasing margins on each sale), these stores have tended to give proportionately more shelf space to other, related consumer items such as DVDs, games, t-shirts and memorabilia.

Online sales of physical product

Another route to market is via an internet store such as Amazon, whose business is primarily as an online retailer of physical goods. Amazon also sells MP3 files but in effect Amazon is a major retailer in much the same way that Walmart and Tesco are major retailers (and who also have online divisions). Amazon, however, has no physical stores. Instead, the store is a website, which potentially places it in the home of every music shopper, and means that Amazon is not subject to limited shelf space in the manner of a physical retailer. In effect, Amazon can stock anything and everything without consideration for where and how this will be accommodated within the retail space. The same is true of CD Baby – an online store that facilitates the sale of CDs produced by independent artists, and which also offers digital download and distribution services. Chris Anderson's book *The Long Tail* (2006) discusses the effect of this phenomenon, and notes the impact that this level of availability has on the overall sales of goods. In particular, the overall economic value of 'hits' to the retailer is challenged in size by the overall economic value of the less popular items, simply because of the sheer number of those items now available for sale. As large as they are, Walmart and Tesco are both unable and unwilling to stock in their physical stores every single item that could potentially be available for sale, as the economics (and scale) of physical retail simply do not allow it.

INDEPENDENT RETAILERS

In contrast to the multinational corporate super-retailers and national music chain stores are the independent record stores (sometimes known as 'mom and pop stores' in the US). These are small- to medium-sized high street retail outlets owned and run by an individual or family, or sometimes small groups of branded stores in a single geographic location. Independent record stores are not called that because they are sellers of independent records (although they regularly do that), but because they are independent from corporate ownership. As such, proprietors of these stores have a much greater degree of autonomy over what they do and do not sell than their counterpart in the local branch of a major department store. This does not mean that they simply 'sell what they like', but that they have the ability to focus on particular genres or on particular demographic communities. For instance, it is not unusual to find independent record stores that specialize in electronic dance music, classical music, or jazz.

The 'death' of the independent store?

The decline, as an economic and cultural force, of the independent music retail sector has been well documented (see Jones, 2010). In addition, record stores themselves have been nostalgically portrayed and romanticized within fiction (see Hornby, 1996), and lauded as a social context for the incubation and propagation of new popular music genres and subcultures (see Ogg, 2009). Yet we should be wary of generalizations when it comes to these independent stores. Each is different from the others by virtue of its clientele and local market, and even the particular tastes and idiosyncrasies of its proprietor. The rhetoric of the 'death' of the independent record store, while used to describe some very worrying trends for the owners, customers and fans of these stores, has been much overstated. While challenged and very much under threat from the economic realities of operating an increasingly niche business, it is important to note that some independent retailers are surviving and even thriving.

Online technologies have created not only problems for independent stores, but also opportunities. Websites such as Gemm.com, Discogs.com and Ebay.com provide a platform through which independent sellers of recorded music products can reach a global marketplace, while retaining their localism and individual character. There may be an overall trend of record store closures, but some continue to survive through a process of adaptation, increased specialization and innovative practices. Moreover, there is considerable support from musicians for independent retailers. For instance, an annual Record Store Day has been held in the US since 2007 and in the UK since 2009. Special merchandise and unique vinyl and CD releases are made available by numerous artists, some of whom also make in-store appearances or give one-off live performances in support of the event (see recordstoreday.co.uk and recordstoreday.com).

SECOND-HAND RETAILERS

Many physical recorded music products, such as LPs and CDs, have a commercial life well beyond that which produced direct revenues for the record label and artist. This is another reason why recorded music itself should be regarded as conceptually separate from the physical artefact or commodity that contains it. The fact is that if you tire of a record, or need to raise some extra cash, it is possible to convert your CD or vinyl record collection into money by trading it in to a second-hand store. Likewise, it is possible to purchase recorded music artefacts at a significant discount, and to find rare, deleted, collectible and otherwise-unavailable records for purchase.

The 'first-sale doctrine'

This exchange, trade and redistribution of physical product is only made possible by an act of law that allows for a limitation on copyright after the first sale of a lawfully made copy. The 'first-sale doctrine', as it is known in the United States, makes it possible for owners of records and CDs to re-sell them freely without needing to make a further payment to the copyright holders. The first-sale doctrine does not strictly apply in Europe, yet a similar legal framework is in place, which allows a legitimate market in second-hand records and CDs to exist. This is significant not only because of the sheer economic value of the second-hand record (and CD) market, but also because of the (current) impossibility and implausibility of a second-hand digital music market that could operate in a comparable manner.

An 'underground' economy

Many second-hand record stores sell a combination of new releases (sourced from record labels and their distributors) and previously owned records from individual consumers and other sources. Due to the nature of second-hand record stores (including charity shops that sell donated vinyl and CDs, and flea markets or car boot sales) their retail activities are not recorded in official music industry statistics. There is, therefore, a significant disconnect between the amount of money consumers spend in this underground economy each year and the quantity of sales and revenues reported in the accounts of record labels.

ONLINE MUSIC DISTRIBUTION

Digital distribution of recorded music is an important area of analysis. The differing ways that these distributors operate, and the extent to which they generate revenue for the industry, are subjects of much debate in public discourse. Moreover, such discourses are increasingly driving public policy regarding copyright legislation and regulation of the internet. It is also an important area for examining how people discover, purchase and make meaning from music, and how they order, share and experience it (see Chapter 8). Indeed, understanding digital distribution is central to an understanding of the changes that are affecting the entire ecology of the music industries in the twenty-first century, as traditional notions of distribution and retail are changing considerably.

Distribution as administration

One way of thinking about online distribution is to consider the institutions involved. For instance, Apple's iTunes Store has become a significant (if not the most significant) online analogue to physical retailers. So in consideration of digital distribution, as opposed to physical distribution, it is possible to think of iTunes as one of the key destinations that record labels wish their music to be placed. Of course, getting music from a record label to iTunes does not involve mass production of discs, warehousing, moving things around in trucks, or any of the other things that we associate with physical distribution of recorded music. In fact, digital distributors require only one copy of a music file in order to distribute that recording to a wide range of music retailers, including the iTunes Store. Because of the nature of digital media, the recorded file is endlessly and perfectly replicable, so distribution becomes more of an administrative activity than it is a process of moving things from place to place.

While the technologies and processes are radically different, there is still a need for specialist industry knowledge, and this allows new types of middlemen and new kinds of music business to emerge and fulfil these roles. Typically, digital distributors are not physical distributors who have learnt a new skill or offered a new service, but entirely new entrants to the marketplace or newly created divisions of existing companies such as the major record labels. This is especially significant when considering the changing nature of the music industries in the age of digital media. While it is common to think of online retailers as being like physical retailers, and online distributors as being like physical distributors, from the point of view of professional practices they are engaged in almost none of the same activities as their predecessors.

How does digital distribution work?

Digital distributors (or digital aggregators, as they are sometimes known) build relationships with a range of different online music retailers, and work with the systems, formats, and reporting procedures used by them to ensure that music recordings are made available for sale. The most prominent companies offering digital distribution are The Orchard, CD Baby, Ditto Music and TuneCore, yet these businesses operate business models that can vary greatly. Each organization has its own methodology for managing, distributing and working with the catalogues of its clients. For instance, TuneCore is designed as a one-stop tool for artists and record labels to distribute their music to a host of online stores and streaming sites. In contrast, Ditto Music takes a more hands-on approach by offering other services such as promotion and marketing. The retailer and the distributor will normally take a percentage per sale, though some digital distributors charge set-up and maintenance fees instead, or offer additional services.

Local specificity

It is important to remember that even in an age of connectivity, global distribution and online services, music businesses are largely organized at the level of the nation-state. Release schedules for an album can differ from country to country, and licensing deals can mean that some releases are under the control of different organizations in different geographical contexts. There is no technical reason why the iTunes store or Spotify should be regional, but licences with major record labels mean that the online service necessarily differs from place to place, and some recordings may not be available to purchase (or stream) in certain countries. This regional variation may also be used to facilitate different marketing campaigns in different places in order to accommodate local tastes and industry practices.

Unlimited inventory

The main online retail sites, such as iTunes, prefer to deal with digital aggregators and distributors rather than with individual bands or labels. This greatly simplifies their accounting procedures, especially if we consider the effects of the 'long tail' (Anderson, 2006). In the digital realm, there is unlimited inventory as digital files take up no physical space except as data files recorded onto computer hard drive, and there are inevitably a large number of files that are only rarely, if ever, downloaded. It is highly inefficient for an online retailer to have to manage and monitor individual distribution deals in relation to all of those files on the off chance that they are actually purchased through its store. Indeed, it is also rather inefficient for digital distributors to maintain and administer a broad range of music genres, artists and labels. This has led to the development of companies that service particular musical niches and that build focused catalogues of music in order to target specific types of retailer, website and consumer. This suggests that the long tail can only work beneficially where there is marketing or other support to guide potential consumers towards music that they might not otherwise be aware of. This issue will be considered again in Chapter 6.

Music recommender systems

One of the problems of an unlimited inventory is that it becomes difficult for consumers to discover new music amongst the many millions of individual songs that are available to them. A solution to this problem is to introduce music recommender systems that can suggest appropriate songs to listen to, or automatically add those songs to an online stream. Three main systems are in place (see Celma, 2010 for a full discussion), which are used by a host of recommendation services (see Box 5.2).

Box 5.2
Types of music recommender system

Content-based filtering systems collect and collate descriptive information about the audio content of songs. This is then used alongside data collected about individuals' service usage to suggest appropriate songs. The internet radio service Pandora uses a system of this sort, and describes individual songs in terms of nearly 400 separate attributes. One problem of this system is that it could recommend songs that are too similar to music that the listener already knows.

Collaborative filtering systems work by comparing an individual's music preferences to those of other users to make suggestions based on similarities and differences between them. They are used, amongst many others, by the internet radio service Last.fm and by the online retailer Amazon. A key criticism of this system is that it works poorly for new or occasional users, since there is little information about their listening habits.

Context-based filtering systems, such as that used by the music intelligence company The Echo Nest, use data extracted from web mining and social tagging including online reviews, ratings, blogs, charts and so on to examine similarities between songs at a cultural rather than an audio level. One problem with this system is that its reliance on web mining means that lesser known or new artists with little online discussion will be described in a less full manner than well-known artists, so are less likely to be recommended.

In practice, many sites use elements of two or more of these recommender systems in hybrid approaches.

Direct-to-fan distribution

The internet also enables individual artists and record labels to become retailers themselves, either on their own websites or using online services designed to facilitate the sale of recorded music. Two primary examples of the latter are Bandcamp and Topspin. Bandcamp allows artists to create their own page on the Bandcamp website, and then advertise, host and sell their music online at prices controlled by the artist. In return, Bandcamp receives a small proportion of the sales revenue generated. Topspin offers an alternative model by providing e-commerce tools that can be integrated into an artist's own website. Again, Topspin charges for this, but because of the largely 'hands off' nature of this kind of distribution, the fee is much lower than would be expected if a digital aggregator and a retailer were to be involved. Despite these alternatives, the overwhelming majority of online music sales still occur through online music retailers such as iTunes.

STREAMING SERVICES

In addition to online retail, there has been a marked growth in other methods of online music distribution that less closely resemble traditional retail models. For instance, We 7, Spotify, Deezer, Pandora and many others are music delivery platforms that offer advertising supported (ad-supported) music streaming services. That is to say, instead of paying for permanent downloads of recordings of music, consumers listen to music that is 'streamed' online. This is analogous to listening to music on the radio, though a consumer can choose his or her own playlists of music, or allow the web service's music recommendation system to select songs based on his or her listening preferences. When listening to the music, advertising messages will be inserted into the audio stream or be shown on the web service's internet page. The business model that underpins these services is called a three-part or two-sided market (Anderson, 2009: 252), where the online platform (the website) serves both listeners and advertisers (its two markets). In such cases, the advertisers are paying for the service that the listener receives for free. In return, the advertisers gain access to a targeted audience and hope to convert that access into future sales through direct links to their own websites. They may also receive statistical information about audiences, which can assist in future planning, targeting and marketing.

A legitimate alternative to music piracy?

Ad-supported music streaming services are a relatively new phenomenon, but they may help to reduce internet piracy by offering a legitimate way to access broad catalogues of music online. The major recording companies were initially reticent in licensing their music to these services, but have now embraced the potential of the streaming model – even though revenues from these services are relatively small. Many of the services offer additional paid features, such as sub-scriptions that remove the advertisements or permit access to the service via an internet-enabled mobile phone. The services may also link through to retail sites so that listeners can legally purchase the music that they have listened to. As with other online music systems, effective marketing and music recommendation systems are required to make the most of any potential 'long tail' effect, which is why such companies are now seeking alliances with social media platforms such as Facebook that can offer an online version of 'word of mouth' advertising.

MUSIC MEDIA DISTRIBUTION

We will discuss music in media such as radio, television and the press in Chapter 6, yet we should be clear that music distribution outside of a live context always occurs through processes of mediation. By mediation, we mean that music is communicated by its inclusion in some sort of transmissible or transportable form. Compact discs are a form of media, as are radio broadcasts, television and films, and so on. Rather than simply being a platform for promotion, these media environments are ways through which music companies distribute their music to audiences and, importantly, extract revenues by doing so. While it may seem that a radio listener is not paying for the music he or she is consuming, there are in fact a number of processes at work to ensure financial compensation for copyright holders (in much the same way as the online streaming services noted above). The law surrounding copyright will be discussed further in Chapter 9, so this section focuses on how music delivery and distribution via media platforms can generate revenue streams for the music industries.

Public performance and synchronization

When music is publicly performed, whether live, on the radio or in television programmes and movies, the broadcaster or programme/film-maker must make payments for the use of that music. This is because the use of music 'adds value' to the experience and helps attract audiences and revenues to the media outlet. For instance, commercial radio stations charge money for advertising. Those advertisers seek to connect with large numbers of people, so in effect commercial radio is in the business of selling access to audiences, and those audiences are attracted through the provision of music. Over time, financial settlements have been reached that vary between different places around the world, but which ensure that a proportion of the money made by the commercial radio stations is returned to the music industries (see Chapter 9 on public performance royalties).

Audiences may believe that the music they consume through media channels such as commercial radio is effectively 'free', yet they are actually paying for it by listening to advertising (it is another example of a two-sided market). Music distributed by its inclusion in films, computer games and other media is also deemed to 'add value' to the overall experience, hence usage fees and/or royalties (known as 'synchronization fees') will need to be paid to the relevant copyright holders. These fees are generally the subject of negotiation, hence highly variable, though television channels in the UK have organized blanket licences to keep costs down and administration simpler.

UNAUTHORIZED DISTRIBUTION

Distribution is a vital part of the music industries, yet not all forms of music dis- tribution are welcomed. In particular, peer-to-peer and BitTorrent distribution methodologies (see also Chapter 9) facilitate the unauthorized distribution of copyrighted music, and are viewed as highly problematic. Yet, the technologies in themselves are not illegal (in the same way that photocopiers are not illegal even though they are often used in breach of copyright), and some artists and websites have even used them legally. Examples include Digital Global Mobile (the progressive rock band King Crimson's online shop), the social media sites Facebook and Twitter (for server updates) and the online games developer Bliz- zard Entertainment (for patch updates to its games).

Public discourse about file-sharing tends to focus on whether piracy is theft and if people who download or upload music through unauthorized channels should be punished in one way or another. Sometimes, the discussion centres around whether the corporate music industries are attempting to over-reach the boundaries of what is fair, or whether changes in technology 'make people' behave in certain ways online. We must, therefore, distinguish between discussions about technologies of distribution and those about the ethics, morality and legality of how those technologies are used.

CONCLUSION

Music distribution practices are a complex and interesting area of the music indus- tries. Distribution takes place through a wide range of mediation methodologies with some having an informal dimension to them. Moreover, distribution does not simply mean distribution for sale, but encompasses practices such as online streaming and music media synchronization, though, as with radio, there is still a strong commercial dimension to many forms of 'not for sale' music distribution.

FURTHER READING

Graham Jones is one of the founders of the British independent music distributor Proper Music, and his *Last Shop Standing: Whatever Happened to Record Shops?* (2009) offers an entertaining and personal tale of the history, decline and survival of independent record stores in the UK. Chris Anderson's *The Long Tail* (2006) is useful for understanding the commercial impacts of unlimited inventory made possible by online music storage, while his *Free* (2009) discusses the ways that ad-supported and other internet-based services may use the public perception of music as 'free' for commercial and marketing ends.

6

MUSIC PROMOTION

Music promotion, and its intersections with marketing, media, sponsorship, retail and the internet, has taken an increasingly central position within the music industries. The unlimited inventory of the internet and the ease with which artists can record, release and distribute music mean that it has become more difficult for record companies and artists to get their message across. This chapter discusses the management of promotional campaigns and the changing operations of both traditional and online media.

KEY FINDINGS

- Music industry gatekeepers are increasingly augmented by fans as opinion leaders.
- The volume and immediacy of music on the internet has resulted in a multitude of potentially viable niche markets.
- There are symbiotic relationships between music companies, advertisers, sponsors and media.
- Traditional music media are losing some of their power base to interactive Web 2.0 media.

MARKETING, BRANDING AND GATEKEEPING

Marketing and market segmentation

In general terms marketing is about 'satisfying customer needs or desires' and requires that a company defines and understands both its potential 'market' and the 'needs' of that market (Hull et al., 2011: 229). This is in some ways more difficult for the music industries, since their primary product, recorded music, is characterized by emotional and experiential responses/needs rather than strictly utilitarian ones. In addition, consumer preferences and markets can be difficult to predict and define. Nevertheless the music industry seeks to define its market through musical genres (like rock, rap and country) and demographics (including age, gender, ethnicity, income and geography). This kind of categorization allows for market segmentation and the demarcation of target markets: sets of consumers who are believed to share common characteristics and/or common needs (Baskerville and Baskerville, 2010: 305). A clear example of this market segmentation can be seen in the system of commercial radio formats used in the US (discussed later).

Branding

Marketing is closely connected to the concept of branding. In its most basic form branding is a symbol, name or logo that differentiates one product from another, yet branding is far more complex than this. The brand name and logo imbue a product with a broader set of meanings: the brand is, therefore, a shorthand for expressing a wider set of values that link to the beliefs, interests and needs of consumers. The question becomes: does the brand owner's conception of its own brand value (its identity as a brand) match consumer perceptions of that brand (its image)?

The gap between brand identity and brand image can be adversely affected by matters beyond the brand owner's control. For example, British soul singer Craig David's core brand identity was located around his position as a multi-Grammy Award winning songwriter, while his outward image became defined by third party intervention: the comedian Leigh Francis, who frequently mocked David on his television sketch show *Bo' Selecta!*. David's brand image was altered among his British audience and despite several attempts by his management and record label, his brand identity remains some distance from its image. Of course, where the music industries are concerned, it is not only third parties who affect the brand. As artists are effectively their own brands, their personal and professional activities may also damage, change or in some cases enhance their public image.

The marketing mix

The 'marketing mix' is a range of activities, tools and strategies that a company uses in order to communicate with and satisfy the perceived needs of a defined target market (Brassington and Pettitt, 2006). Various models have been created to help organize and manage those activities including the 'extended marketing mix' – see Box 6.1.

Box 6.1
The extended marketing mix

The extended marketing mix was introduced by Bernard Booms and Mary Bitner (1980) and builds upon an earlier '4Ps' model (product, price, place and promotion) developed by E. Jerome McCarthy (1960). Three additional elements (people, physical evidence and process) were added to focus attention on service industry aspects of marketing. The full '7Ps' model is outlined below:

- Product – all aspects of product development and design (including intangible services), such as brand name, image, genre, and packaging. New products should be appealing, cost-effective to produce and different from the competition.
- Price – the amount of money (or time) a consumer is willing to exchange to receive a product/service. For instance, decisions about how to price CDs, downloads and concert tickets, or calculations regarding advertising income to be received from consumers clicking on banner advertisements (known as 'click-throughs').
- Place – distribution or delivery of a product/service to the consumer. This may relate to the choice of physical and online retail spaces, to concert and festival venues and so on.
- Promotion – using a variety of tactics to inform people about the existence of a product/service and to motivate them to consume it. These tactics are discussed in greater detail later in this chapter.
- People – some products/services are delivered by people, and the influence of those people on the consumption experience should not be overlooked. For instance, a poor live performance by an artist may stop audience members from attending another concert by that performer, while overly aggressive security staff at a venue may deter some people from returning to that venue.
- Physical evidence – in the music industries, physical evidence of a service may include, for example, physical merchandise like a ticket stub from a concert, or a wristband from a festival.
- Process – this idea refers to the manner in which a service is managed. For instance: whether there are long queues to gain entrance to an event or on-site bar, the ease with which a download can be bought and delivered to the purchaser, or the arrangements that have been made for dealing with customer complaints.

The extended marketing mix can be criticized for not focusing enough on the consumer and for not being entirely applicable to digital products, yet it is still useful in helping companies think through the different elements of their campaigns and to plan appropriately. It is also useful as a research tool for understanding how campaigns have been organized and managed.

Gatekeeping

Drawn from media studies, gatekeeping is a filtering process through which 'gatekeepers' make key decisions and/or control the flow of information between producers and consumers. Gatekeeping can be seen throughout the music industries (see, for example, Hirsch, 1990) in activities like A&R managers selecting new artists, the prioritization of certain artists over others when allocating production budgets, and the international department deciding who is likely to 'travel well' (see Chapter 2) and so be supported in non-domestic markets. In this chapter we are interested in gatekeeping processes related to promotional activities, and in particular the need to influence key opinion leaders or taste-makers: those who are situated between the music industries and the public.

The gatekeeping relationship between music industry professionals and key media content producers (taste-makers) sits at the core of promotional campaigns. Taste-makers are identified by press and promotions teams as individuals with high 'subcultural capital' (Thornton, 1995) within their music scene or genre market: in other words, those with an in-depth knowledge of, or relationship with, a particular scene or genre, and whose opinion is likely to influence others. Press and promotions personnel subsequently groom these taste-makers through a high level of personalized attention, which may include the provision of rare promotional items, invitations to exclusive parties and increased access to an artist. The aim is to make the taste-maker a compliant gatekeeper who will promote the record company's acts.

Taste-makers include freelance music journalists, magazine and newspaper editors, radio and television presenters and producers, club DJs, independent record store owners, internet bloggers, and any other people considered to be in a position to influence public opinion and/or the editorial content of media presentations. For the promotions industries this system has proven effective in promoting new artists and new scenes through which artists may be promoted.

THE PROMOTIONAL CAMPAIGN

In larger record companies, the promotional campaign will be created and managed by a product manager working within the company's product development or artist relations/artist services department. The product manager will coordinate the campaign across a number of departments and/or with external publicists and other companies. This process may even begin prior to an act being signed, as the potential of an act to gain press, radio and television coverage may be an important determinant in the decision of whether to sign or not (Negus, 1992: 64).

Where the promotional campaign is handled 'in-house' (entirely within the record company structure), the promotional budget will not usually be recoupable from the artist, but if external parties are employed, the costs are likely to be either part or wholly recoupable (Harrison, 2011: 214). It is important for the success of the campaign that the materials created by each department or external organization support the same overall promotional messages about the artist and product. The project team will therefore discuss the musical style, direction, visual identity and potential audience of an act, as well as the most relevant promotional techniques and media to target (Negus, 1992: 64).

Visual identity

An artist's visual identity is often fundamental within the genres of pop and rock, as magazine/internet coverage and promotional video are critical marketing routes and rely heavily on the visual to attract interest. A concise image can represent an act's 'entire identity and music' and 'articulate the authenticity and uniqueness of an artist' (Negus, 1992: 72). Franco Fabbri (1982) suggests that image is also an essential aspect in our understanding of musical genres. This extra-musical aspect of genre identification extends into the design, photography and iconography used in every aspect of a campaign. Image is as essential for major artists as it is to new or emerging talent since it relates directly to the target market and the need to both match expectations and provide difference. For some artists, such as Madonna, Lady Gaga or Kylie Minogue, image can be a major driver for press coverage.

News value

Promotional campaigns in support of new products (album or singles, concert tours, DVD releases and so on) are driven by notions of 'news value', and so are dictated by the demands of news-driven media – whether that media is a television or radio programme, a major daily newspaper, a weekly or monthly magazine, or a website. Fresh and engaging news angles are required to target appropriate media for debuting acts, as well as to revitalize previously established careers: in essence, answering the question 'what makes this artist or release special and newsworthy?' To this end, a series of promotional tools are produced by the press office, promotions division and creative video department.

The press office (or publicity department)

The press office supplies artist biographies in which the news value, or angle, of an artist or product is clearly defined. Subsequent press releases extend, or underline this angle, and can form the focus of an attention-grabbing headline. Each press release gives full contact information, answers the questions of who, what, when, where, why and how (Hutchison and Allen, 2010: 212), and guides journalists and commissioning editors towards the angle that the press officer wants highlighting.

   The aim of the press officer is to get maximum coverage in multiple publications during or in the immediate lead-up to the week that a record is released.

An up-to-date database of quality contacts is perhaps the most important tool to develop (Hutchison and Allen, 2010: 210) so that press releases and press kits (incorporating the biography, discography, promotional photographs, videos and notable reviews/statistics) can be disseminated in a timely and effective manner.

The promotions division

The promotions division produce Audio EPKs (electronic press kits) in which an audio interview with an artist is recorded, but all questions removed. The recording is disseminated to radio show producers, who can program an interview with the artist based on a selection of pre-recorded answers. The radio presenter reads questions from a script and plays the recorded answers to create the illusion of the artist being present. Audio EPKs are particularly prevalent in the process of breaking an artist in non-domestic territories since they offer a cost-effective illusion of 'live' presence within those territories. The promotions division may also request radio edits and remixes of tracks that are constructed to support the specialist programming and consumer tastes of different territories or consumer segments. For instance, it is not uncommon for entirely different edits of songs to be created for mainstream US and European territories, or for 'club' remixes of pop and rock tracks to be created. The edits and remixes are supplied by the A&R department and can give the artist access to new and broader audiences.

Creative video

The creative video department commissions videos for individual tracks, or occasionally entire albums. These videos are subsequently used to gain exposure on television channels or through online social media channels such as YouTube and Vimeo. The same department also commissions and supplies audio-visual versions of EPKs in the form of short (normally 11 minutes long) documentary-style films, which are available to television channels to broadcast for free. These have become a staple of the late night schedule of the British terrestrial television station Channel 4, which broadcasts them on condition that they do not appear to simply be adverts for new products.

Free promotional items

In support of these creative tools a number of associated free items will be produced for use across all divisions. These range from low cost items like artist/product branded t-shirts and hooded sweatshirts, to expensive items such as snowboards, games consoles and signed lithographs of album artwork. These campaign-related promotional items can subsequently become highly collectable, and through resale at occasionally inflated rates, may continue to underline an artist's cultural value.

Club promotions

The club division makes selective use of the above tools, but primarily focuses on supplying upfront mixes (traditionally known as 'white labels') to key DJs. These mixes will often be exclusive to the club campaign and may never receive official release from the act's label. In this situation, selected club DJs are recognized as taste-makers whose support can produce a future chart hit. Underlying this kind of gatekeeping activity is one of the defining ideologies of the dance music industry: its need to remain at the cutting edge of the popular music zeitgeist. The upfront mix is an essential tool in this process, as it allows DJs to play tracks that have not yet been released commercially. Clubbers often follow the trends and trajectories suggested by opinion-leading DJs and their response to a mix will indicate its potential value for the record company. As such, the upfront mix is both a test marketing exercise and a chance for DJs and clubbers to gain the kudos (or subcultural capital) of hearing something first.

The divided campaign

Each part of the promotional campaign should be coordinated to ensure that the same messages about an artist/product are given through each promotional route and do not contradict each other. In practice, this might not always be the case. For instance, when commissioning a video, a number of directors may be asked to pitch their ideas (or 'treatments') for a particular song. In so doing, they bring an autonomous creative vision to the project that may be at odds with the campaign as a whole.

The campaign may also lose cohesion when the practices above are extended to the global scale. The major recording companies are structured as a series of markets (or 'territories') that may each have their own priorities. A local promotional team may feel it necessary to adapt a campaign from another market to suit the perceived promotional needs of its particular territory, so moving away from the original vision. The internet has brought these differences to sharp focus since global campaigns are necessary for artists to exploit specific consumer niches. Accordingly, global coordination has become more important than in the past. We can see this not only through the street-level global marketing of underground artists like The Prodigy, but also through the mass media impact of major mainstream global Disney stars like Selena Gomez. In each case, every aspect of the promotional campaign is carefully constructed and managed to optimize potential consumer markets.

MUSIC JOURNALISM

On the face of it music journalism appears to be the act of writing reviews, feature articles and news stories about music and musicians, yet as Tara Brabazon suggests, 'it is writing that grants meaning, importance, relevance and the survival of sounds' (2011: 36). It connects audiences to music and helps create artistic and commercial value for particular artists and releases. Despite this, there has been relatively little popular music scholarship about the field (Jones, 2002: 1) and even less about the intersection between music journalists and the music industries. Notable exceptions include Eamonn Forde (2001), who investigated music journalists' relationships with record company press officers, and Matt Brennan (2006), who explored musicians' perceptions of the role of the music press. This section addresses both print and online music journalism and the role of the journalist as taste-maker.

The development of rock and pop music criticism

Professional rock and pop music journalism emerged in the 1960s with writers positioning themselves as 'enlightened fans' (Lindberg et al., 2005: 60) who developed a countercultural ideology of rock criticism (Frith, 1981). This ideology placed emphasis on 'authenticity and originality' and considered rock music to have artistic value (Atton, 2009: 53), especially in contrast to 'throwaway' pop music. At the same time, some music journalists presented their own work as similarly authentic and original, and these 'personality journalists' or 'name journalists', such as Lester Bangs, Nick Kent and Everett True attained a fame that rivalled that of the artists they wrote about.

During the 1970s and 1980s in the UK, freelance journalists and editorial staff of magazines such as *NME* and *Melody Maker* considered themselves to be a part of the Left-leaning, alternative, underground activist media, despite the fact that they were published by a global corporation. However, by the 1990s, music journalists were conforming to standardized homogenous writing styles, especially in adult-oriented rock magazines (Forde, 2001). The highly personalized and individualistic style of the name journalists was lost (Atton, 2009), yet the romantic illusion of music journalism persevered through the process of 'synthetic personalization' (Talbot, 2007). Here, journalists engage in an illusory conversation with their readership implicit to which is the unspoken acceptance that the journalist is living the fans' dream. To acknowledge the music journalist's professional role within the context of the wider music industries is to shatter this illusion but, as Simon Frith notes, a journalist's work is almost always 'determined by companies' publicity and promotion plans, tied to support record releases and concert tours' (1981: 173).

Fanzines

Fanzines are important for promoting music communities and gatekeeping music tastes; and, as Simon Frith has suggested, they may be regarded as 'central to the history of rock criticism' (2002: 240). Rock music fanzines emerged in the late 1960s, and were typically written, compiled and designed with no financial recompense. This position promoted a sense of authenticity of opinion and fanzines quickly became a fundamental expression for music fans. Indeed, authenticity is essential to the ideological position of fanzines where critical opinion is assumed not to have been bought through industry favour or financial reward.

Fanzines enable 'a democratic conversation between music lovers, a social celebration of a particular kind of musical attention and commitment' (Frith, 2002: 243). As such, fanzines have become synonymous with the early mediation of new subcultures and scenes. For example, *Sniffin' Glue* covered early British punk bands as well as rock bands considered authentic by the punk scene (Perry, 2000), while American hardcore and punk was discussed in *Maximum RocknRoll* (Waltz, 2005). Although fanzines are most often associated with punk, others genres have close links to non-professional publications, including riot grrrl, progressive rock and dance music's rave scene (see Leonard, 2007; Atton, 2001; and Waltz, 2005 respectively). In each case music audiences were able find coverage of emerging or marginalized music cultures that were not covered by commercial magazines.

In the mid-2000s a number of highly stylized fanzines (known as prozines) emerged in the face of internet activity. These discussed marginalized music in a format usually associated with the mainstream press and subsequently gained considerable advertising support from a music industry seeking to access niche audiences. Examples include Everett True's *Every Good Boy Deserves Favour* and *Loose Lips Sink Ships* by music journalist Stevie Chick and photographer Steve Gullick. Fanzines have now been surpassed by ezines (online fanzines) and personal blogs as the primary expression of the fan voice (discussed later).

Record companies and the press: a symbiotic relationship

The relationship between the music press and the recording industries may be described as symbiotic (Negus, 1992: 125). Magazines need music to write about in order to attract the advertising income that supports them, while record companies need magazines to positively promote their products. To convince magazine journalists and editors to give coverage to their acts, the press departments of record companies (or independent publicists working on behalf of a company) may offer 'freebies'. These range from free CDs and entry to gigs and festivals, to free clothing and all-expenses-paid trips to any number of countries where an artist might be touring. Despite claims that the critic's opinion is being bought in this process (Marr, 2004), the promotional 'freebie' is represented as acceptable compensation in a low paid job role (Frith, 1981) and has become part of the myth of the music journalist (Mueller, 1999).

Perhaps more importantly, a record company press office may commission a journalist who has given a positive review of an artist to write album sleeve notes, an artist's Twitter feed and Facebook page, or a press biography (or EPK) in support of that artist's promotional campaign. The biography will, as noted earlier, use the artist's story and promotional campaign to suggest interesting or newsworthy angles for magazine features, and so encourage magazine editors to commission features that naturally follow the focus of the record company campaign. In following the chosen angles, the journalist and commissioning editor will buy further favour from the press office. This is perhaps most clearly seen in the 'new artist' sections of music magazines where the commissioning editor will promote new artists at the request of a press officer in return for access to higher-profile artists. What emerges is a trading system that sees magazines and journalists extending their brand value through association with a range of cutting edge and established artists. Artists similarly develop their cultural capital through association with key taste-maker journalists and magazines.

The death of the printed music magazine

With occasional exceptions, a downward trend has been a feature of the music magazine market since the 1990s. It is tempting to relate this decline to the growth of the internet, which has increasingly become the first choice destination for consumers looking for news and reviews. Yet it would be overly simplistic to argue that the internet is responsible for the death of the music magazine and the end of the music critic, since the print media were under threat long before the internet emerged as a 'millennial cultural force' (Sterne, 1999: 258).

One of the key reasons for this is a shift in the editorial stance of newspapers and broader entertainment and lifestyle magazines. Writing in 1981, James Curran discussed research by newspaper publishers which showed that current affairs news appealed to a limited market of older men, while human interest and entertainment features appealed to both women and younger men. Consequently, newspapers began to target wider audiences with texts such as music and the lives of musicians that 'have a universal appeal, transcending differences of sex, age and class' (Curran, 1999: 720). This process became especially clear in mid-1990s Britain when the genre of Britpop gained regular coverage in daily newspapers, lifestyle magazines and specialist titles. Its almost universal appeal meant that demand for access to artists outstripped supply and availability. It became normal for the biggest artists to undertake only two interviews with music magazines per territory in their campaigns: typically for *NME* and *Q* in the UK. As a result, bands came to be seen as the 'property' of these dominant titles, which made it difficult for other magazines to compete.

The 1990s also saw changes in the contracts available to freelance journalists. In particular, the ability to syndicate (sell) stories to more than one magazine was eroded and then largely removed. This development significantly impacted potential income streams for freelancers and led to 'name journalists' moving to broadsheet newspapers instead.

Print magazines, advertising and homogenization

Music magazines are not only tied into relationships with record companies; they must also answer to advertisers whose revenues financially support them.

Advertisers use magazines to target particular demographic groups, so need magazines to feature stories and reviews that are appropriate, attractive and interesting to their target demographic. This system means that magazines have to work closely with record company press departments to gain relevant content, which puts the balance of power in favour of the recording industry. Critical reviews may be stifled since access to higher-profile artists will often be on condition that lesser-known artists on the label's roster are featured and given a positive reception. This kind of bartering may create a sense of homogenization across the music press since the same artists appear to be getting coverage all the time, a process compounded by declining music magazine circulations. Press officers may feel unable to justify the time needed to work with music magazines when greater impact may be achieved through newspapers and lifestyle magazines.

Online magazines and ezines

In the mid-1990s major and independent music magazines began developing online presences that allowed them to explore the possibilities of audio and audio-visual presentation. At first they followed the same processes as their print counterparts with similar power relations between press and advertising departments. Within this context the critic's role as taste-maker remained critical to the promotion of new music while the editorial hierarchy and its relationship with the music business dictated content. In this sense, online magazines were often little more than an extension of their print counterparts. Even early internet-only magazines, such as Playlouder.com, followed the print magazine structure of heavy reliance on name band features, new music reviews and critic-driven content.

The 1990s also saw the emergence of online fanzines (or ezines), including artist-focused sites, where artists could break news and provide key information directly to fans. For these artists, official websites became important promotional spaces that lay outside the gatekeeping practices of the traditional press and gave direct contact to highly targeted niche markets. Artists have increasingly developed their own websites to do this (initially through platforms such as MySpace), but there is always the problem of 'preaching to the converted'. Ezines are therefore useful in exposing new or non-mainstream artists to new readers/listeners who may then be motivated to visit official artist websites.

Interactivity, Web 2.0 and the rise of the blog critic

The promotional possibilities of the internet expanded further with the arrival of a set of developments commonly referred to as Web 2.0. The term refers to the growth of read–write applications that foster interactivity and communication between users, such as social networking and blogs. This differs from what is retrospectively termed Web 1.0 where websites were largely read-only and under the control of a single webmaster. Under Web 2.0, it is possible for multiple users to upload (and in some cases edit) information and content to a single site, and for sites to be automatically updated via 'feeds' from other sites.

Ezines, blogs, message boards and so on have become important promotional targets for record companies and artists at all levels. Individual artists can talk to and directly interact with fans, while record companies may attempt grassroots promotion (discussed later) by using messages to create and foster interest in an artist. An artist that is successfully promoted in this way can gain credibility and authenticity in a manner analogous to the notion of 'paying your dues' in the live music industry.

Internet blogs have, perhaps, become the primary driving force in online publishing and journalism. Independent blogs in particular represent a powerful critical voice that echoes the non-commercial ideology of the fanzine (Frith, 2002). A number of artist-, genre- or theme-based blogs, eased from commercial pressure, have found critics able to express their opinions again, in addition to allowing space for readers' comments to be freely published in response. The resulting conversation can result in an angry exchange of views (a 'flamewar'), though this is in itself an effective tool for raising interest among a niche consumer base. The rising importance of the blog critic has led, perhaps inevitably, to music promoters providing the same kinds of exclusive content and free products that were once the preserve of the mainstream printed press, and with the same anticipated outcomes: positive reviews and editorials. Furthermore, campaigns may be built using music industry insiders, or 'weasels' (as they are sometimes known), who use message boards and blogs to drive grassroots conversations about artists and products.

RADIO

Music radio continues to be a 'key channel for promotion and one of the main ways in which we experience popular music' (Wall, 2003: 114; see also Howard, 2011). This section focuses primarily on the US and UK radio industries, the role of the weekly sales and airplay charts and the impact of content quotas.

US radio industry

In the US, commercial music stations are formatted according to genre and demarcated by terms such as R&B, country, rock, hip hop, gospel, Latin and Christian. Within these terms are further divisions; for example, within the 'rock' format there is adult oriented rock (AOR), adult contemporary (AC) and adult album alternative (AAA).

Each commercial radio format has been established to deliver 'very specifically defined audiences to advertisers' (Negus, 1992: 102), which may relate to both demographics and geography. As Keith Negus (1992) notes, the practice of formatting may affect both the fortunes of artists and record company practices. For instance, artists may become defined according to particular formats. This characterization may in turn limit their cross-over potential to other audiences by affecting how record company personnel think about and work with them. Some artists may even fail to be signed because they do not readily fit an existing radio format and so are difficult to promote. In other cases, promotional campaigns may be targeted geographically or multiple mixes of a song produced to target different radio formats.

Since the 1990s, labels and artists have enjoyed increasing levels of success with so-called 'cross-over' artists and genres, where music may be playlisted on more than one radio format at the same time. For instance, 'Latin' music acts like Ricky Martin, Jennifer Lopez and Enrique Iglesias as well as 'Classical' acts like Il Divo, Katherine Jenkins and Russell Watson have all seen mainstream pop success. In the US, the country music genre has been especially successful in creating cross-over artists, from Shania Twain, Garth Brooks and Faith Hill in the 1990s to Taylor Swift and Lady Antebellum in the 2000s.

The US also has a series of non-commercial radio networks, which are funded primarily through sponsorships, grants and donations from the public or business entities. Such networks include NPR (National Public Radio), PRI (Public Radio International) and Pacifica Radio. These operate under the public service remit of non-commercial radio while seeking to create compelling programming content. They also help to serve traditionally under-represented communities, musicians and music genres, so go some way towards redressing the gaps caused by the commercial genre-formatting process.

Radio in the UK

In the UK, formatted commercial radio stations do exist but generally the lines of division are far more blurred than in the US, with programming on mainstream radio distinguished according to time of day rather than genre (Hendy, 2000). The specialist genre shows are programmed after 7pm, with indie and rock shows in the early evening and subgenres of dance and hip hop appearing later (due to their associations with the night-time economy). Dance music is invariably the weekend music of choice. In each case a playlist (discussed later) exists, though the evening specialist shows have a greater degree of autonomy than those in the daytime.

The duality between night and day is not arbitrary but rooted in the history of public service broadcasting in the UK (the BBC) and an ideological division that separates casual music listeners from serious music fans (Wald, 2009). Daytime's disposable pop offers a pre-masticated format, which acts as an unchallenging background to work (Adorno, 1990), while evening programming is classed as 'serious' leisure time. The former is grounded in frivolity, while the latter represents passion and knowledge. This ideological split also supports the BBC's 'Reithian values' (named after the first director general John Reith): that the broadcaster should seek to 'educate, inform and entertain'. These values have lain at the heart of the BBC since its inception in the 1920s, and are evidenced in its radio programming by a commitment to new, cutting edge and specialist music in the evenings.

On any one evening a huge array of styles will be played, though it is noticeable that the specialist shows will often program mixes of tracks that later become playlisted in the daytime. This practice supports the ideology of an evening show being ahead of the game, and of the BBC being responsible for discovering new talent. In 2008 the BBC extended this notion of discovery and ownership through the introduction of its 'Sound of...' list. This is a list of artists to watch out for in the coming year and is selected by personnel from the music and media industries. Artists promoted through the list in turn promote the BBC by association and further enhance its brand value. This major gatekeeping exercise has in turn become a key promotional route in record company campaigns since it links directly to playlisting and to wider media profiling. Further initiatives include 'BBC Introducing', which promotes new and unsigned acts, and live events such as 'One Big Weekend' that are strongly connected to daytime playlists.

The charts

Each week, lists of the most popular songs and albums in the country are compiled from sales charts, radio airplay and other metrics (depending on the methodology used in a particular region). The charts form the subject of music radio programmes that 'count down' to the number-one most popular song in a given country, and are often used in music magazines and trade publications as indicators of success for a particular song or album. Of course, for the vast majority of music released into the marketplace, the charts are of little relevance. Nevertheless, the charts are an important source of market intelligence for major record labels and larger independents working with potential mass-market artists, and form a focal point for their marketing campaigns. They can also provide support and leverage for distributors to request prominent product placement within retail outlets.

While it may not take much critical analysis to conclude that any one song's popularity relative to another is not necessarily an indicator of its superior quality, or even of its long-term profitability as a product, it does provide a snapshot of the activities of the larger recording industries and their promotional successes and priorities.

Who compiles the charts?

In the United States, chart information is provided by a number of organizations including Nielsen SoundScan, MediaBase (part of Clear Channel) and CMJ (formerly College Music Journal) (Allen, 2010). Nielsen SoundScan takes point of sale information from bar code scans in retail outlets across the US. From these, it calculates sales figures for albums and songs, and generates a ranked list that is the basis for the Billboard Top 200 chart. The Billboard Top 100 chart adds online music sales and radio airplay to the calculation (the latter sourced from Broadcast Data Systems). MediaBase creates airplay charts for national newspaper *USA Today*. Its station coverage is similar to that of Broadcast Data Systems, while CMJ focuses more on non-commercial and college radio stations and publishes charts on its own website.

In the UK, chart information is compiled by the Official Chart Company, which is a joint venture between the British Phonographic Industry (BPI) and the Entertainment Retailers Association (ERA). It tracks bar codes at over 6,000 retailers in the UK including independent stores and internet retailers and publishes data weekly. The charts are used by the press and by BBC Radio 1, which has a weekly Top 40 count-down programme.

Charts are created by organizations within most countries around the world, and there are also a large number of online providers that can offer a global overview of popularity. For instance, iTunes has real-time updated charts that show global trends, while YouTube has daily charts of the most popular music videos. Specialist sites such as Beatport also publish charts, and all of the above produce information that is further delineated by genre or subgenre.

The data collected by these companies is used by record labels, artist managers, concert promoters, retailers, music media and distributors not only to determine which acts are selling well or not, but also to direct marketing campaigns, ticket pricing strategies and so on. The categorization of the charts into different genres or territories aids greatly in this, whilst also catering to niche consumer markets. For some artists, the failure to achieve the sales targets and chart positions set by the record label can lead to a loss in company support and marketing budget, and even lead to their being 'dropped' (losing their recording contract).

Promoting to radio

The relationship between the radio and the recording industries is, like the print media industry, a symbiotic one: radio stations need musical content and record companies need exposure for their new songs. To gain that exposure, radio promoters (also known as pluggers) need to develop personal relationships with the key decision-makers at a radio station. Those decision-makers may be individual radio presenters (or DJs) who have developed a reputation for 'discovering' new artists, but it is more likely to be radio producers or programme directors, as these have the power to 'playlist' songs (discussed later). Programme directors have set times per week when pluggers can formally meet with them to lobby on behalf of their acts/songs, but pluggers also use numerous other tactics. They may arrange lunch meetings, offer access to artists for interviews, or provide promotional giveaways for personal use, or for use in radio competitions (Allen, 2010: 197). Through these mechanisms, radio presenters and programme directors are encouraged to feel part of an exclusive community. This sense of exclusivity is subsequently embedded into a show structure and presentation style which supports the audience feeling of communal exclusivity.

Payola

Competition for air time is fierce, as there are many new releases vying to be heard and only a limited time per day in which they can be played. This has led to some morally questionable tactics as major record labels need to get their songs played in order to achieve mainstream mass sales success. For instance, in the 1940s and 1950s it was routine for DJs to receive money from promoters in return for playing songs. This practice, known as payola, changed form in 1960 after the US Congress ordered that gifts and money could only be taken if disclosed to the public on air, and if the record companies involved also formally reported it.

By the late 1990s and early 2000s, record companies were exploiting a loop-hole in the law that allowed them to employ third party independent pluggers to induce airplay through promotional payments and gifts. This arrangement was challenged by a legal investigation in 2005–06 which led to multi-million dol-lar out-of-court settlements against the major record labels and broadcasters. Since this time the practice has been controlled more stringently (Allen, 2010: 199–200), though independent pluggers are still used and may even be hired by radio stations as playlist consultants (Howard, 2011). The overall effect is that mainstream commercial radio in the US is dominated by those companies that can afford the high rates charged by independent pluggers: the majors.

Playlists

Weekly playlists define what songs are to be played on the radio and how often. In the UK, they are divided into 'A', 'B' and 'C' lists, with 'A' list songs played at least once a show, and songs on the other lists played less regularly (Wall, 2003: 115). In the US, the playlist is defined as 'heavy', 'medium' or 'light' rotation on a similar basis. The playlists take into consideration the target market of the radio station and, if a commercial organization, the potential advertising and sponsorship revenue that may accrue. Failure to playlist a song can lead to significant knock-on consequences for an artist. For instance, the marketing budget may be cut and the support of record company staff may ebb away because the act is no longer considered a 'hot property'. Alternatively, if monitoring tools such as blog and chat room traffic are suggesting potential, the promotional campaign may be enhanced (Allen, 2010: 198).

'Going for adds'

In the US, 'going for adds' is a promotional campaign aimed at creating a national buzz around a track through coordinated airplay. It is most commonly found for artists or songs that a record company has prioritized. The company will place an advertisement in the major radio trade magazines stating that they are 'going for adds' in a specific week for a particular song. This is followed by a concerted campaign to influence programme directors to playlist the song in that week. If enough stations do so, strong airplay statistics will aid the song's chart position and potentially drive sales.

Content quotas

In some countries, content quotas have been introduced that require radio stations to devote a certain percentage of their airtime to 'domestic artists'. These quotas aim to support and promote domestic music industries and to counteract fears of cultural domination of the airwaves by foreign countries (especially the US). This reading of cultural impact as a one-way flow of influence and dominance (sometimes referred to as Americanization) is overly simplistic, since musical styles and influences travel in more complicated ways, and local cultures often adopt and adapt foreign styles for their own purposes (Tomlinson, 1991).

Nonetheless, fears of cultural domination, loss of national identity, and the inability of local industries to compete with the cultural and financial power of transnational global conglomerates have driven many countries to adopt media-focused content quota legislation, including Canada, France, Portugal, Australia, Nigeria, Ukraine, and the Philippines. Quota regulations vary from country to country. For example, France requires that 40 per cent of music broadcast during peak hours be French-language recordings, half of which should be either new releases or from new artists. In Australia, the popular music quota for Australian composers/performers is lower: 25 per cent for contemporary hit radio, mainstream rock and alternative stations.

Issues surrounding content quotas

Content quotas have been seen to support and invigorate domestic music output. For instance, the French quota system led to the growth of French hip hop as Francophone rappers gained airtime on radio stations that needed the music to fulfil their quota obligations (James, 2003). Yet there are issues with such regulations, with perhaps the most important being their legality according to international trade agreements such as the 1995 World Trade Organization General Agreement on Trade in Services (GATS). In relation to radio, the agreement prohibits any form of quantitative restrictions and requires non-domestic services and service suppliers to be treated no less favourably than domestic ones. In other words, if domestic quotas are imposed, those quotas must also be applied to foreign products (Bernier, 2003: 7–8).

This trade agreement prevented the introduction of quotas in New Zealand when the radio sector was deregulated in the late 1990s. In consequence, New Zealand-produced music fell to just 2 per cent of broadcast content. In response the New Zealand government introduced grants for domestic music and radio pluggers were supported in raising the profile of local music. New Zealand's commercial radio stations now play a significant proportion of music written, performed or produced domestically even without a quota system in place (Stein-Sacks, 2012).

An important threat to content quotas in general is the growth of internet radio and the increased use of social networking and blogs as primary sources for new music. National quotas now seem inconsistent with cultural and techno-logical change, and are not applied to internet radio stations due to the nature of global listening patterns. This development has led to a two-tier system in those countries that have content quotas and, as in Australia, calls that quota systems be abandoned in order to level the playing field.

TELEVISION

Television is an important promotional route for some artists, since television appearances and adverts can increase sales for mainstream acts. The downsides are that advertising on television can be prohibitively expensive (Harrison, 2011: 216) and that the main commercial channels will only really be interested in personal appearances from acts that are likely to draw significant audiences for their advertisers (typically those backed by major recording companies). There are, however, increasing opportunities for the broadcast of audio-visual EPKs in specialist programming slots, and internet television is a growing area for niche genre providers. An example of the latter is GuitarTV.com, created by the guitarist and composer Steve Vai, which streams guitar-focused music videos, performances, interviews and other content.

Synchronization

Television synchronization presents a significant route for revenue generation and promotion for artists and their record companies. As discussed in Chapter 3, synchronization involves the licensing of an artist's music for use in film, television, advertising, animation and so on. Licensing songs to movies and television has clear benefits for both artists and the film/television production companies involved, due to the potential for cross-marketing and brand linkages. For example, the *Trainspotting* (1996) movie used licensed songs to help drive story development, and exposed associated artists to a previously untapped mainstream audience. A prime example is Underworld's 'Born Slippy (.NUXX)' that was used in the movie's highly stylized final sequence and went from being an obscure single B-side to a huge global hit.

Artists have also found promotional opportunities through the synchroniza-tion of tracks as theme songs or background music for long running television series. A case in point is 'Woke Up This Morning' by the British act Alabama 3 (known as A3 in the US) that was licensed as the theme to the US drama *The Sopranos*, thus raising the band's profile globally through the show's huge suc-cess. Artists whose music has been licensed as a show theme have found their careers financially supported, yet also run the risk of being overshadowed by the constant presence of their best known song.

Advertising

Manufacturers and brands seeking a youth demographic will often use music in their television and radio advertising. Notably the jeans brand Levi's has run numerous music-based campaigns since the 1980s, drawing both on heritage acts like Sam Cooke and The Clash, and new artists such as Freakpower, Pepe Deluxe and Babylon Zoo. The positive cross-marketing associations of the Levi's campaigns have often led to hit singles, yet there are less positive aspects to these relationships. For instance, the act may only remain popular for as long as the advertising campaign is live and fail to achieve career longevity.

POINT OF SALE (POS) MARKETING AND IN-STORE MUSIC

POS marketing

Customer buying behaviour in bricks-and-mortar and online retail stores suggests that customers are significantly influenced by what is seen or heard during their retail experience. Point of sale (POS) marketing is therefore an essential aspect of the promotional campaign for mass-market products in particular. Product placement is at a premium and it can cost huge sums of money to gain promotional space at, for instance, a shop entrance, the end of an aisle (known as an endcap), a listening post, or at the point of purchase. Stores will also use a defined chart space for the promotion of new releases according to chart popularity. The online equivalent is the store homepage, which may provide chart listings of top-selling acts in different genres, or show striking marketing images that link directly to editorial reviews and audio samples of specific artists. Most will also make use of some form of music recommender system to attract additional sales (see Chapter 5).

POS marketing can be problematic for artists on independent labels, as these can afford neither racking nor promotion in key spaces so are less likely to benefit from impulse buying. In these cases in-store playback may be an essential marketing and promotion tool.

In-store music

Research suggests that in-store music can have a positive impact on customer shopping behaviour (Yalch and Spangenberg, 1990). This is supported by research into in-store radio at the UK clothing outlet Principles, where the customer-focused in-store radio channel helped to foster double-digit sales growth over times when no music was playing (Vision One, 2009). Such figures underpin the public performance licensing system (see Chapter 9), but as yet there is only anecdotal evidence that playing a song in-store may lead to increased sales for that artist. Nevertheless, it should be noted that music stores are often staffed by music fans, and those working in independent stores often have a strong knowledge and interest in local music scenes and underground genres. They can determine the in-store playlist and are able to discuss records in detail with customers, thus potentially raising interest in marginal, underground or independent music.

SPONSORSHIPS AND ENDORSEMENTS

Sponsorship is a business arrangement through which a company provides funds, logistics, services or other forms of support. In return the sponsor expects to receive benefits ranging from advertising space and media coverage (commonly found in live music and festivals – see Chapter 7) to product endorsements and other rights that may be used to provide commercial advantage. For instance, an artist's name, image, logo or reputation may be used to connect the sponsor company with a particular target market, or to contribute to or enhance the sponsor's brand image.

Sponsorships and endorsements have become increasingly important as revenue from record sales has fallen and artists have sought other ways to fund tours and earn income. There are even sponsor agencies that exist to bring brands and artists together – usually in return for 5–15 per cent of the sponsorship income generated (Harrison, 2011: 251). There are risks to these arrangements since sponsors may occasionally find themselves linked to detrimental values through negative press associated with sponsored artists, while artists may feel constrained by the need to consider the sponsor's views and needs.

Product endorsements

Endorsements have long been a part of the music industries, and take numerous forms. For instance, an artist might use instruments and equipment provided free or at a discount from a particular manufacturer. In return they may prominently display that equipment on stage, appear in manufacturer advertisements, give in-store demonstrations, or acknowledge the manufacturer in the liner notes of a CD.

Artist endorsements are often linked to television advertising and the use of an artist's music, though this is not always to the benefit of the artist's ideological stance and personal beliefs. For example when Moby's *Play* (1999) album became the first to license every track to TV and film, much was made about the large number of car manufacturers that used his music, despite the musician's much publicized anti-car stance (James, 2001). A more sophisticated endorsement is that between car manufacturer Vauxhall and the singer Katie Melua (see Box 6.2).

Box 6.2
Katie Melua – 'environmental brand ambassador' for Vauxhall Motors

In 2010, it was announced that Katie Melua would be the 'environmental brand ambassador' for Vauxhall Motors (owned by the US company General Motors) because of her role 'as an advocate for environmental protection and charitable activities' (Vauxhall, 2010). Peter Hope, Vauxhall's Marketing Director, stated that '[Vauxhall is] passionate about consistent environmental awareness and social responsibility; as a subject very close to Katie's heart, this only makes our partnership more fitting' (Vauxhall, 2010). The deal included the sponsorship of the singer's 2011 European tour where she was accompanied by the Vauxhall Ampera – the company's new model of electric car that was yet to be commercially launched. Through this arrangement, which is essentially a product endorsement, Melua gains publicity, finance for touring and an ideological link to the brand's progressive environmental values. In return, Vauxhall can associate its new environmentally friendly product to an artist whose target market is squarely aligned with its own.

GRASSROOTS MARKETING

Grassroots marketing encompasses a range of strategies that differ markedly from the traditional mass-marketing approaches of press, radio and television. We will discuss three types here: word of mouth, viral, and guerrilla marketing.

Word of mouth marketing

Word of mouth marketing (also known as buzz marketing) is the practice of providing certain individuals with information and products and then encouraging them to circulate and promote them through various forms of social communication. It has become particularly important for online and mobile social media. The individuals targeted are described by Malcolm Gladwell (2000) as 'mavens' and 'connectors'. Mavens are those people who have a respected knowledge of scenes and are recognized as taste-makers or opinion leaders within a social or community group. Connectors are those people who have access to a wide range of contacts across disparate groups of people. In the music industries, word of mouth marketing is often highly effective when targeted through artist fan clubs, as these clubs (whether online or offline) attract fans who have the characteristics of both mavens and connectors. Key individuals can be targeted to disseminate information prior to general release, or to offer products for competitions (Allen and Hutchison, 2010). In this way, such individuals increase their cultural capital and respect within a group, which increases the trust relationship with other members.

Viral marketing

Viral marketing is the online equivalent to word of mouth marketing in that it encourages individuals to pass on marketing messages to their friends, colleagues and acquaintances, thus creating the potential for exponential growth in the exposure and influence of that message. It is most commonly achieved through email and social messaging platforms such as Twitter. In order to have the greatest impact, viral messages need to be interesting, memorable and succinct, easy to transfer to others, and timed carefully to support the schedule of a promotional campaign. It also helps to have some free product or service that can drive interest (see Box 6.3).

Box 6.3
Viral marketing successes

Notable viral marketing successes include an integrated campaign for the Nine Inch Nails album *Year Zero* in 2007. This started with a concert merchandising t-shirt that sported an internet address. Visitors to the website were offered a chain of clues that eventually led to an alternate reality game that expanded on the album's storyline. In addition, USB flash drives containing new recordings were left in concert venue bathrooms, and leaked onto the internet by fans who effectively participated in enhancing the pre-release buzz for the album. The album subsequently sold nearly 200,000 copies within the first week, peaking at number 2 on the Billboard charts. Viral gaming campaigns have also been used by Lily Allen, Gorillaz and Iron Maiden (Harrison, 2011: 213).

Guerrilla marketing

This strategy employs low-cost and unconventional means to create a buzz around an idea or a product at a local community level, with the basic requirements being time, energy and imagination. For example, the little known New York City band Atomic Top performed one of their songs on a subway train using iPhones rather than real instruments. The subsequent YouTube posting received 2 million views and the track featured on the iTunes front page due to download activity.

Another common approach is to use 'street teams' to get involved in street-flyering, sticker-bombing and graffiti. They are especially important for non-mainstream artists who cannot afford or gain mainstream media coverage, and are usually drawn from an artist's local fan base or network of friends and family. Street teams may also act online by posting messages, reviews, and pictures to internet message boards, blogs and chat rooms or requesting that songs be played on the radio. Their effectiveness is such that mainstream record companies now use street teams as part of their promotional campaigns by recruiting through artist websites. As with the more traditional gatekeepers of the press and radio, street teams need to be compensated and rewarded for their activities through such things as free concert tickets and special promotional items.

SOCIAL MEDIA/MOBILE MEDIA

The development of social media platforms has had a profound impact on music promotion. Individual artists are now able to take control of their own interactions with fans in ways that would have been difficult or impossible prior to Web 2.0. Social media tools are at their best when linked through a dedicated website. YouTube videos, SoundCloud tracks and Twitter feeds should be embedded within an artist's webpage or blog rather than directing visitors outside the site.

When using social media for promotion, artists need to become both mavens and connectors within their online communities. Free rewards are required at every stage and can include interesting or exciting information, new tracks and mixes, filmed performances or personal messages from the artist. Sites should be highly interactive, with members able to use message boards to talk to each other as well with the artist, to upload and tag photographs, or to get creative in competitions. These help to enhance participation and inculcate a sense of inclusiveness and distinction for community members, thus providing subcultural capital and a sense of belonging and loyalty. To work successfully and in the medium and long term, communication must be continuous, interesting and add value for community members; they must not feel as if they are simply being marketed to.

The downside of social media

The instant nature of social media can pose problems for an artist's image and subsequently have a negative impact on their relationship with fans. Ill-considered tweets can cause huge damage in the short time before they are deleted, creating a crisis management challenge for publicists. For example, in April 2012, Lady Gaga tweeted, 'Just killed back to back spin classes. Eating a salad dreaming of a cheeseburger', and added the hash tag #PopSingersDontEat. Some fans understood this to mean that the star was encouraging eating disorders, especially in light of a press conference given a few months earlier in which she admitted to suffering from bulimia when she was a student. The reaction on Twitter was hugely negative.

Smartphone apps

Effective online social media strategies have become ever more important with the advent of smartphones that allow high levels of data processing such as music, video and games streamed directly to a phone. The smartphone has become a primary entertainment source and method of accessing digital content and this shift has been supported by the development of apps. Global mobile statistics show that over 300,000 mobile apps were developed in the three years from 2009 to 2011 (MobiThinking, 2012), with many of these apps developed as promotional tools to support products and brands. For example, Daft Punk's iDaft app turns the band's best known hit 'Harder Better Faster Stronger' into an interactive game, while rapper Nicki Minaj has an Android app called Nictionary that details her highly personalized street slang.

The importance of apps is underlined by a partnership announced between EMI and The Echo Nest (an online platform for app developers) in late 2011. Under the terms of the deal, app developers gain access to 'sandboxes' provided by EMI and administered by The Echo Next. Each sandbox contains a range of digital content such as audio tracks, photographs, videos, artwork, discographies and other information and tools related to an artist (such as Robbie Williams, AIR, Evanescence and Gorillaz) or a catalogue of music (including Blue Note and EMI Classics). Developers may use this material to create and pitch app ideas to EMI. If accepted, EMI will deal with the rights clearances, market the app, and split the revenues (Healey, 2011; Echo Nest, 2012). The partnership offers a relatively low-risk and affordable way of harnessing the creative power of freelance developers and may help to drive future sales of EMI products.

CONCLUSION

As with other areas of the music industries the internet has had a significant impact on music promotion. The huge choice, immediacy and interactivity it has created leads to an environment of promotional noise through which artists and music companies must use increasingly inventive and community-focused methods to be heard. The relationship between artist and fan has been renegotiated, in turn impacting upon the roles and industrial relationships of professional taste-makers. This shift has seen a change in traditional media forms such as print magazines and radio that have ceded some of their power base as primary taste-makers to internet radio, targeted blogs and social media.

Yet the continuing power of mass media platforms (press, radio, television) as promotional tools, and the relatively few examples of non-major label viral marketing successes, suggests that the resourcing required for a full and effective mass-market promotional campaign requires the financial backing and resources of the corporate industry. In addition, social media has developed not necessarily as a direct rival to traditional media, but as a complement to it, and music industry marketers and promoters are increasingly integrating their campaigns through all available and relevant routes.

FURTHER READING

Although dated, Keith Negus's *Producing Pop* (1992) still provides a fascinating insight into the individuals that operate behind the scenes of the music industries, while Tom Hutchison, Amy Macy and Paul Allen make a detailed investigation of record company marketing through traditional and new media channels in *Record Label Marketing* (2010). Steve Jones's edited collection *Pop Music and the Press* (2002) offers an illuminating investigation into the complex relationships between print media, the music industry, critical practice, and rock music culture. Also recommended are David Jennings's *Net, Blogs and Rock 'n' Roll* (2007), which maps the notion of digital discovery, and Malcolm Gladwell's *The Tipping Point* (2000), which unpicks the ways that ideas, products, messages and behaviours spread like viruses.

7

THE LIVE MUSIC INDUSTRIES

Live music offers a rich and unique experience for audiences and performers, and is often regarded as crucial to the establishment of new music scenes and styles of music. In addition, live music offers new artists the chance to develop their songs, build grassroots fan bases, and attract record company interest. This chapter begins by outlining a history of the live music sector before discussing the roles and responsibilities of personnel involved in creating and managing events. It then examines a range of issues including motivations for touring, the authenticity of live music, the changing roles of sponsorship and ticketing, and the shifting relationship between the recorded and live music sectors.

KEY FINDINGS

- The sector is dominated by major transnational corporations, though there are still independent promoters and venues at a local, regional and national level.
- There is a growing gap between the top-selling and 'heritage' acts and the rest of the live music market.
- Ticketing is a crucial area of change for the live music industry.
- There is convergence between some areas of the live and recorded music sectors.

THE RESURGENCE OF LIVE MUSIC

The twentieth century saw the emergence of recorded music, in a variety of formats, as the foremost commodity of the music industries. As the music industries came to be organized primarily around recorded products, so live music became a promotional tool to drive record sales. This relationship has changed in recent years as revenues from recorded music have declined and been paralleled by increased income from live performance. For instance, statistics prepared for PRS for Music suggest that total revenues from live music exceeded those of recorded music in the UK during 2008, 2009 and 2010 (Page and Carey, 2011). These figures not only include tickets sales, but also tour and venue sponsorships, media licensing income and other ancillary revenue streams. As ever, care should be taken when examining the statistics produced by music industry trade bodies.

Of particular note is the expansion of the music festival sector since the turn of the millennium, with more attendees, more events and more media coverage demonstrated year on year (Anderton, 2007, 2009). This is particularly true of the UK, which has a rich history of open-air music festivals, but also increasingly true of Europe and the USA, with festivals becoming important tourist destinations for music lovers. The festivals market is highly volatile, with many events failing to achieve longevity due to poor ticket sales in a crowded marketplace. Other problems include adverse weather conditions such as floods, the loss of sponsorship support, and the increasing costs of security, policing, insurance and licensing (Getz, 2002; Anderton, 2009).

It is perhaps surprising to learn that the history of live music is poorly researched within academia. In part this is because of the primacy of recorded music – an art form that leaves tangible and easily examined traces for historians and journalists to study. As a result, the history of twentieth century popular music has been told principally through recorded artefacts, though some key moments and events in the history of live music have received special attention, such as: Bob Dylan 'going electric' at the 1965 Newport Folk Festival; the Monterey, Woodstock and Altamont festivals of the late 1960s; and the Live Aid concert of 1985. It is noticeable that such moments and events were captured on film (hence, there is a tangible record) and regarded as vital to the development of specific popular music artists and broader political issues (for example, see the essays collected in Inglis, 2006).

A BRIEF HISTORY OF THE LIVE MUSIC INDUSTRY

Histories of post-war popular music tend to focus on the recorded medium rather than live performance, leaving a gap in the literature that has only recently begun to be investigated in detail (Frith 2010). Matt Brennan (2010) distinguishes three broad 'eras' in the history of the UK live concert industry since the emergence of modern popular music in the mid-1950s: 1955–69, 1969–96 and 1996 to date. These eras have some parallels with US experience and to developments in the music festival sector, so have been adopted for discussion below.

1955–69

Brennan argues that this era was marked by an 'absence of corporations and ancillary industries'. Instead, there was an 'informal network of venues, agents, managers and promoters' who offered 'variety' shows that packaged musicians, comedians and magicians into a single night's entertainment (2010: 5; see also Cunningham, 1999). In the UK, this era saw a huge surge in amateur music-making in the jazz, folk, skiffle, rhythm & blues and rock 'n' roll genres, together with the growth of live music clubs, pubs and venues which could cater for them (Brennan, 2010: 5).

Live music technology was weakly developed during this first era, but amplification systems began to improve towards the end of the 1960s, with US festivals such as the Monterey International Pop Festival in 1967 benefiting from a bespoke sound system. The late 1960s saw the development of dedicated rock music venues and clubs, as the hippie counterculture of San Francisco spread and developed globally. These included Bill Graham's Fillmore East and Fillmore West in the USA, and Middle Earth, UFO and others in the UK. Mega-festivals (over 100,000 attendees) also emerged, such as the US Woodstock Festival in August 1969, the Rolling Stones at Altamont Speedway in California in December 1969, and the Isle of Wight Festival 1970 in the UK. Dave Laing (2004a: 8–10) argues that the success and prominence of the Woodstock Festival in particular was a catalyst for creating a 'specific rock performance business', with artists demanding higher fees: for instance, Jimi Hendrix's fee rose to US$75,000 from the US$18,000 he was paid for the Woodstock Festival (2004a: 9).

1969–96

Brennan's second era, from the late 1960s to the mid-1990s, sees record companies subsidizing the tours of rock and pop music artists in order to promote new acts and drive record sales. In the early 1970s, a circuit of live music venues emerged in the UK, based around university student union clubs, the pre-existing network of town hall venues (originally built to accommodate orchestral music performances), and new indoor rock venues such as The Rainbow (Cunningham, 1999; Brennan, 2010; Long, 2011). The common touring practice of having a main headliner plus support acts also emerged at this time though some bands, such as Deep Purple, were able to tour without support (Cunningham, 1999: 14). In the US, arena-based concerts grew in importance at the same time, since they offered a greater profit potential and economies of scale in terms of production (Cunningham, 1999: 16). It took somewhat longer for a similar circuit of large-scale venues and arenas to develop in the UK, though a number of events were staged at sports stadia in the early- to mid-1970s. It was not until the 1990s that bands were able to tour the UK 'using similar equipment, standards, and economies of scale that they did in the US' (Brennan, 2010: 8). During this era, technological developments led to improvements in sound quality and staging, plus the introduction of lasers, projection screens and lighting control systems such as Vari*Lite.

In Britain, the 1970s and 1980s also saw the formation and growth of post-hippie 'free festivals'. These were not-for-profit, volunteer-run events, strongly associated with the post-hippie counterculture, and what might be referred to as a generalized 'Woodstock Nation' or 'Glastonbury ethic' of environmentalism, social consciousness, and left-of-centre politics (see McKay, 2000; Worthington, 2004). The free festival scene outnumbered the commercially run festivals by the end of the 1970s, with the Stonehenge Free Festival attracting tens of thousands of attendees. Police action to prevent the 1985 Stonehenge Free Festival from happening led to legislative measures and restrictions that largely crushed the movement. There was a brief revival in the late 1980s and early 1990s, alongside an outdoor acid house rave scene, but this led to further legislation in 1994 (see Collin and Godfrey, 1997).

Since that time, all outdoor music festivals in the UK must be licensed by local authorities and abide by the licensing terms imposed. This development has led to a professionalization of the festival industry, which has been paralleled in the live concert industry. For instance, a number of organizations have been established to share best practice, lobby the government, and improve the stereotyped image of concert promoters as 'being aggressive wheeler-dealers, making excessive profits, and occasionally running off with the takings' (Negus, 1992: 130). These include the Concert Promoters Association (est. 1986), and the International Live Music Conference (est. 1988).

1996 to date

Brennan (2010: 9) argues that the most recent era of live music is marked by changes in market economics and corporate ownership. In the mid-1990s, concert ticket prices began to exceed the rate of inflation while recorded music revenues began to decline as a share of consumer leisure spending (Page, 2007). New concert promoters and venue owners also entered the market in the mid-1990s, and there has been a great deal of consolidation since that time. This consolidation has led to the creation of large transnational promoters such as Live Nation and AEG Live, which also own their own venue operations and festivals (see Box 7.1). These companies are able to organize major international tours through a single deal, making them highly efficient for touring artists. Such tours also spread the promotional risk of booking concerts that later fail to sell out, since any losses could be offset by the more successful concerts of the tour. The ticketing business has also consolidated since the 1990s, with Ticketmaster emerging as the leading international ticket sales provider, followed by the German company CTS Eventim in mainland Europe.

Box 7.1
Live Nation Entertainment and AEG Live

Live Nation Entertainment (LNE) is based in Los Angeles and was formed in 2010 from the merger of Live Nation and Ticketmaster. It operates in a range of music industry areas including concert promotion, venue operation, ticketing, sponsorship and artist management. A range of ownership, part-ownership and joint ventures gives LNE a stake in British music festivals and venues such as Glastonbury, Reading, T in the Park and Wembley Arena, as well as European events such as Rock Werchter (Belgium), Popaganda (Sweden) and Lowlands (Netherlands). LNE also owns or operates well over 100 live music venues in the US, including the House of Blues chain.

AEG Live (a subsidiary of the Anschutz Company) is based in Los Angeles. It operates the Coachella Valley Music and Arts Festival in California (in association with Goldenvoice) and owns a large number of arenas and venues across the US. It also operates worldwide, with British subsidiary AEG Live UK established in 2005. AEG Live UK now owns or operates a number of British festivals and venues including LED Festival, RockNess, and London's O2 Arena. AEG Live is also involved in global merchandising and sponsorships and is developing arenas in China.

National, regional and city-based concert promoters are also found. An example from the UK is SJM Concerts, which organized Take That's stadium tour of 2011, and has shareholdings in DF Concerts, the V Festival, and the Academy Music Group (Palmley, 2011: 40). Independently run festivals, such as Bestival and Summer Sundae in the UK also exist. Many of these events have joined the Association of Independent Festivals (est. 2008), which has members across the UK, Europe and US. In addition, the festival market has attracted the attention of venture capitalist trusts (VCTs) such as Ingenious Media and Edge Media, which have each raised more than £100 million to invest in events such as Field Day, Creamfields, and Underage Festival in the UK (Masson, 2011).

The festival industry has seen a number of other changes since the mid-1990s, driven by corporatization, professionalization, and the customer service demands of a changing festival audience (see Anderton, 2009 & 2011). This development has led to the creation of 'boutique' festivals such as Camp Bestival. These are relatively small events of up to around 10,000 attendees that cater for a family market and offer a variety of activities beyond music. This is partly in response to a demographic shift away from the historic core market of 16- to 34-year olds to older patrons and those with higher incomes. This latter market demands higher quality facilities and entertainment, which has allowed festival promoters to charge premium prices. For example, entrepreneurs such as Tangerine Fields and Camp Kerala offer new services such as pre-erected tents and luxury camping options costing several thousand of pounds. Dedicated parking and camping areas, plus exclusive access to food concessions, showers and flushing toilets are also available at most of the larger festivals.

Licensing and regulation

The professionalization of the music festival industries has been paralleled by the growth in legislation and regulation to which festival organizers must adhere in order to gain an entertainment licence for their events (Anderton, 2011). In the UK, these are collated in the Health and Safety Executive's *Event Safety Guide* (1999), which summarizes over 100 separate regulations, standards, laws and best practice advice relating to event organization and safety. Examples include venue and site design, the management of crowds, waste, noise and transportation, and requirements for sanitation, fire safety and first aid. In addition, festival associations like Yourope (est. 1998) and A Greener Festival (est. 2006) have been established to share best practice and research resources with regards to issues such as environmental sustainability and event safety.

The live concert industry in England and Wales is also subject to licensing regulations in the form of the 2003 Licensing Act, which categorizes live music concerts of all scales as 'a form of regulated entertainment' requiring a licence (Cloonan, 2010). This means that clubs, pubs and venues wishing to host live music events must first apply for a licence to do so. However, lobbying by the Musicians' Union and UK Music (amongst others) has led to a new licensing exemption for venues with audiences of up to 200 people (enshrined in the 2012 Live Music Act). It is hoped that this development will stimulate the growth of grassroots music-making in the UK by increasing the number of potential live music venues.

Economic recession and new markets

There are indications that the live music sector's success in expanding revenues during the 2000s is beginning to falter in response to global economic recession. The American trade magazine *Pollstar* reported a 17 per cent year-on-year drop in the revenues of the top 100 US tours in the first half of 2010, with the larger, higher priced, tours faring worst (Smith, 2010). Concerts were cancelled due to poor sales, and tickets offered at discounts to fill the larger stadia and amphitheatres. Sales picked up in 2011 due to tours by U2, Roger Waters and Bon Jovi (Smith, 2011), which suggests that the industry is reliant on the touring schedules and availability of big-name artists. This idea is supported by statistics from the UK, where live music revenues fell in 2010 in part due to economic recession, but also due to supply factors: there were fewer major stadium tours in that year in comparison to the previous year (Page and Carey, 2011). Concerns have been raised about the rate with which new artists are graduating to stadium and arena level, as it is these artists that drive the profits of the major national and international promoters.

Due to the relatively poor performance of the core American and European markets, promoters are increasingly looking towards the 'emerging territories' referred to as BRICA (Brazil, Russia, India, China, and South America). These countries not only demonstrate strong demand for Western artists but have rapidly expanding social and mobile media usage, making concert promotion easier and cheaper than in the past (Simon, 2011: 15).

MOTIVATIONS FOR LIVE CONCERT TOURING

Artists and bands tour for a variety of reasons and at a variety of scales. These range from 'house concerts' and gigs organized by fans and others within a small-scale music scene such as hardcore punk, riot grrrl or folk music, to local and regional live music clubs with typical audience capacities of 100 to 500 people, and national and international tours and festivals attracting anything from a thousand to tens of thousands of people. These sectors and their motivations are discussed below.

Grassroots sector

At the small or grassroots scale, the musicians might make little or no money or even make a loss. Despite this, the tour may be regarded as an essential promotional route and a necessary investment for the future. In some cases, these tours may be organized as intimate invitation-only 'house concerts' hosted by music enthusiasts (see Box 7.2).

Box 7.2
House concerts

House concerts are generally held indoors, often in a host's living room, and attended by up to 50 or so people who are personally invited by the host and who are encouraged to pay a donation to the performer. Their status as private parties, together with the use of a donation system, allows these small-scale events to be held in compliance with local laws. The artists tend to perform acoustically or with limited amplification and are usually solo acts, duos or small groups. The intimate setting helps to foster a sense of connection between the performers and the audience, and in addition to donations, the artists may also achieve good merchandise sales. Regular hosts build a network of contacts for booking acts and inviting audiences, and usually offer free accommodation and food to the performers. Online networking and advice sites, such as houseconcerts.com and concertsinyourhome.com have also been created to help artists and organizers. The phenomenon is well established in the US, where house concerts have been held for well over 30 years, but may also be found in the UK and across Europe. Networking musicians can link house concert performances together to create short tours that, due to free accommodation, donations and merchandise sales, may be relatively affordable or financially successful, as well as useful for cultivating a broader fan base.

Music-making may also be regarded as 'art for art's sake', as a contribution to a particular scene or genre or, indeed, as just plain fun. Such musicians enjoy meeting new people and gain pleasure and enjoyment from the act of performing and from the trials and tribulations to be overcome in making gigs and tours happen: from sleeping on people's floors to scrounging for equipment, food and transport. At the club level there are bands whose members hold down day jobs in order to experience the excitement and fulfilment of live performance. Many hope to attract a grassroots following and/or the attention of press, media and record companies – 'cultural mediators' (Negus, 1992: 131) – who can help to take the band to the next level and allow them to leave their day jobs behind.

Mid-range sector

Mid-range artists with recording contracts and an existing media presence will use live tours to promote their records, maintain grassroots support, win new fans, and gain features in the music press. Some may be able to use ticket sales as an income stream, though it is more likely that they will focus on ancillary revenues such as tour merchandise. For instance, t-shirts, posters, tour programmes, CDs, DVDs, button badges, hats and so on can be highly lucrative, with artists typically receiving 25–35 per cent of gross sales (Frascogna and Hetherington, 2004: 171). In the US, touring is often used to persuade local and regional radio programmers to broadcast a band's music, raising public awareness, which drives both ticket and record sales. The importance of touring is illustrated by the practice of 'buying on' to a tour, where an up-and-coming act will pay to be the support act for a major touring artist. The act often makes a financial loss on the tour, but gambles that the additional exposure will drive record sales and produce new fans to support the band in the future.

In contrast, an artist may be using live performances to capitalize on current popularity, due to a hit single or exposure through a television programme, film soundtrack or advertisement. This type of artist may not have the longevity of other acts who have 'paid their dues' on the live circuit (who achieved success by touring and building a grassroots following), but may nevertheless make a good income while they can, or use the opportunity to attract and develop a longer-lasting fan base.

Large-scale sector

In the 2000s, music festivals with media licensing deals have become increasingly important to both established and up-and-coming bands, since radio and television coverage may extend the potential reach of an artist's performance. Festivals also allow acts to perform to bigger audiences than they would normally attract on a concert tour and the festive atmosphere can make audiences more receptive to hearing new acts. There is also significant demand for mid-range artists to flesh out larger festival programmes. Exclusivity deals (where an artist agrees to play only one festival in a region or country in any one year) were less common in the late 2000s. As a result, festival headliners and other top-billed artists could play a string of festivals in place of a tour. This led to complaints from festival-goers and journalists about generic festival line-ups, aimed as much at headliners as at mid-range acts. Some festivals have responded by re-introducing exclusivity deals in order to retain the distinctiveness of their programmes, though this has had the knock-on consequence of raising artist fees.

Large-scale acts can now demand very high fees for their tours and festival appearances, with sums in excess of £1 million not uncommon for top acts and events. In part this is because of increased competition, but it is also due to the increased production costs of staging tours: from giant television screens and special stages to bespoke lighting and sound equipment and so on. Increasingly, top-end artists (and some mid-range acts too) view tours as 'projects' (Auslander, 2008: 29) where the net income from all revenue streams will determine the profit potential of a tour. These revenue streams include ticket and merchandising sales, sponsorship deals, media rights for broadcasting, and subsequent live albums, DVDs and so on. To produce great quality, live recordings and DVDs require the live production to sound and look fantastic so some artists have responded by creating lavish live experiences (see Box 7.3).

Box 7.3
U2's *360° Tour* and Kylie Minogue's *Aphrodite: Les Folies*

2011 saw U2's *360° Tour* (2009–11) become the highest grossing (over US$736 million) and most expensive (an estimated US$100 million) tour in history (Waddell, 2011). At the heart of the tour was a purpose-built stage called 'The Claw': a huge four-legged structure incorporating a cylindrical video screen, lighting effects and a sound system in each leg. The stage had a total weight of 600 tons, required extensive ground reinforcement panels to prevent land damage to the host venue, and took 120 trucks to transport (Perpetua, 2011). The tour was sponsored by BlackBerry (Research in Motion) and a concert DVD/Blu-Ray was released in 2010.

It is not only rock stars who have elaborate and expensive stage shows: Kylie Minogue's *Aphrodite: Les Folies* tour of 2011 included not only sumptuous sets and costumes, but also onstage fountains and water effects needing 44,000 litres of water. The tour had 60 full-time staff, 25 drivers and 28 performers, and benefited from sponsorship deals with Lexus in the UK and Xbox in continental Europe (IQ, 2011). Part of the Lexus deal was that Kylie appeared in a television commercial for the car manufacturer, and recorded exclusive video diaries for the brand's website. The Xbox deal (linked to the Kinect *Dance Central* game) also included exclusive backstage videos of Kylie (released on the brand's European Facebook page), an online video dancing competition, and an on-site presence for the brand at Kylie's concerts (Dring, 2011).

These examples suggest the difficulties that up-and-coming or mid-range artists will have in attempting to break into the large-scale touring market. As recorded music revenues fall, so tour support from labels has reduced, promoter risks have increased, and sponsorship become ever more important. Accordingly, it is difficult to convince promoters to take on the risk of an artist unproved at the top end of the market, and it may also be difficult to convince concert-goers to pay the high ticket prices required.

Heritage acts

Rising production costs and artist fees have exacerbated the gulf between a limited number of superstar earners and a 'long tail' (Anderson, 2006) of artists at the lower end of the market, where making a living from touring has become ever more difficult (Page and Carey, 2009). It is commonly argued that the top earners are primarily 'heritage acts': those who became famous in the 1960s, 1970s or 1980s. Their tours may be significant income generators in and of themselves due to high ticket prices and consistent demand, whilst also acting as promotional campaigns for both new (if available) and back catalogue recordings available as physical merchandise at the shows.

There are concerns that there are too few major artists coming through the ranks to challenge these older heritage acts in terms of live music sales. For instance, analyses of the top grossing artists of the decade up to 2010 show that well over half (based on age of lead singer) will be aged 50 years or more by 2011 (Page and Carey, 2011). Statistics produced by the US live music industry magazine *Pollstar* give some hope for the future in that the top-ten highest-grossing US concert tours of 2010 included the Dave Matthews Band, Michael Bublé, The Black Eyed Peas, Lady Gaga and John Mayer, with Michael Bublé and Lady Gaga also making it into the top-ten for worldwide tours (Reinartz, 2010). Nevertheless, a glance at major festival headliners underlines the importance of heritage acts to driving ticket sales.

AUTHENTICITY AND LIVE PERFORMANCE

Audiences have certain expectations regarding live music that, as Philip Auslander (2008: 82) suggests, may vary considerably between different genres, venues and environments. Our expectations of an 'authentic' heavy metal performance will, therefore, be different from those of an 'authentic' blues performance or pop concert. Furthermore, he suggests that live performance is crucial to traditional notions of musical authenticity in a number of ways. First, an artist may be considered authentic if they have a history of 'paying their dues'. Such artists are regarded as close to their audiences, and as having proved themselves in the live environment. Second, it is in live performance that audiences can determine through first-hand experience whether or not an artist is authentic. As Simon Frith (2007: 8) notes, 'the live show is the truest form of musical expression, the setting in which musicians and their listeners alike can judge whether what they do is "real"' (see also Moore, 2002). In live performance, the audience can see the work that goes in to the show – they can see and experience the emotion of the singer and the musical proficiency of the artists, and know that it is them making the music (Auslander, 2008: 90–1). Live concerts may also allow the audience to see an artist develop, to hear new songs, and to witness something unique, including the potential for accidents and mistakes that further prove the authenticity of the live event and performer.

Challenges to authenticity

For Auslander (2008), authenticity has been undermined by contemporary uses of technology. For instance, artists may use sequencers, backing tapes or samplers in their live acts, employ additional musicians on or off-stage to provide musical parts that were overdubbed on record, or have an entire show linked to computer-sequenced lighting and effects that makes improvisation and flexibility impossible. Moreover, pop music acts may be judged on an entirely different basis to rock artists. For instance, pop stars may be recreating their promotional videos on stage and so be judged on how well their performances match the expectations created by their videos in terms of clothing, backing dancers, stage sets and so on. Similarly, lip-syncing to backing tracks (pretending to sing while previously recorded vocals are played back with the music) may be viewed as acceptable if it allows an artist to undertake dance routines that would otherwise make singing almost impossible. In other musical genres, such as dance music, authenticity may arise from the ability of the DJ to 'work the crowd' – to understand the dynamics and mood of the audience in order to heighten or control their emotional and physical responses to the music.

Community and symbolic capital

Related to authenticity is the belief that live music may build a sense of community: that being part of an audience is to share a unique emotional experience. This idea links with notions of being 'lost in the music' or 'lost in the crowd' – an intense, spontaneous, immediate and shared experience that the symbolic anthropologist Victor Turner (1969, 1982) calls communitas: time seems either to stop or to flow endlessly and there is complete immersion in the concert experience, together with an intensification of feelings and actions (Turner, 1982: 56–8). Communitas may be experienced at a really good gig, in the midst of a music festival crowd, or by dancers at an all-night rave (see Malbon, 1999); however, the value of the live music experience might simply be that of 'being there'. For instance, there is great 'symbolic capital' (Bourdieu, 1984) in saying that you were at a particular performance, or at a particular festival. This may be why people use mobile phones to film or take photos of gigs, which they then upload to personal websites, blogs and online communities: it is proof that they were there, even if making the films or taking the photos actually detracts from the immediate experience of attending. Such souvenirs are as important to attendees as leaving festival wristbands on for weeks after an event is over.

LIVE MUSIC SPONSORSHIP

The value of live music in terms of authenticity, community and heightened experience has not been lost on advertisers and sponsors, who subsidize, promote and support bands, concerts, venues and festivals. In essence, they are paying to reach a receptive target audience and to associate their particular brand, product or service with an act, venue or event (Frith, 2007: 7). Sponsors hope to capitalize on the 'good times' of what are memorable and exciting leisure experiences in order to raise awareness, drive sales, increase market share or help to reposition the brand in relation to the market. For instance, in 1996 the Virgin Group became the headline sponsor of the newly launched V96 Festival with the express intention of reasserting the youth branding of Virgin's line of products (see Anderton, 2009). Tour and festival sponsors need to be chosen carefully to avoid conflicting with the image or ethos of the band or event (see Anderton, 2011). Otherwise there may be accusations of 'selling out', which can be damaging to success.

Sponsorship can take a variety of forms. Some companies underwrite tours or individual shows by providing upfront cash advances, or by paying for radio and television advertising. In return, the sponsor may require a promotional presence at the concerts, special 'meet and greet' VIP tickets, product tie-ins (using the artist's name and image), or participation by artists in their advertising campaigns. An alternative is to acquire 'naming rights' for venues, tours and festivals (or stages within festivals). Examples include the O2 Academy venue chain, the Nokia Theater L.A. Live, the Vans Warped Tour, and the Wireless with Barclaycard festival of 2011. It is noticeable that many festivals are sponsored by corporations specializing in financial services, drinks and electronics – especially computer games/consoles, and mobile phone handsets and network providers – which clearly see the festival market as primarily about young adults with disposable incomes. Yet, as noted earlier, the demographic for festivals is aging, so new sponsor types and opportunities are likely to emerge in the future.

ROLES AND RESPONSIBILITIES

The live music industry encompasses a great many job roles and responsibilities, including tour managers, stage/production managers, sound and lighting technicians and directors, and areas such as catering, transportation and insurance. The largest international tours may operate with over 50 staff on a day-to-day basis, while at the other end of the market an artist (or friend) may act as tour manager, perhaps with a van to transport musical equipment to venues. Common at most scales of the industry (see Figure 7.1) are the roles of booking agent, promoter and venue operator discussed below.

Booking agents

Artists performing in small venues or at the start of their performance careers may contact venues directly to organize shows or short tours. If they want to perform at larger venues, secure opening slots for higher-profile acts, or attract sponsorship, they will need to have a manager and work with a booking agent.

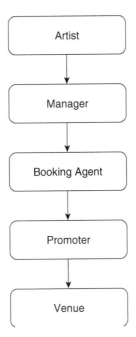

Figure 7.1 Key roles in live music

The agent will work with an artist's manager to agree the basic terms of the show or tour, and to set the minimum ticket price. They then approach promoters and venue operators to secure appropriate venues, and issue performance contracts for promoters to fulfil. As such, the booking agent occupies an intermediary position between artists and managers on one side and promoters/venues on the other, and attempts to broker deals that are of benefit to both sides. In return, they earn a fixed or percentage fee commission of around 10 per cent of the performance guarantee (discussed later).

Booking agents act as a kind of talent scout, since they need to know that the artists they work with have a press profile or buzz in order for them to take them on. In addition, they need a good working knowledge of the venues they work with, the genres of music that are successful in those venues, and the likely success of an artist in any particular venue/location. Agents exist at all scales of the industry from strictly local (a single city) to international. New artists often move from one agency to another as they gain success and attract the attention of larger agencies or as they try to find an agent with the right knowledge of promoters, venues and audiences to make them a success. As booking agencies work on a commission basis, the major agencies usually work only with artists who have secured major record label support. The leading agencies for international tours are the US-based Creative Artists Agency and William Morris Endeavor Entertainment.

Promoters

Concert and event promotion is a high risk occupation, as a promoter's income is largely determined by (uncertain) ticket sales, and because they may need to pay substantial guarantees to secure artists to play. Promoters may rent venues or own their own, and it is not uncommon for venues to act as promoters themselves (known as in-house promotion) or for regional and national-level promoters to manage chains of venues. New artists embarking on small tours may well work with different promoters at each venue, while larger concert tours at the theatre and arena level are likely to be handled by national promoters that manage every date of a tour. As with booking agents, promoters act as talent scouts. They seek to develop sustained relationships with up-and-coming artists so that they can capitalize on any future success.

The promoter works with the booking agent and artist manager to set the ticket price per gig, then advertises and sells tickets to the public. If the show is successful, the promoter stands to make a substantial profit, but if not, the promoter will make a loss even though the band and venue get paid. Larger promoters are able to spread their risk across multiple shows and benefit from economies of scale, which is a distinct advantage over the smaller, local promoters.

Venue operators

Venues range in size from pubs and clubs with capacities of less than 100 people to major amphitheatres, stadia and festival sites that allow attendances in excess of 50,000 people or more. Venue operators usually earn a percentage of ticket sales, or a flat fee plus a percentage of ticket sales. They may also gain a percentage of merchandise sales (up to 50 per cent in some cases), and can earn additional revenues from parking charges and food and drinks sales. Smaller venues, such as pubs and clubs, promote live music in order to drive increased sales of drinks, and a 'free gig' model has become increasingly common in the UK. Here, artists and venues aim to make money from bar sales and merchandise rather than from ticket sales. An alternative is 'pay to play' where artists buy discounted tickets from the promoter/venue then sell them on to friends and fans at full price. This reduces the potential risk for the promoter and venue (as they have already been paid), and places the onus on the artists to sell tickets and make the gig a success.

When promoting their own in-house events, venues may use street teams to hand out flyers or use social networking opportunities to publicize their shows. Conversely, when hiring to an external promoter the venue may provide only limited promotion, such as putting up posters or adding the concert to their own internet concert listings. Ticketing may be handled in-house or through online ticket providers such as Ticketmaster and See Tickets.

LIVE PERFORMANCE CONTRACTS

Live performance contracts can vary considerably, particularly as the scale of a concert or tour increases, but two basic varieties of contract may be distinguished: fixed-fee deals and guarantee plus percentage gate deals.

Fixed-fee deals

In a fixed-fee deal the artist will receive a guaranteed sum whether or not the gig sells out. This is most common for the 'free gig' model and for other events that are offered free to the public, as well as for support acts or smaller clubs (with the latter sometimes offering a share of bar sales instead). The booking agent and/or manager will charge their commission from this fixed sum.

Guarantee plus percentage gate deals

In a guarantee plus percentage gate deal the artist will be guaranteed a fixed sum payment plus a percentage of ticket sales (the 'gate') if the promoter breaks even on the night. Here, the booking agent and manager will take their cut from the total income received by the artist. The percentage gate varies from 50 to 90 per cent (superstars attracting the highest rates), while the guarantee is dependent on a combination of artist expenses (they must at very least break even in terms of transport, accommodation, and other costs) and the potential profitability of the concert. If an artist is attracting a following or is already a major draw or national-level touring act, the artist will negotiate a higher guarantee, and seek a higher percentage gate. The promoter must then ensure that enough tickets are sold to pay the guarantee, meet expenses and make a profit for themselves.

The performance contract and rider

The booking agent issues the live performance contract in two parts. The first gives the basic shape and details of the show. This includes the date, time, location and length of the concert, confirmation of the act's place on the bill if more than one artist is performing, and details regarding how the agreed artist fees will be calculated and paid. The second, known as the rider, includes requests on behalf of the artist, and in relation to the artist's technical requirements. Artist requests include travel and hotel arrangements, catering needs, and specifics regarding dressing rooms, such as access to wireless internet. One of the most notorious rider clauses comes from Van Halen's 1982 tour in which the band requested a bowl of M&Ms sweets with the brown ones removed. Cited as an example of rock's excess, the request was added as a test of concert promoters' professionalism: if the brown ones had not been removed, the promoter may not have read the rider properly and could have missed something much more important in the technical rider (TSG, 2008).

The technical rider details the needs of the show itself, for example with regards to lighting rigs, amplification, special effects, power supplies, the need for local musicians and crew and so on. This part of the rider becomes increasingly important as the artist becomes more successful and tours with a more complicated show. The requests and terms of the rider are negotiated in advance with the concert promoter whose contractual responsibility it is to ensure that all terms and requests are met appropriately.

CONCERT AND FESTIVAL TICKETING

Primary ticketing

Primary ticketing refers to the total face value of tickets sold directly to concert-goers by venues and promoters through a venue box office or website, or indirectly through the use of a specialist ticket agency. Additional service charges may be levied on top of the face value of the ticket, with a percentage of that charge payable to venues and promoters as ancillary income. This practice has been criticized for a couple of reasons. First, the service charge can significantly increase the price of the overall purchase transaction, yet must be paid in order to acquire a ticket. Second, the ancillary income derived from the service charges does not need to be passed on to performers, who will not benefit from it.

Ticketmaster is the world's largest ticket agency, and has come under particular criticism not only for its high prices and service charges, but also for its dominant market position. As a result, the company's merger with Live Nation was challenged (though eventually agreed) by the Competition Commission in the UK and the Justice Department in the US. In the US, the merger was agreed on condition that the Ticketmaster software was licensed to its rival AEG Live, and on agreement that Live Nation Entertainment would not retaliate against a venue should it wish to sell/promote with a non-Live Nation company (Knopper, 2010).

Pricing strategies

Since demand uncertainty is high for most concerts, setting the right price is essentially a gamble. If a concert is underpriced it may sell out quickly and allow touts and scalpers (see below) to make a profit. If overpriced, the concert may fail to break even due to low attendance. Ticket prices are determined after examining the headlining artist's current popularity, media presence, past performance, audience demographic and other factors, generally on the basis of an estimated 60 per cent attendance. Companies such as Ticketmaster are looking at ways to increase the accuracy of their pricing strategies and are using digital data collected through online sales in order to do so. For instance, LiveAnalytics was launched by Ticketmaster in 2011 to mine the company's ticketing data on behalf of artists, promoters, and managers.

Differential pricing

Differential pricing, also known as 'scaling the house', occurs when venues price different sets of seats in different ways, with the more popular seats commanding higher prices. For instance, the 2010 Eagles arena tour had a 16-point pricing system ranging from US$30 to US$250 (Knopper, 2010). 'Added value' tickets might also be offered, such as bundling a programme or a drink into the ticket price. The system allows cheaper seats to be, in effect, subsidized by more expensive ones, thus making the concert more affordable to a greater number of people and potentially enhancing sales.

Dynamic pricing

Dynamic pricing has been used for many years in the airline industry. In this system, ticket prices change in relation to demand. A baseline price-per-seat is set internally to ensure that the concert can break even, but seat prices are not themselves published at a fixed price. Instead, the seat price only appears during the online booking process and will alter in the run-up to the concert: increasing when demand increases or decreasing when demand falters.

Paperless ticketing

Two main types of paperless ticketing systems may be identified: bar codes sent to mobile phones, and RFID (Radio-Frequency Identification) microchips embedded into wristbands or mobile phone handsets. One benefit of these systems is that tickets cannot be transferred to a third party, thus stalling the secondary ticketing market (see below). RFID also supports contactless access control at music festivals, which may significantly reduce access times and gate staffing costs. In addition, the wristband microchip can be pre-charged with credit so that it can be used to purchase food and drinks on-site without the need to carry cash.

Secondary ticketing

Secondary ticketing is the practice of purchasing concert and festival tickets before subsequently re-selling them to a third party. This may be because the original purchaser is no longer able to attend a concert. Alternatively, it may be carried out by scalpers or touts. Scalpers buy in bulk then re-sell at inflated prices once a gig has sold out, while touts are people who loiter outside venues in order to buy and sell tickets from and to people waiting in the queue. Scalping is a particular problem for larger festivals and arenas where the likely popularity of an event can more readily be ascertained. One example of this is the Glastonbury Festival, which has adopted innovative solutions to prevent secondary ticketing (see Box 7.4).

Box 7.4
Ticketing at Glastonbury Festival

The Glastonbury Festival has an iconic status within the global music festival industries. First held on Michael Eavis' farm in the early 1970s, it embodies a countercultural and ethical ideology that sees annual donations to charities such as CND, Greenpeace, Oxfam and Water Aid. During the 1980s and 1990s, official attendance figures rose to around 90,000, with live television coverage from 1994 giving a promotional boost to a more mainstream audience. Throughout this time there was a tradition of 'fence jumping' by which route many thousands more people gained access to the site without a ticket.

Matters came to a head at the 2000 festival where approximately 250,000 people were on-site. The festival was fined for breaching the terms of its licence, leading to the construction of an impregnable 'superfence' for the 2002 event, and the involvement of the Mean Fiddler concert promotion company to handle ticketing. Audience capacity was limited, by local authority licence, to 140,000 people, so demand for tickets was greatly in excess of availability. This led ticket scalpers using online auction sites such as eBay to receive up to £800 for sales of individual tickets. In keeping with its ethical principles, festival organizers sought to prevent such scalping in the future.

In 2004 and 2005, ticket sales were limited to two per person and the names and addresses of the attendees printed on the tickets. On arrival at the site, ticket holders had to present a government approved photo ID such as a driving licence to prove they were the legitimate ticketholders. In 2007, the organizers went a step further by adding a pre-registration form that required purchasers to submit a photograph prior to applying for tickets. The printed tickets now included the submitted photographs and postcodes, making it even harder to fraudulently transfer them to another person. Online registration was introduced in 2009, and the two-person limitation removed. Purchasers can now buy any number of tickets, but the registration numbers, photographs and postcodes must all match, making it almost impossible to defraud the system (www.glastonburyfestivals.co.uk).

Secondary ticketing has been legitimized to an extent by the emergence of online re-sellers who match up sellers and buyers of tickets in return for commission. These first emerged in the US (for example StubHub, est. 2000), and have been operating in Europe since the mid-2000s (for example, Viagogo, Get Me In! and Seatwave). The primary ticketing agencies were initially hostile to the secondary market but have since warmed to the idea. For instance, Ticketmaster bought TicketsNow and Get Me In! at the beginning of 2008. Legislative proposals to control the secondary ticketing market have thus lost the support that the ticketing industry had previously offered (Cloonan, 2010: 20). Some blocks of tickets may even be held back by primary ticket sellers, promoters and artists specifically for sale on the secondary market, though few artists are keen to publicize this fact, as it would seem they are exploiting their own fans by doing so.

Ethical ticket exchange

Concerns about the secondary market have driven the creation of 'ethical' online ticket exchange companies such as Scarlet Mist, Swap My Ticket, and The Ticket Trust that do not allow tickets to be re-sold at inflated prices. Ticketmaster joined these initiatives in 2011 by launching TicketExchange – a site that enables fan-to-fan transactions of tickets originally issued by Ticketmaster, including its own paperless tickets. The latter allows the company to maintain control of the secondary market in its paperless tickets whilst simultaneously undermining secondary ticket sellers who require physical tickets to operate.

Direct-to-fan and social ticketing

Individual artists may benefit from online sales by selling their own tickets directly to the public through websites such as Bandcamp or Topspin, and by collecting information about their fans themselves rather than having it stored by a big ticketing company. This will enable the artist and artist manager to better understand the geography of their fan base, to plan tours more efficiently, and to market the tour and cross-sell other products more effectively. An alternative is to encourage fans to become ticket sellers on behalf of an artist through the use of online social ticketing platforms such as Fatsoma, Eventbrite and FanFueled. These sites charge lower service fees than Ticketmaster and offer additional rewards programmes that range from service charge rebates to discounted or free tickets. The aim is to maintain and expand the fan base of an act at the same time as marketing events and selling tickets. This is effectively an extension of the long-established 'street team' promotional concept whereby fans are used to spread the message about an artist or event by putting up posters or handing out flyers.

THE RELATIONSHIP BETWEEN THE RECORDED AND THE LIVE MUSIC INDUSTRIES

Tour support

Record companies may provide financial support to underwrite tours that run at a loss, though this is less common than it was in the past. The rationale has been that the tour is an important promotional opportunity that will increase exposure and so drive record sales. The aim is that the tour support monies will then be recouped from income due under the recording contract from record sales and so produce a profit overall. This is one reason why multiple rights recording deals (also known as 360-degree deals) have become more common – as any tour support can be recouped not just from record sales but potentially from ticket and ancillary income from the tour.

For some acts, tour support is essential since they may not have a mass media presence: their tours are the primary route through which they engage, maintain and expand their fan base. In addition to underwriting tours, record companies fund advertising campaigns and promotional support, engage corporate sponsors, and give away tickets to influential taste-makers such as radio DJs and magazine journalists in host cities. The belief is that the goodwill fostered by these actions will lead to positive reviews, drive further ticket sales and help further an artist's career.

Cover-mounts and 'bundles'

Another innovative form of promotional involvement is the use of cover-mounts. This is a practice where an album is given away for free with a newspaper or magazine in order to raise awareness of upcoming concerts. For example, in 2007 Prince distributed three million copies of his *Planet Earth* CD in the *Mail on Sunday* (UK) in order to support a string of 21 shows at the O2 Arena in London promoted by AEG Live UK. It is estimated that the shows grossed £11 million (Wikström, 2009: 137–8), though Prince will also have benefited by selling the CDs to the paper. Whether or not a cover-mount drives live sales, the revenue generated from the paper may still be considerably more than might be achieved by selling through traditional physical sales routes.

Another innovation in this area has been to 'bundle' albums and tickets into a single package/purchase, which has been tested by artists such as Stereophonics and Snow Patrol. Research conducted for IPC Inspire (publisher of the *NME* and *Uncut*) suggests that such bundling does not, however, offer a strong incentive for its readership. Instead, price sensitivity remains crucial to purchasing decisions (see Cardew, 2010).

Convergence and multiple rights contracts

A relatively recent phenomenon is for live concert promoters to become involved in the recording industry by signing multiple rights deals (see Chapter 2). Live Nation Entertainment is the most prominent of these, having signed a deal with Madonna in 2007 worth an estimated US$120 million over ten years and three album releases. Jay-Z made a similar deal with Live Nation in 2008 to form the sub-label Roc Nation, while U2 brokered a worldwide deal with Live Nation for touring, merchandising and control of the band's website. In 2011, AEG Live announced its first multiple rights deal, with the UK artist Saint Saviour. The company will help to finance and then release the singer's debut album in return for exclusive long-term promoting rights and a share of revenues from areas such as publishing, merchandising and brand licensing (CMU, 2012a).

Record companies have tended not to move into the live music market as promoters, but to capitalize on the expansion and success of live music in other ways. For instance, the major labels have established (or more often purchased) merchandising companies and artist management companies, and have increasingly shifted to multiple rights recording deals. Such diversification is not new. Ironically, some major record companies had moved into the concert production and merchandising markets in the 1990s before selling their holdings at the end of that decade as CD sales started to fall. As Dave Laing notes, their 'first thought was to raise cash and preserve profits by selling off "non-essential" parts of their companies' (2004a: 11): a strategy that with the benefit of hindsight now seems rather unwise.

CONCLUSION

The live music industry is undergoing considerable change as it adapts to and embraces a variety of new technologies and sponsorship deals. The mid- and large-scale sectors of the market have become increasingly dominated by large transnational companies with complex patterns of ownership. At the same time, grassroots performances and venues remain an important part of the industry, particularly for up-and-coming artists who are seeking not only to 'pay their dues', but also to harness the potential of their fan bases through internet-based methods. New strategies for both primary and secondary ticketing are emerging, with the latter causing ethical concerns and leading to a range of alternatives. Convergence between the live and recorded music industries has also been seen, and is likely to continue as musicians and promoters explore other ways to make recorded music available to the public, and record companies seek to diversify their income streams.

FURTHER READING

For more information on the history and development of the British live music market see Matt Brennan's 'Constructing a rough account of British concert promotion history' (2010). For a highly readable discussion of music festival development, see George McKay's *Glastonbury: A Very English Fair* (2000), and for an understanding of how cultural history affects contemporary sponsorship, see Chris Anderton's 'Music festival sponsorship: between commerce and carnival' (2011). Philip Auslander's *Liveness. Performance in a Mediatized Culture* (2008) is a useful source for discussing the authenticity of live music, while Dave Laing's 'The three Woodstocks and the live music scene' (2004a) offers a discussion of the corporatization and commercialization of US arenas and festivals.

8

MUSIC AUDIENCES

In the post-internet environment, the active consumption of music and music media by audiences and consumers has had a profound impact on the music industries. The increasingly fragmented nature of audience profiles, and the focus on individuals as opinion leaders within social networking platforms, have seen the relationships between artists and their audiences become an ongoing conversation that may appear to sidestep music industry control. In addition, personal listening devices enable a controlled auditory experience that places emphasis on individual, rather than group, taste. This environment has seen a growing importance in the individual's relationships with music and its location to personal biographies, which in turn has spawned a renewed interest in heritage music.

KEY FINDINGS

- Audiences operate as active consumers in a fragmented musical landscape.
- New media technologies have placed audience conversation at the centre of music mediation.
- Music audiences consume history as an always-present past through gaming, collecting, nostalgia and heritage.

UNDERSTANDING MUSIC AUDIENCES

Roy Shuker describes audience research as concerned with 'the who, what, where, how and why of the consumption of individuals and social groups' (2012: 18). Historically, popular music audiences have been investigated through three general approaches: neo-Marxist critiques of passivity and fanaticism, subcultural (and post-subcultural) theory, and consumption practices (see Wall, 2003: 167).

Passivity and fanaticism

The initial approach of passivity and fanaticism is closely linked to neo-Marxist concepts of mass culture and articulated by, for example, Theodore Adorno (1990) and Theodore Adorno and Max Horkheimer (2002). Although considered in greater detail elsewhere (see Negus, 1996 or Wall, 2003), it is worth briefly examining the basis of the mass culture critique. In essence, the mass culture argument suggests that music produced by the popular music industries requires little effort to engage with and so leads to 'deconcentrated listening' (Adorno, 1990) and consumer rejection of music that is not immediately familiar. This produces an infantilized consumer who enjoys music through the recognition of repetitive refrains (melodic hooks and phrases). Adorno (1990), writing during the height of Tin Pan Alley pop music in the 1930s and 1940s, described this as 'quotation listening': a passive listening state created by the standardized songs promoted by the music industries. Furthermore, Adorno believed that disengagement from active listening resulted in audiences becoming dislocated from an understanding of their social position. In effect the soporific nature of popular music depoliticized listeners, and kept them in a compliant state that fostered full acceptance of their subordinate place in society.

Keith Negus (1996: 10) notes that many of Adorno's critics have focused on his assertion that there are two types of listener: one that is lost within a crowd and thus easily manipulated (the majority), and the other who is identified by their alienated, poorly socialized obsessive individualism (the minority). Adorno suggested that both types were passive, though later studies and theorists moved to the position that audiences are active rather than passive: that they do not unquestioningly consume the products of the music industries (see Negus 1996: 13). Instead, music consumption extends into areas such as style, identity, social interaction and resistance – areas that form the focus for subcultural theory and popular notions of subculture.

Subcultural theory

Subcultural theory was proposed and explored by a number of academics working at the University of Birmingham's Centre for Contemporary Cultural Studies in the 1970s (for instance Hall and Jefferson, 1976; Willis, 1978; and Hebdige, 1979). A number of criticisms have been made of subcultural theory (see, for instance, Huq, 2006), and these underline the key concepts or assumptions upon which such studies were based: heroic style, homology and resistance to a working-class parent culture.

Within the context of subcultural theory, personal style (including clothing, hairstyles, body piercing, and attitudes to others) was deemed 'heroic' in the sense that it visually demarcated the subculture from its parent culture. In this context the 'spectacular' styles of teddy boys, rockers and punks became central for subcultural theorists. Related to this was the notion of homology, which suggests that there is a natural 'fit' between particular music genres and the styles, lifestyles and values that are associated with them. A core value was identified as class-based resistance: a politically motivated oppositional stance made by working-class males against middle-class parental aspirations. Taken together, these concepts and assumptions placed 'a hermeneutical seal around the relationship between music and stylistic preference' (Bennett, 1999: 599) – one that cannot account for the fluidity with which subcultural identities are used by audiences. Nevertheless, and as noted below, the concept has entered popular usage and is useful for its marketing potential for the music industries and journalists.

Popular usage of 'subculture'

The notion of subculture became popularized in popular music culture in the 1980s when artists like New Order and The Pixies recorded songs named after the term, and music journalists began referencing the concept. It first became common vernacular in mainstream media during the emergence of grunge and the mainstreaming of alternative rock music via MTV's *120 Minutes* show. Here, it became shorthand for underground or marginalized youth cultures and a useful way to bypass the dichotomy presented in the mainstreaming of the margins. For instance, American grunge artists such as Nirvana could be mediated and marketed through a veneer of outsider culture despite major label and mass media support. The notion of 'subculture' became romanticized as a form of opposition and still pervades, even if not articulated by name, in popular media discourses that attempt to deal with disparate or marginal groups of music fans.

Post-subculture

Traditional subcultural analysis places the subculture at the heart of individuals' identities: people are defined by their membership of a specific subculture. Yet it is common for a group of people outwardly collected together through style, music and space to share a wide range of musical tastes that actually stretches beyond any particular subcultural code. Post-subculture approaches attempt to address this by thinking about the fluidity of individuals within and between different groups (see Muggleton and Weinzierl, 2003).

Through this broader postmodern approach we can recognize the importance of 'taste', 'distinction' and 'cultural capital', which may be as important for social stratification as the accumulation of financial capital (see Bourdieu, 1984). In her investigation of club culture Sarah Thornton (1995) adapted these ideas to encompass a notion of taste cultures that use various forms of media (flyers, music papers and tabloids) and temporary groups of people (clubbers or ravers) as a way of emphasizing 'subcultural capital': of allocating value to a non-mainstream pastime that may or may not have oppositional connotations.

Fluid identities and neo-tribes

In her work on the apparent stability and 'naturalness' of gender and sexual identities, Judith Butler argued that gender is not an aspect of identity by which people act, but is an enactment that 'produce(s) that which it names' (1999: 225).

In simple terms, a person is not termed masculine because of their biology, but because of how they perform masculinity within a society that has normalized expectations of masculine behaviour. This position presents all identity (not just gender) as constructed, performed and replayed through everyday actions, image, music and other cultural practices. Within this understanding, identities are extremely fluid and profoundly unstable.

Fluidity of identity has also been explored by Michel Maffesoli (1996) in his work on 'tribus', or neo-tribes, through which he argues that group identities are no longer formed along traditional structural determinants (the grand narratives of class, gender and religion – see Chapter 1). Instead, consumption practices enable people to create new forms of contemporary tribe that refer 'more to a certain ambience, a state of mind ... preferably to be expressed through lifestyles that favor appearance and "form"' (Maffesoli, 1996: 98). Through consumption, identities can be put on and taken off according to time, space and environment.

Neo-tribes do not exhibit stable practices of inclusion and exclusion. Furthermore, they encourage fluid and part-time involvement rather than fixed group identities. Within this context, individuals are able to flow between numerous 'performative' identities (Butler, 1999). Neo-tribes therefore allow for the contemporary audience environment, which is embodied by 'the shifting nature of youth's musical and stylistic preferences and the essential fluidity of youth cultural groups' (Bennett, 1999: 614). This is, perhaps, key to understanding contemporary music audiences, most of whom, when asked what they listen to, would argue that their tastes are eclectic and that they 'listen to a bit of everything'.

Consumption practices

Roy Shuker (2001) points to various modes of consumption that connect with our fluid musical identities. These include buying recorded music, listening to the radio, viewing MTV and music videos, home-taping and downloading from the internet. He further defines secondary, social levels of music consumption in the forms of reading the music press, dancing, clubbing, gig-going and putting music-related posters on bedroom walls (2001: 173). To this we can add a further level, that of social media interaction, where online 'sharing' and 'bump' technologies associated with smartphones (see later) exemplify the move from passive audience to active consumer. Moreover, social media interaction underlines the increasingly central position of the audience as a communication hub for music promotion and distribution.

Consumers as producers

John Fiske (1992) suggests that popular culture is created by combining the products of the cultural industries with an audience's creative productivity, which he distinguishes as semiotic, enunciative and textual. Semiotic productivity relates to the ways that people make sense of the world around them and incorporate their experiences internally. Music industry products, images and recordings are imbued with meaning by active consumers who find value in them, and make them part of their personal identities and biographies. These meanings take on public form through face-to-face interaction: Fiske's enunciative productivity. Factors such as fan talk, or hair and clothing styles, are included within this form of production, which for Fiske exists only in the 'moment of speaking' (1992: 39). However, with the advent of the internet, we may extend this to include interactions through web-based discussion groups, chat rooms and other social media. Finally, audiences (and fans in particular) may create their own unofficial products for circulation amongst their peers. This textual productivity creates new artefacts that differ from 'official' culture in that they are generally neither mass marketed nor for commercial gain (Fiske, 1992: 39). Unofficial products include, for example, internet websites (Watson, 1997), fanzines (Duncombe, 1997) and unofficial concert recordings (Anderton, 2006).

MUSIC ON THE MOVE: FROM THE WALKMAN TO THE IPHONE

Elijah Wald (2009) suggests that in the mid-1960s a divide in value emerged based on methods of music consumption. His assertion, formulated around The Beatles' *Sgt. Pepper's Lonely Hearts Club Band* (1967), is that the private home listening experience of the concept rock album came to represent a serious activity, while dancing to live or public music was judged to be an act of frivolity. In this assessment he draws a divide between public and private music spaces. This divide underlines many consumption practices since that time and in particular the personal stereo which was popularized with the launch of the Sony Walkman in 1979.

The Walkman

Michael Bull (2000) describes the Walkman as a tool used by 'urban' dwellers that enables them to extend their mediated behaviour into many environments previously inaccessible to privatized listening. The device used compact audio-cassettes, a small portable playback device and headphones to enable users to enjoy the private experience of discreet music listening in public spaces, thus enabling a different sensory experience of the everyday to the other people inhabiting those same spaces. That experience could be managed by the use of self-recorded mix tapes that allowed users to actively match or control their personal moods through planned music choices. For instance, research by Bull (2000) revealed that many commuters would play the same tapes every day thus forcing 'their environment to mimic the straightjacket of their own mindset' (2000: 344).

Another aspect of the Walkman as form of music consumption was its aesthetic use value. On its launch the Walkman was promoted to the youth market with a host of brand values that extended the value of the music being played. Ownership of the listening device itself suggested connotations of the serious 'private' music listener alongside such social values as financial success, mobility, enjoyment and kudos. The Walkman's success can be seen in the growth of cassette tape sales that outstripped vinyl album sales during the device's peak in the 1980s.

When the CD became the market leader in the 1990s, portable CD players were also produced. Unfortunately there was a tendency for discs to skip when used on the move, and as recordable CD technology was not widely available when these devices were launched, consumers were unable to create their own music compilations as they had with cassettes. Far from improving and enhancing the mobile listening experience, portable CD players were less flexible than their predecessors and it was the creation of the MP3 file format and portable hardware MP3 players in the late 1990s that really began to expand the possibilities for mobile music. Nevertheless, broad consumer acceptance of such players only really came with the introduction of the Apple iPod in 2001 and more significantly iTunes in 2003. These products and services changed the consumer relationship with personal listening devices and placed online media stores as a vital space for music consumption.

The iPod

The iPod's appeal when launched was manifold. It had the ability to store an unparalleled number of songs as digital files within one device and to play music for greater periods of time than its competitors due to its much longer battery life (Bull, 2005). Its user-friendly interface and stylish design has now made the iPod almost synonymous with the notion of the MP3 player, and it consistently outsells rival products from Creative and Microsoft. Digital music players such as the iPod allow individual users to build personal playlists from sound files stored on the device in a much quicker manner than the cassette-based mix tapes of the past. Like the cassette Walkman, users create a 'privatized auditory bubble' (Bull, 2007: 68) through which public spaces become extensions of the private listening experience, and personal emotions, moods and experiences of time can be managed.

An interesting feature of the iPod is the shuffle setting. Here, the device will randomly select tracks from a user's entire music library, so creating playlists of songs that have not been specifically chosen by the user. The result is a constant rediscovery of the listener's musical past and present, which can in turn create a biographical narrative that draws on memories and associations raised by these randomly selected tracks. The iPod also has social uses, as listeners may share headphones to play music to each other, while 'dock' systems allow the device to be attached to home stereo equipment. Nevertheless, the primary function of the iPod remains as a solitary experience defined by the privatized auditory bubble: a private space in a public environment.

The iPhone

The smartphone has a central role in music consumption as a media form thanks to its ability to act not only as a mobile phone, but also as a media player with internet connectivity. Success came with the introduction of devices by Palm, Windows, and BlackBerry, yet these were initially focused on online interactivity and personal organizer features. In contrast, Apple's iPhone gave music playing capabilities a more central role, though it is through the development of iPhone apps that the device's popularity has grown.

The introduction of the iPhone presented a clash of user values. Like the iPod, it has the potential to reorder the user's experience of time and space. However, where the iPod relies on continuous immersion in the private space of the auditory bubble, the iPhone represents a discontinuous private space, punctuated by absent others interrupting with phone calls and texts. The combination of social and solitary aspects, together with other smartphone applications, web-browsing capabilities and an in-built camera has resulted in a huge growth in their popularity, and consequently their use for music consumption. Users are also able to 'bump' files between iPhones using Bluetooth and other technologies, which matches consumers' internet-driven need for immediate satisfaction. Smartphones similarly offer a link to games and music apps that enable the consumer to enjoy a different experience of music consumption.

iTunes

A number of online media distribution and retail platforms have emerged in recent years (see Chapter 5), yet Apple's iTunes store has gained market prominence due to its links with the iPod and iPhone, and is interesting due to its role as a consumer-driven guide. Album releases on the site are accompanied by biographies supplied by allmusic.com, and by a user-generated customer review system that allows discussion about the release and enables all users to become critics. Vasant Dhar and Elaine Chang (2007) suggest that user-generated content should be considered seriously by record labels especially in light of pre-release blog coverage through which audiences are able to discuss and evaluate new albums. By examining these variables, the authors suggest that record companies could predict future sales well in advance of an album's in-store availability. Similarly, customer reviews on iTunes allow audiences a direct impact on the reception and sales of an album once released.

MUSIC AND SOCIAL MEDIA CONSUMPTION

Online video

In the 1980s the creation of MTV turned the music video into a primary site of music consumption, and this has now translated into online video. For instance, a survey of 26,644 online consumers in 53 markets across the globe during September 2010 revealed that the 'watch' habit represented the most popular form of music consumption, with 57 per cent of respondents having watched music videos on computers during the research period. Furthermore, 20 per cent of online global consumers had watched a music video on a mobile phone (Nielsen Music, 2011).

Typically online video sites such as YouTube are used as test marketing for the music industries with official videos uploaded to artist channels, and viewing figures and comments used to inform marketing campaigns. There are also advantages for consumers like the instant availability of a huge range of music for free and the ability to share links via Twitter and Facebook or embed videos into personal blogs. Music discovery and recommendation can therefore be accomplished by consumers and this may be a strong grassroots marketing opportunity for individual artists and the music industries as a whole. Consumers are also able to upload their own user-generated video, photo, animation and music content, so sites such as YouTube offer multi-functional capabilities that recognize and support the creation and maintenance of online communities.

Gamers as a music audience

Consumers also access music through computer gaming, and the use of video games as a promotional tool is well documented (see Box 8.1).

Box 8.1
Music in video games

Holly Tessler points to the power of football games like EA's *FIFA* series, which saw 3,000 to 4,000 songs being pitched to the developer for inclusion on the soundtrack of the 2005 edition of the game (2008: 15). This is not a new phenomenon. In 1996 the much publicized UK electronica invasion of the US was trailed by the promotion of music by artists like The Prodigy, Chemical Brothers, Fluke and Underworld on the soundtracks of high-profile Sony PlayStation 1 games like the Psygnosis racing game *wipE'out 2097*. For gamers who might not have had knowledge of UK dance music, the high octane beats that accompanied their gameplay offered the perfect complement to the adrenalized gamers' aesthetic. Electronica quickly became bound with the futuristic sheen of home console gaming, and UK dance music magazine *Muzik* introduced a PlayStation league featuring a variety of renowned electronic music artists and DJs. Indeed, The Prodigy's Liam Howlett has suggested that the album *Fat of the Land* (1997) was delayed by over a year due to his obsession for some of the games used in the league: a fact that the band's audience fully appreciated and, despite their frustration at the lack of new music, even applauded (James, 1997).

An important aspect of the consumption of music through gaming is that it places music as a secondary pastime since the soundtrack invariably augments game-play.

In contrast, games such as *Guitar Hero* and *Rock Band* shift the relationship once more by combining music memory skills with reward gaming. They allow the audience to imagine themselves in spaces where they are able to simulate the act of performing music without the necessary musical skills or knowledge. As a cultural phenomenon such games fuse fantasy with reward. The gamer/fan takes on the role of fantasized performer, while their reward for excellence in playing the hand-to-eye and memory coordination game is to unlock the original song (Tham, 2010).

Consuming through social networking

The development of social networking sites runs parallel with file-sharing and both have had a profound impact on the music industries. Platforms like Facebook, Bebo and Twitter have had a democratizing effect on users, giving them the illusion that they control their own private spaces and allowing them to build their own friendship communities who may share that space. Conversely, users have to log on to a holding website and divulge key demographic information in order to access their pages. This information then allows the host platform to place adverts on each user's pages that align with their user profile and key words that are being used in their conversations. In effect the users are delivering themselves as individuals to advertisers.

The democratizing effect of these platforms is purely in the area of information, whereby users are encouraged to place themselves at the centre of taste communities and friendship groups, and to upload media content (sound files, videos, images and internet links) that connect those communities together. Sharing is encouraged in a variety of ways and the whole process allows music audiences to become both critics and consumers in a gatekeeping activity that locates the individual at the core. The possibilities for an audience to engage in and have a direct impact upon the music promotion process are profound and may drive success for an artist, which is why record companies have been approaching fans with successful social media fan sites to act as 'mavens' in their marketing campaigns. Ironically the fans themselves become 'weasels', but are accepted as being an authentic voice associated with the band (see Chapter 6).

HERITAGE AND NOSTALGIA

When Harmonix Music Systems developed the console game *The Beatles: Rock Band* in 2009 the release was squarely focused on the user's nostalgic desire to perform their own musical biographies. To 'play' The Beatles in the game is in some sense to be The Beatles, and new technologies increasingly unlock historical musical artefacts in order to bring the past as an always-there presence, into the present. The constant desire to gorge on the past in a contemporary context can also be seen in the enduring presence of music-related styles such as goth, and the constant reinvention of music scenes like emo and punk.

Classic albums revisited

It can also be viewed through the rediscovery of 'classic' albums: those that have passed into the accepted canon of a music genre, or are a highlight of a particular heritage act's career. This rediscovery exists in the remastering, repackaging and re-release of albums with studio outtakes, interviews, live performance recordings and film footage, and also in the live music industries. For instance, there has been a rise in one-off classic album performances by heritage acts such as Iggy and the Stooges (*Funhouse* and *Raw Power*) and Primal Scream (*Screamadelica*). The promotional value for these artists can be considerable, yet for the audience it allows the extension of a fantasized past and of personal biography. These were the shows that audiences thought they would never be able to witness again. In reality of course, these are shows that had never been performed in this way in the first place, as with the exception of some progressive rock bands like Pink Floyd, ELP, Jethro Tull or Yes, it is rare to find heritage acts that originally played entire albums during a single show. These modern performances are therefore a simulacrum (Baudrillard, 1994) of an idealized past that are staged to satisfy nostalgic desire, to reward fandom, and to generate ticket sales and renewed interest in an act.

The ever-present past has also become an aspect in the consumption of the live music concept where the impossible is made possible. For instance, when Take That reunited as a four piece in 2006, rumours spread that original member Robbie Williams would make a surprise return for the live tour. As it transpired he returned as his younger self in virtual form as a huge holographic image projected onto the stage. Similar holographic performances have also seen Japanese pop star Hatsune Miku perform as her virtual self in 2010 to underline her manufactured style, while rapper Tupac Shakur (2Pac), who died in 1996, came back from the grave in a 2012 Coachella festival performance with Dr Dre and Snoop Dogg.

Old technologies

The continued audience desire for nostalgia can also be seen in the ongoing (and in some cases growing) popularity of 'old technologies'. In 2011 the Official Chart Company reported a 40 per cent year-on-year increase in sales of vinyl (Official Chart Company, 2011). The same phenomenon was noted in the US where 2011 sales of vinyl increased by 14 per cent on the previous year, with over 2.8 million units sold. This represented the highest vinyl sales since 1991 (Caulfield, 2012). During the same period, audio-cassette tape sales were also reported to be on the increase in the US, with Nielsen SoundScan reporting that music-related cassette album sales were 46 per cent higher than in 2010 at 22,000 units sold (Rose, 2011).

These figures suggest that some audiences still place value on physical formats of music, and that they are consequently prepared to pay a premium to receive a tangible product. Audiophiles have long argued that the quality of vinyl is superior to that of MP3, yet the same cannot be said of audio-cassettes, which suggests that packaging may be the major draw for consumers.

The medium is the message

There are also clear links between the medium of product formats and the message of music scenes: the choice of vinyl or cassette has meaning in and of itself (McLuhan, 1964). For instance, 7-inch vinyl singles are strongly associated with do-it-yourself punk scenes, while 12-inch vinyl has strong ideological links with dance music culture. Hip hop has origins located in the iconic image of the boombox playing cassettes for MCs, break-dancers and graffiti artists to practice their art forms to, and it was through mix tapes that the message of hip hop spread from borough to borough and coast to coast in its earliest days. Audio-cassettes have also been important for 'underground' genres, and may encode ideologies that relate to those genres (see Box 8.2).

Box 8.2
Dave Grohl and audio-cassette culture

Punk, hardcore and lo-fi noise music all have a long history of cassette-only releases, with many artists distributing their music for free or at cost price through 'underground' networks of fanzines and independent stores. When Dave Grohl released his debut album *Late!* (1992) under the pseudonym Pocketwatch he did so on the Arlington, VA cassette-only punk and hardcore imprint Simple Machines, despite being signed at the same time to major label Geffen with his band Nirvana (James, 2004). The album was a second-generation tape copy but the low-quality, hissy sound fit with the lo-fi nature of the music. In signing with Simple Machines, Grohl sought to realign himself with his Washington DC hardcore roots through ideological association and was tapping into a tradition of labels that had been associated with punk, hardcore, riot grrrl and sound collage since the 1970s.

The vinyl and audio-cassette formats each carry connotations of authenticity, with investment in old technologies implying a fracture between serious, high-quality 'paid for' home listening music, and frivolous, low-quality 'free' music for use on personal stereo or mobile music devices. In each case the actual music can be the same, but its format carries different economic, cultural and ideological values.

RECORD COLLECTING

Will Straw (1997) has speculated on the psychology of record collecting as a social practice and identified several characteristics that relate to the marginal nature of many collectors' interests: hipness, connoisseurship, bohemianism and the adventurous hunter. These point towards the stereotyping of record collectors as obsessive, which in turn harks back to Theodor Adorno's (1990) assertion that popular music fans are either an easily manipulated mass or alienated and poorly socialized loners. In such a reading, record collectors would be classed as the latter.

The gendering of collecting

Tim Wall (2003) points out that the act of collecting encompasses not only the ownership of products, but also various processes of archiving and display, and that these are typically identified as masculine activities. Roy Shuker (2010: 5) notes that while little work has been undertaken on the role of ethnicity or class within the context of collecting, 'the "gendering" of collecting has attracted considerable attention'. For instance, studies by Susan Pearce (1997) and Russell Belk (2001) show that while male and female children are equally likely to be avid collectors, collecting declines significantly among adolescent girls. Shuker also notes the 'tendency for men to renew collecting in middle age – a trend not seen to the same extent in women' (2010: 5).

Types of record collector

Susan Pearce (1997) distinguished three modes of relationship between collectors and the items they collect, and these may be applied to the act of record collecting: souvenir, fetishism, and systematics. 'Souvenir' represents the application of personal biography to the life story of the object, thus providing personalized meanings: the record carries the past life of the collector into the present. Fetishism relates to how record collecting creates the identity of the collector. The historical and cultural context of the records are secondary to the act of collecting and what a collection as a whole may say about the collector. An obsessive urge for complete-ism is often found as collectors seek every artefact relating to a genre, record label or scene through which they define themselves. This leads to the third area of systematic collecting where the collector rationalizes obsessive complete-ism through systematic archiving, and deep knowledge of the records themselves. For instance, collectors of Northern Soul records can identify a record's value through a memorized knowledge of the vinyl's run out scratch marks and other pressing information.

Bootlegging and 'official bootlegs'

The act of bootlegging and bootleg collecting is an area that reveals Pearce's (1997) three traits in action. Bootlegging (see also Chapter 9) can be viewed as an active expression of fandom through which live performances, radio sessions and unreleased studio recordings are distributed without, in many cases, the permission of the copyright owners. Bootlegs may be produced by commercially motivated companies flouting copyright legislation or by fans who distribute the recordings non-commercially and may be creative in designing artwork and/or remastering often poor quality recordings (Anderton, 2006). Fans and bootleggers have pointed to the legitimacy of bootlegging as an expression of fandom for individuals who already own all official products, and also an important process for documenting a musical history of artists that may not be supported through officially released products (Marshall, 2005; Anderton, 2006). In some cases, demand for bootleg recordings of this sort has been so high that record companies and artists have subsequently released official versions (see Box 8.3).

Box 8.3
'Official' bootlegs

Official bootlegs are most often seen in the form of unreleased studio albums or demo recordings such as Bob Dylan's *The Basement Tapes* (1975), which included demo recordings made with The Band in 1967. Many had previously been available on what is considered to be the first commercial rock bootleg, *Great White Wonder*, released in 1969 (see Heylin, 1994). Other examples include the Buzzcocks *Times Up* studio sessions (bootlegged in 1977 but not available officially until 1991) and Prince's *Black Album*. The latter was an album originally scheduled for release in 1987 but withdrawn a week before release. Promotional copies came into the possession of bootleggers who issued an illicit version of it. It was subsequently given a limited edition official release in 1994, which has itself become a collectors' item.

Record companies and independent artists have continued to address the desires of collectors by including extra live and studio material within re-release packages of classic albums, or as bonus discs or downloads available with new releases. These extras are used as promotional hooks to target the fan-as-collector and are a particular feature of the reissue industry that has emerged around the heritage music market. In some cases, bootlegged recordings have been sourced from fan collections. For instance, the entire content of Tangerine Dream's *Bootleg Box Vol. 1* (2003) and *Bootleg Box Vol. 2* (2004) (ten concert recordings across 14 CDs) was sourced from an archival remaster project organized through an unofficial online fan forum.

Blogging and out-of-print records

An interesting development in the unauthorized distribution of music recordings is the creation and growth of online music blogs that digitize and distribute otherwise unavailable back catalogue music. Some have become central to online communities of fans that focus on specific genres and subgenres of music. An example of such a blog is the now-defunct *The CTI Never Sleeps* (formerly at http://cti-kudu.blogspot.com). This site was dedicated to making the entire back catalogue of the soul/jazz label CTI/Kudu Records available for download since the vast majority of that catalogue had not been re-released on CD or through legal download channels. Similarly, there are blogs dedicated to old library music recordings (originally intended as background music for adverts, films and television, and not commercially available for the public to buy), and to obscure audio-cassette-only labels and magazine cover-mounts. Of notable interest is the hugely eclectic *NME* compilation cassette series, which included the mail-order release *C86* (1986). Compiled in conjunction with the independent label and distributor Rough Trade, *C86* helped to create the notion of 'indie music' in mid-1980s Britain.

The fans who contribute to these music blogs are record collectors who specialize in out-of-print (OOP) recordings: those that are no longer manufactured by a record company (in physical or digital form) and are unavailable for legitimate purchase except through second-hand retailing (and often at highly inflated prices). These recordings are often 'ripped' (recorded into a digital format such as MP3 or FLAC) and made available via internet cyberlocker links posted to the blog (cyberlockers are online storage sites that can be accessed by multiple users). Quite often the person who 'posts' the recording will provide an in-depth discussion of the value of the work, details about the musicians who performed it, and so on. Many of these blogs have multiple authors who may not be known to each other on a face-to-face level, but solely through their online identities. Nevertheless, through the sharing of these files, a series of social and cultural practices have emerged, communities developed, and individual statuses increased through the sharing of particularly rare and hard to find recordings.

Given that these out-of-print recordings are often unavailable for legitimate purchase, the enthusiasts who use these blogs assert that while this form of dissemination infringes copyright, it does not negatively impact upon the commercial activities of the record industries. In addition, they maintain that it helps to preserve and propagate cultural forms that might otherwise become endangered or remain unheard except by a privileged few. They also commonly remove links to albums that are subsequently commercially released, and may even add links to online stores to facilitate purchase (whilst simultaneously acting as a form of marketing due to the written reviews and information that they provide). Of course, there are also many other blogs whose authors are less than altruistic, and who do not take pains to limit themselves to out-of-print albums, or may actively post brand new or pre-release recordings. As both sets of bloggers use the same cyberlocker hosts, legal action against cyberlockers affects all of them irrespective of their particular intentions (see Chapter 9).

CONCLUSION

The consumption of music has undergone considerable change with the development of digital and mobile technologies. Music is consumed and conversed through blog comments, Facebook feedback and Twitter chatter, and 'played' through the internet, mobile devices, and video and app gaming. There has been a shift from the top-down mass-market model of the music industries to a focus on individual consumers as opinion leaders situated at the heart of a continual and pervasive conversation. Music listening has become an extension of media products and it is increasingly accessed as a personalized experience through devices such as iPods and smartphones. The impact of this has been to allow consumers to manage their audio-sensory experience of the world around them, and to mobilize their entire music collections in a user-friendly manner.

Throughout this period of change, collecting has remained a constant part of the consumption and use of music, though archiving has now shifted to online platforms where obscure and rare performances and recordings are made more readily available. Despite the free availability of music files, audiences have continued to buy physical products. These are lauded for their greater collectability, better sound quality and packaging, and the sense of investment that these products offer in cultural, subcultural and ideological terms. Associated with the continued purchase of music (physical and digital) has been the growth of a nostalgia industry associated with vinyl records, cassette tapes and classic album performances by heritage acts.

FURTHER READING

Roy Shuker's *Popular Music Culture: the Key Concepts* (2012) offers a comprehensive dictionary of key ideas and concepts in popular music culture. These are explored in further detail by Tim Wall's *Studying Popular Music Culture* (2003). Rupa Huq's *Beyond Subculture* (2006) provides a useful analysis of the theories surrounding subcultures, scenes and neo-tribes, and investigates the cultures of hip hop, bhangra, grunge and Britpop. In *How The Beatles Destroyed Rock 'n' Roll*, Elijah Wald (2009) presents a thorough and fascinating study of developments in music consumption practices from the dawn of recording through the 1960s, while Michael Bull (2007) investigates the impact of the iPod on music consumption in his *Sound Moves: iPod Culture and Urban Experience*. Karen Collins's edited collection *From Pac-Man to Pop Music* (2008) includes thought-provoking essays on the intersection between computer gaming and mobile media technologies. Finally, Roy Shuker's *Wax Trash and Vinyl Treasures* (2010) investigates the various contexts and discussions that surround the practice of record collecting.

9

COPYRIGHT AND MUSIC PIRACY

Copyright law is a complex yet vitally important area of the music industries. This chapter will examine the main areas of copyright law affecting songwriters, musicians and record companies in the UK, and the changes brought about by Britain's membership of the European Union. It will also draw parallels and contrasts with copyright law in the US to show how copyright laws differ between nations. A secure knowledge of copyright law is critical to understanding the effects of music piracy, and the actions and reactions of both the music industries and the artists to the challenges of the online environment.

KEY FINDINGS

- Copyright law in Europe and the US was created to encourage new works that enrich the cultural life of a nation.
- Anyone wishing to exploit (make use of) a song, recording or performance needs permission from the relevant copyright owners prior to exploitation.
- The public domain has been eroded by successive copyright legislation.
- Artists and music industry lobbyists have each responded to the issue of digital music piracy in varied and contrasting ways.

INTRODUCING COPYRIGHT

Copyright is defined by the International Federation of the Phonographic Industry (IFPI, n.d.) as 'the means by which a person or a business makes a living from creativity'. In commercial terms, it is argued that copyright acts as an incentive for people to create new works, safe in the knowledge that they will have exclusive rights to exploit (make money from) their work for a set period of time: the copyright term. It is also argued that copyright should enrich the cultural life of a nation and act as a public good. For that reason, a work will pass into the 'public domain' upon expiry of its copyright term, where it becomes a collectively owned and shared cultural asset available for use by anyone, for any purpose and without seeking permission from the original copyright owner.

These commercial and cultural justifications underlie the world's first copyright act, the British Statute of Anne (1709), and the first American law in this area, the Copyright Act 1790 (Marshall, 2005: 10, 19). These laws were introduced to protect the publishing copyrights of artistic and literary works in printed form (including lyrics and sheet music). Later laws and international agreements have been enacted to expand protection to sound recordings and performers.

Copyright legislation has created a collection of authorial and related rights that will be discussed in detail later. These rights are crucial to the financial dealings of the traditional music industries as they create numerous income streams for record companies, songwriters and performers. In consequence, unauthorized sale and free downloading and streaming of copyrighted music recordings is a cause of great concern to those traditional music industries, since a digitized recording may be 'copied, shared, and distributed without diminishing its value' (Rodman and Vanderdonckt, 2006: 248). In other words the digital copy is identical to the original and the question becomes: why buy the original? Independent artists may also be concerned with the effects of music piracy, though they may not be as reliant on traditional copyright for their income.

Why is copyright the way it is?

Copyright laws are not natural laws but ones that have been settled upon after a process of negotiation between artists, music companies, legislators and others. These negotiations have been significant to the establishment of copyright as it is today and to arguments over how it should be in the future. Copyright laws vary from country to country and change over time, though it is common to find that the commercial interests of record companies and music publishers do not entirely align with the notion that copyright should emphasize the public good. When examining the copyright laws of a given country, we must first seek to understand why those particular laws exist in that specific time and place, and second, consider how changes in the cultural, technological, social, and political environment may invite a reconsideration and resettlement of them.

This chapter will explain some of the main components of the current copyright settlement in the UK and USA, but it is important not to simply 'learn the rules'. Instead, those rules should be contextualized through the perspectives of political economy, media ecology and popular music subcultures (as discussed in Chapter 1). Copyright laws are dynamic and fluid in nature, and while the music industries seek to extend and enforce copyright laws ever more strongly, there are dissenting voices who argue against such control, and those who fight to protect the public domain. These and other aspects are examined below, together with an exploration of music piracy and the many issues that it highlights.

COPYRIGHT BASICS

Copyright law does not protect ideas, but the expression of those ideas (Stokes, 2005: 3): to gain legal protection, ideas must be expressed and 'fixed' in a tangible fashion, whether written down or recorded in some other way. Under UK legislation, there is no need to register a song or recording with an official body, though it is recommended that creators of musical works (songwriters and lyricists) should assert their ownership by including a copyright notice (see below) on their products and by registering their work with the UK Copyright Service (UKCS). In the US, registration is provided by the US Copyright Office and, while not technically a condition of protection, it would be difficult to take legal action without it. This is because copyrights are 'negative' in nature: they give the 'right to restrain others from exploiting work' without the permission of the copyright owner (Sparrow, 2006: 33). If there is no proof of the existence of a copyright, it is difficult to argue that it has been exploited without permission (known as copyright infringement). A fee is charged by both organizations, and up-to-date information can be found at http://www.copyrightservice.co.uk/ and http://www.copyright.gov/.

Copyright notices

The copyright notice consists of either the word 'copyright' or the symbol ©, followed by the year of publication and the name of the copyright owner. Sound recordings can similarly be given protection. This is known as a phonogram copyright notice and indicated by the ℗ symbol. Both notices will normally be found on the packaging of a CD, where ℗ refers to the sound recording and © to the underlying musical composition and/or any printed materials that form part of the packaging (such as artwork and printed lyrics). The wording of these notices may be extended, with common examples being 'All rights reserved' and 'Unauthorized duplication is a violation of applicable laws'.

What does the consumer own?

Copyright is widely misunderstood and many people do not realize that when they buy a CD or download a track (legally), they do not actually own the copyright. Confusion is fostered in part by differences between physical and digital products. A CD or LP can legally be re-sold as 'second-hand' because what is being sold is a physical artefact that is not 'copied' in the process. In contrast, digital tracks are always copied when they are transferred between computers or other digital devices, so any unauthorized distribution of digital tracks (whether for money or for free) will automatically infringe the underlying copyright. This is why the internet (and internet-enabled mobile phones and other digital devices) is a key battle ground for those parts of the music industries reliant on copyright revenues, and why the recording and publishing industries are so active in lobbying governments for legislative action to combat music piracy.

National treatment and international agreements

Copyright is viewed as a national property right, and while international agreements have been created to harmonize the terms and protections of copyright laws across nations, those agreements must be adopted into national legislation to be effective. The earliest agreement – the Berne Convention 1886 – protects songwriters and lyricists and, in addition to moral rights (discussed below), provides 'that each signatory country must grant the same copyright treatment to nationals from other member countries as they do their own nationals' (Schulenberg, 2005: 412). This is important when cases of copyright infringement are being fought, as each case will be determined according to the law of the country where the infringement is said to have occurred. This leads to problems where internet distribution is concerned, as it may be difficult to decide which national laws are applicable when launching a legal case (Stokes, 2005: 7–9).

There are a number of multi-lateral international treaties offering legal protection to copyright owners. Since 1995, these have been overseen by the World Trade Organization. Dave Laing (2004b) argues that American corporations were highly influential in this and other changes that push 'Western' style copyright law upon countries that did not previously offer the same levels of copyright protection. A year later, the 1996 WIPO (World Intellectual Property Organization) treaties were introduced to extend copyright protection into the digital environment for the first time. These treaties have since been adopted into the national legislation of most European countries, as well by the US (through the 1998 Digital Millennium Copyright Act).

Public domain

On expiry of the copyright term a composition will, as noted earlier, enter the public domain and be available for anyone to use without requiring permission or payment. This recognizes that musical creativity is often rooted in an 'unconscious process of borrowing from and referring to other works' (Hesmondhalgh, 2007: 153), and that future creativity should not be unduly restricted by copyright law. However, a version or arrangement of a public domain lyric or musical composition may be granted a copyright in its own right. This is commonly seen in folk music where the abbreviation © Trad. Arr. (Traditional Arrangement) is used to indicate the copyright owner of the version/arrangement.

Orphan works

If the author of a work is unknown (despite attempts at identification) then that work will be classed as an orphan work, and will retain copyright protection indefinitely. It cannot enter the public domain and cannot be used commercially since its use would automatically infringe copyright (as there is no one to give permission). The internet allows works to circulate online very easily, and there is a very real potential for many new orphan works to appear.

KEY TERMS IN UK COPYRIGHT LAW

The Copyright Designs and Patents Act 1988 (hereafter CDPA 1988) is the primary legislation for music and music-related copyrights in the UK, though it has subsequently been amended and/or supplemented by a number of international agreements, and in response to technological developments and the lobbying of music industry organizations. The key terms of the Act are discussed below.

Works

The CDPA 1988 protects 'works' that are 'recorded in writing or otherwise', hence are 'fixed' in some tangible (physical) or electronic form. A song lyric is protected as a literary work, while any musical accompaniment is protected as a musical work, defined as 'exclusive of any words or action intended to be sung, spoken or performed with the music'. Vocal-based songs therefore attract two separate copyrights: one for the lyric and one for the music. In addition, any sound recordings of the literary and/or musical work will be protected separately by phonographic rights (discussed further below). It should be noted that works not fixed in tangible or electronic form gain no protection.

Originality

According to the CDPA 1988, a copyrighted work must be 'original', though it does not offer a definition of this term. Legal cases suggest the work must express the skill and labour of the author and not simply copy a pre-existing work in a mechanical fashion, but otherwise the applicable standard for originality is 'very low' (Stokes, 2005: 24–5). There is, for instance, no requirement for the work to be novel or inventive. This is quite different from patent law where a new or innovative idea must be demonstrated in order for protection to be granted.

Author

The CDPA 1988 provides protection to the 'author' (or 'authors') of the work, which in turn determines who owns the copyright and how long the copyright will last (Stokes, 2005: 26). For musical compositions and lyrics (see later for phonographic rights) the 'author' will be the songwriter or lyricist, though they commonly assign or license their rights to music publishers in return for a royalty (see Chapter 3). When assigned, the publishing company takes the place of the author (or copyright owner) for the purposes of the Act. This means that the publishing company gains all the copyrights associated with being an 'author', and in turn allows whole catalogues of songs to be bought and sold between companies.

Authors' rights

A number of exclusive rights are available to authors of lyrical and musical works under the CDPA 1988. These are 'restricted acts' (Stokes, 2005: 35) as they prevent others from doing the following without the copyright owner's permission/licence (see Box 9.1).

Box 9.1
Authors' rights

- Copying the lyrical or musical work in any material form;
- Issuing copies of the lyrical or musical work to the public;
- Renting or lending the lyrical or musical work to the public;
- Performing, showing or playing the lyrical or musical work in public;
- Broadcasting the lyrical or musical work;
- Including the lyrical or musical work in a cable programme service;
- Making an adaptation of the lyrical or musical work;
- Doing, in relation to an adaptation, any of the above.

Where permission is granted, licence fees, royalties and/or other payments will normally be payable to the copyright owner. These include performing rights income, related to the public performance of the musical composition and/or lyrics, mechanical rights income, related to the reproduction of the composition or lyrics in any material or electronic form, and synchronization, where the composition or lyric is used in relation to visual media such as television adverts, videos and films. These income streams are monitored and administered by collection societies and are discussed later.

Duration of protection

The current copyright term for literary, dramatic, musical or artistic works in the UK (since 1 January 1996) is the lifetime of the author plus 70 years (see later for phonographic rights). If the work is authored by more than one person, the copyright will be linked to the death of the last of the joint authors to die. This is the case even when assigned or licensed to a music publisher. Once expired, the work enters the public domain. As the duration of protection is now the lifetime of the author plus 70 years, much popular music of the mid-late twentieth century will remain protected for some considerable time to come. This erodes the 'public good' justification of copyright law and is a key area of interest for copyright reformers and those who make use of samples.

Authors' moral rights

The CDPA 1988 confers non-economic moral rights to the original authors of literary and musical works (see Box 9.2). These rights cannot be assigned or licensed to anyone else and last as long as a work is in copyright. The Performers (Moral Rights, etc.) Regulations 2006 extends these rights to performers.

Box 9.2
Moral rights

The main moral rights are the right of paternity and the right of integrity, though authors may also be protected from having a work falsely attributed to them, or from having private or privately commissioned photographs made public, for instance, by a tabloid newspaper.

The right of paternity is the 'right to be identified as the author' of a work whenever that work is published commercially, performed in public, communicated to the public in some other way, or issued to the public in a film or sound recording.

The right of integrity gives authors the 'right to object to derogatory treatment' of their work. This includes any additions, deletions, alterations or adaptations of a work where those changes are deemed to be prejudicial to their honour or reputation.

Authors' rights and interests are often mentioned by music industry organizations when lobbying for greater protection in the online environment, yet moral rights have yet to be fully addressed by legislators. Furthermore, the recording and publishing industries successfully sought a waiver clause to the CDPA 1988 that allows authors to relinquish their moral rights by signing a written document to that effect (Harrison, 2011: 324–5). This gives maximum control of songs and sound recordings to publishers and recording companies, but is contrary to the spirit of the Berne Convention that specifically prohibits authors from assigning or licensing their moral rights. Nevertheless it is common practice in music industry contracts, and only those artists with greater bargaining power are likely to retain their moral rights (Harrison, 2011: 325).

Related rights

A number of other copyrights are enshrined within CDPA 1988. These are known as related rights (or neighbouring rights) because they are separate from, yet related to, authors' rights in musical and literary works. They developed during the twentieth century when sound recordings of music, rather than sales of sheet music and live performance, became the predominant economic driver of the music industries. Two sets of these rights are discussed here: phonographic rights and performers' property rights.

Phonographic rights

Phonographic rights relate to sound recordings. Here, the 'author' is identified as 'the producer', who is defined by the Act as 'the person by whom the arrangements necessary for the making of the recording ... are undertaken'. As record companies usually make and pay for these arrangements through producer contracts, the record company will often be the 'author' of sound recordings and assert their rights through the use of the ℗ symbol (discussed earlier). As the 'author', the record company gains the full protection of the Act with respect to phonographic rights: essentially the same as those listed earlier for composers and lyricists, except that the 'work' protected is a sound recording.

Duration of phonographic rights

In the UK the duration of phonographic rights is 50 years from the end of the calendar year in which the recording was made, or 50 years from the end of the calendar year in which it was first published or made available to the public. Record industry bodies have lobbied hard to extend the duration of this copyright, with the EU term extension Directive finally confirmed by the EU in 2011. This Directive, which is due to be implemented by all EU member states including the UK from 2014, extends the protection period for sound recordings and performers on sound recordings to 70 years. This is less than the protection given to composers and some 25 years shorter than the protection for sound recordings under US copyright law. Copyright extension will mean that sound recordings made in the 1950s and 1960s that were due to pass into the public domain will now have their protection reinstated. This will allow older performers and phonographic copyright holders to continue collecting royalties on record sales and performances for an additional 20 years. While this is good for record companies and older artists, it further undermines the 'public good' justification that underlies copyright law.

Performers' property rights

These rights protect the musicians who perform on sound recordings (see Box 9.3).

Box 9.3
Performers' property rights

A performer's rights are infringed when any of the following actions occurs without permission being granted:

- Makes a recording of a performance;
- Broadcasts a live performance;
- Records a broadcast of a live performance;
- Makes a copy of a recording of a performance;
- Issues a copy of a recording of a performance;
- Rents or lends to the public a recording of a performance;
- Makes available to the public a recording of a performance through electronic transmission.

Under the CDPA 1988, performers' property rights last for 50 years from the end of the calendar year in which the performance takes place, or from the end of the calendar year in which the performance was 'first published, played or shown in public or communicated to the public' with consent. This will be extended to 70 years of protection from 2014.

The CDPA 1988 also gives the right for a performer to receive 'equitable remuneration' when a published sound recording is played in public or communicated to the public with the performers consent. This right can be assigned to a collection society which arranges for any income due under the right to be collected and distributed to relevant performers.

Fair-dealing provisions

The CDPA 1988 also details a number of 'acts permitted in relation to copyrighted works', and a similar list of permitted acts in relation to performers' rights. These are more commonly known as 'fair-dealing' provisions. Permitted acts include: the use of copyrighted works for the purposes of criticism and news reporting, and their use for private study and non-commercial research. Format shifting (copying a legitimately bought CD to MP3 in order to play the music on a portable device) is not permitted under fair-dealing provisions in the UK, though it is a common practice facilitated by computer manufacturers that include CD 'ripping' software as a function of their free media players.

Copyright infringement

Copyright infringement occurs when someone copies a protected work without permission or licence from the copyright owner. This will be the case whether or not the whole or a 'substantial part' of the work has been copied, though there is no clear definition of 'substantial part' within the CDPA 1988. The penalties offered under the Act vary depending on which particular right is infringed. Copyright owners may sue for damages, serve court injunctions, demand delivery and seizure of infringing works, and/or be awarded financial damages. Some cases may lead to criminal charges leading to a fine and/or a prison term of up to ten years.

US COPYRIGHT LAW: KEY DIFFERENCES

The 1976 Copyright Act is the primary legislation in the US, though it too has been amended since it first came into force in 1978 and is also affected by legal interpretation through a number of court cases. As in Britain, US copyright protects 'original works of authorship' (music, lyrics, and sound recordings) with regards to a number of restricted acts, and requires that the music and lyrics be recorded in a tangible or electronic format. The terms and definitions largely parallel those discussed for the UK above, though some of the key variations are discussed here.

Works for hire

In the 1920s and 1930s it was standard practice for music publishers to employ songwriters on a salary basis. As they were employed to write songs as part of an employment contract, their songs were regarded as works made for hire, so the publisher owned the first copyright in any works produced (Baskerville and Baskerville, 2010: 89). This is much less common today, though may be found where a songwriter/composer is commissioned to write music for film or television. As the copyright is owned by the commissioning company, these works for hire attract one-off fees rather than ongoing royalties. Sound recordings might also be considered 'works for hire' given that they are made under contract to a record company. This has implications regarding the duration of protection as noted below (Hull et al., 2011: 55).

Duration of protection

The copyright term for music and lyrics is the life of the author plus 70 years, starting from the death of the last co-author. If the work is considered to be a work for hire, the copyright will last for 95 years from publication or 120 years from creation (whichever is shorter). These terms apply equally to sound recordings, and significantly increase the length of time before those copyrights will enter the public domain.

Moral rights

The US joined the Berne Convention in 1989, though strong lobbying by the US film industry ensured an opt-out in relation to the moral rights elements of the treaty

(Baskerville and Baskerville, 2010: 504). As a result, authors of literary and musical works in the US do not automatically benefit from moral rights as they do in Europe.

Performance rights

The 1976 Copyright Act excluded public performance rights in sound recordings, so American performers and owners of sound recordings missed out on a lucrative income stream (principally airplay on broadcast radio) that was available in the UK and much of Europe. This occurred due to intensive lobbying by US broadcasters in the early 1970s who claimed it was unfair for record companies to derive income from 'promotional' airplay and then again from retail sales (Hull et al., 2011: 95). This argument has become increasingly difficult to sustain. For instance, the 1995 Digital Performance Right in Sound Recordings Act provides US record companies with an income stream related to digital audio transmissions including online audio streaming services. As online uses of sound recordings are now treated differently from over-the-air broadcasting, there have been renewed calls to amend US copyright law and level the playing field.

An interesting development in 2012 was a deal made between Clear Channel Radio (the largest owner of radio stations in the US) and the independent country music label Big Machine. Under the deal, Clear Channel will reportedly pay Big Machine a revenue-share royalty for over-the-air broadcasting of its music in return for more favourable online royalty rates. In doing so, Clear Channel may be anticipating the future implementation of performance royalties for broadcast as well as online radio (CMU, 2012b).

Copyright infringement

The remedies available under US law are similar to those in the UK in as much as the copyright owner may apply for injunctions to prevent or restrain infringement of their copyrights and seek damages. In the US the copyright owner may choose to pursue either statutory damages or actual damages. Statutory damages generally range from US$750 to US$30,000 though the courts may increase the maximum to US$150,000 should the infringement be committed wilfully. Actual damages are more likely to be sought on behalf of highly successful artists and can run into multiple millions of US dollars (Baskerville and Baskerville, 2010: 100). Unlike the UK, no legal action can be taken unless the copyright has been officially registered at the US Copyright Office. This registration can be completed at or around the time of publication (for example, the official release date of an album), or even prior to publication. It is especially important if the work is likely to suffer from pre-release piracy (Hull et al., 2011: 60).

COLLECTION SOCIETIES

Collection societies (also referred to as performing rights organizations) administer the various rights that have been discussed above and collect and distribute royalty payments and licence income on behalf of and to authors, performers, publishers and record companies. To do so, rights holders need to join a relevant society which grants 'blanket licences' to users of copyrighted works. Blanket licences cost either a flat or a variable fee (subject to negotiation) and must be obtained by broadcasters, internet services, commercial premises, live performance venues and so on where recorded or live music is publicly performed or broadcast (including shops and restaurants). They are 'blanket' licences due to the inherent administrative difficulties of attempting to record each and every individual performance of a song by each licensee (though some major broadcasters and concert venues will report or sample this information). The blanket licence fees are collected together then disbursed (paid out) to publishers and songwriters according to complicated sharing rules that inevitably benefit some recipients more than others.

Different countries have their own collection societies (for instance, GEMA (Germany), SACEM (France), and JASRAC (Japan)), so bilateral agreements are in place to ensure that monies due from performances in non-domestic markets can be collected, returned and disbursed in the home country.

Collection societies in the UK

In the UK, the main collection societies are 'not-for-profit' organizations that charge commission or administration fees to cover their operating costs: the PRS, PPL, VPL and MCPS.

The PRS (Performing Rights Society) represents authors, composers and publishers of music and lyrics by licensing their performance and synchronization rights. These rights are assigned to the PRS by the copyright holder, and royalties are due for any public performance of the copyright holder's music and lyrics, whether that performance is live or recorded, and whether made on a radio or television broadcast or online. Royalty income is typically split 50:50 between the publisher and the songwriter. The PRS formed an alliance with MCPS (see below) in 1997 in order to share administrative resources. Since 2009 these organizations have been known collectively as PRS for Music (see www.prsformusic.com).

PPL (Phonographic Performance Limited) issues blanket licences for public performances of sound recordings (rather than the underlying music and lyric copyrights), and so represents the interests of record companies and performers (see www.ppluk.com). Similarly, VPL (Video Performance Limited) administers the public performance of music videos, yet only collects and shares licence fee income on behalf of phonographic rights owners (principally recording companies). Performers will only receive a percentage share of VPL income if this is specified in their recording agreement.

MCPS (Mechanical-Copyright Protection Society) issues mechanical licences for sound recordings on behalf of composers and lyricists. In other words, when a record company issues an album or single (on whatever format, including digital files and the synchronization of sound recordings to video and DVD) a mechanical licence must be sought from MCPS. In calculating the cost of manufacturing an album, each individual song will attract a mechanical licence fee, which is then multiplied by the total number of CDs produced. The mechanical royalty rate for CDs is 8.5 per cent of the wholesale price (PPD – published price to dealers) or 6.5 per cent of the retail price prior to VAT deductions. MCPS membership is required even when an artist runs their own publishing and recording companies, though an exclusion agreement is available.

Digital rights collection

The law and collection of digital rights (in relation to online and mobile music services) is still developing both in the UK and further afield. The UK Copyright Tribunal is continuing to review the royalty rates for the use of these rights, which vary depending on the exact nature of the service offered. For example, permanent downloads attract a mechanical licence fee rate of 8 per cent, with a minimum of £0.04 per download (reduced for older tracks and sale of tracks in bundles). In contrast, webcasting (internet radio) attracts a rate of 6.5 per cent, with a minimum of £0.22 per subscriber or £0.0006 per track. It is likely that music industry organizations will lobby hard for higher rates as the market continues to shift from physical to digital product.

US Collection Societies

In the US, public performance rights are administered by three main organizations: the American Society of Composers, Authors and Publishers (ASCAP), Broadcast Music, Inc (BMI) and SESAC. They issue blanket licences to various users of published music (radio stations, bars, restaurants and so on), then collect and disburse revenues to music publishers and songwriters.

In the US the predominant organization for issuing mechanical licences is the Harry Fox Agency, and it also ensures payment and distribution of revenues under those licences to music publishers. The compulsory mechanical licence fee rates are set and reviewed by the Copyright Royalty Board. From 2009 to 2013 the rate for phonorecords (CDs, LPs and so on) and permanent digital downloads is 9.1 cents per copy, or 1.75 cents per minute (whichever is larger).

Since 1995, US performers have benefited from an online public performance right in relation to sound recordings. Royalty income is collected by SoundExchange and paid directly to performers. It is an income stream that lies beyond the terms of an artist's recording agreement and cannot be used to repay it, but as royalty rates and revenues are low, income from this source is likely to be rather small for most acts.

Criticisms of the performance royalty system

Many songwriters receive relatively little from the blanket licence sharing rules that are in place, and many businesses find themselves in a seemingly bizarre position: having to pay a licence fee in order to use a radio on their premises or to play previously bought CDs or MP3s. In such instances, they are not specifically charging their customers to listen to the music (unlike, say, a dance music club), but providing their customers or staff with a musical background while they browse, shop, work and so on.

MUSIC PIRACY

Music piracy is a catch-all term used by the music industries, governments and media to describe a variety of activities that infringe some or many of the copyrights discussed above. It is often referred to as copyright 'theft', yet because copyright is an intangible intellectual property it is more appropriate to refer to piracy as 'infringement' – since the original rights owner is not deprived of the future use of their rights. It is a global problem that involves both the physical production of CDs, DVDs and other media, and the unlicensed sale, distribution or streaming of digital music files through the internet.

Physical piracy predominates when copyright laws are weakly structured or poorly enforced, and where communications technology is less well developed, such as in parts of Asia, Eastern Europe and the developing world. In contrast, online piracy is most common in countries with widespread broadband cable penetration and, most worryingly for the music industries, relatively strong and long-established copyright laws and enforcement measures (Connell and Gibson, 2003; IFPI, 2006; Harrison, 2008). The range of activities commonly referred to as 'piracy' can differ quite markedly in terms of their content, scale and intent, and are outlined below.

Counterfeiting

Counterfeiting occurs when an officially released album (including artwork and packaging) is copied and sold commercially without permission of the rights owners. A counterfeited product is intended to be passed off as the real thing, duping consumers into believing that they are buying a bona fide copy.

Pirating

Pirated recordings may, like counterfeits, consist of entire albums of work, but they are produced and sold without the official artwork or packaging. They may also be in the form of compilations drawn from multiple sources, or as CD and DVD data disks that encompass an artist's entire discography in MP3 form (Marshall, 2005: 111). In some cases, pirated recordings will be released on what appear to be legitimate record labels, with record company names and logos given on the covers. Some companies will even pay the compulsory mechanical fees to a national collection agency in order to give the appearance of legitimacy. However, this only covers the publishing rights in the songs, not the rights in the sound recordings or performances they reproduce (Harrison, 2008: 287). Non-commercial pirating is also found, though usually in the form of small-scale CD-r burning or home taping (Marshall, 2005: 111). In such cases, there is no intention to profit commercially, yet copyrights are still being infringed whether or not the source product is owned by the person copying it.

Commercial bootlegging

Commercial bootlegging involves the 'recording, reproduction and distribution of music that has *never been released* by official record labels' (Marshall, 2005: 111, emphasis in original). The most common sources are audience recordings of live concerts and live concerts recorded from radio, television or the internet. Unreleased or rare studio recordings may also be included. Commercial bootlegs may have specially designed packaging and a sound quality that varies from excellent to poor depending on the source material used (Marshall, 2005; Anderton, 2006).

Non-commercial bootlegging

Non-commercial bootlegging uses the same source material as commercial bootlegging but is conducted on a much smaller scale and on a strictly not-for-profit basis. It developed using audio-cassette technology in the 1970s (and is still sometimes referred to as tape trading), but now uses recordable CD and/or high-quality lossless audio files transferred through the internet (Marshall, 2005; Anderton, 2006). They are produced by and distributed between groups of music fans (see also Chapter 8), with source recordings sometimes being edited and remastered for the best possible audio quality. Some trading groups also produce high-quality artwork that can be printed and inserted into CD cases (Anderton, 2006).

Online piracy

There are three main forms of online piracy. First, there are fraudulent websites that sell or stream music files without making payment to copyright holders. These may have the appearance of legitimate digital music sites, but licensing deals have not been made with rights owners. Second, peer-to-peer (P2P) and BitTorrent software allows users to transfer files directly between personal computers, rather than from a central computer server. Finally, there are cyberlocker sites such as RapidShare and MediaFire that allow multiple users to upload and download large files to and from a central server. Such sites have legitimate applications for transferring very large files, yet are routinely used to store and distribute entire albums of music, rather than single tracks (which is more common for the other two methods of online piracy). Cyberlocker use has grown in popularity because of the inherent problems of P2P downloading, such as incomplete or mislabelled files and the possibility of downloading computer viruses (Rodman and Vanderdonckt, 2006: 256), and because there has been a rise in online music review blogs that provide links to them.

MUSIC INDUSTRY RESPONSES TO PIRACY

Recording industry organizations such as the BPI, RIAA and IFPI make three main arguments when discussing music piracy. These are that piracy is 'killing the business' by replacing legitimate sales, that songwriters and recording artists are losing income, and that record companies can no longer invest in new artists or support niche-market genres. File-sharers are portrayed as 'amoral bandits' (Rodman and Vanderdonckt, 2006: 257) who are stealing from the music industry and its artists and in some cases accused of funding organized crime and terrorism (see also Marshall, 2005; Rojek, 2005). Numerous legal actions against physical counterfeiters, pirates and bootleggers have been successful around the world and are regularly reported on the anti-piracy web pages of the main industry bodies, yet online file-sharing gains by far the greatest news coverage and has formed a sustained focus for legislative lobbying. Six key strategies can be distinguished, and are explored below.

Legal action against file-sharing sites

The first prominent legal case was against Napster.com – a site that provided a 'search and delivery' service for MP3 files through P2P software (Rojek, 2005: 358). Napster was successfully shut down in May 2002, but the publicity surrounding it did little more than alert the wider public to the potential of the internet for freely sharing music. It was quickly replaced by numerous other P2P services, then by BitTorrent software and cyberlocker sites. Several companies facilitating these distribution methods, including Kazaa, Grokster and The Pirate Bay, have also been targeted for legal action. In some cases this has resulted in closure or the implementation of filters designed to prevent unauthorized file-sharing (Harrison, 2008: 285).

The lack of a worldwide consensus on copyright protection and enforcement means, however, that infringing services and websites continue to appear, though research by the NPD Group (2011) suggests that this strategy of legal action may be effective: file-sharing in the US significantly declined when LimeWire (a popular P2P system) ceased operations after a court battle with the RIAA.

Five related strategies have also been seen. First, the Digital Millennium Copyright Act 1998 (DMCA) allows US copyright owners to issue 'notice and takedown' orders to remove infringing content (such as cyberlocker links) from websites. Second, the Prioritizing Resources and Organization for Intellectual Property Act 2008 (PRO-IP Act) gives the US Department of Justice the power to seize internet domain addresses registered in the US without requiring a conviction. Known as 'shuttering', seized websites redirect visitors to a US government page alerting them to the infringing activities the site is alleged to have been involved in. Third, in the US a range of pre-existing laws related to copyright, conspiracy, racketeering and so on can be utilized to take legal action against websites accused of aiding and abetting criminal copyright infringement. For instance, the popular file-sharing cyberlocker site MegaUpload (and related companies) was closed in January 2012 with criminal charges brought against seven individuals connected to the site. In response, several other cyberlockers changed their terms so that users could only access their own files, thus preventing third party downloads and potential legal action. Fourth, music industry organizations are requesting that Internet Service Providers (ISPs) and search engines voluntarily block access to websites believed to be promoting or facilitating unlicensed file-sharing, or requesting court orders to force them to do so. However, new proxy sites are created within hours of ISPs implementing a block, which makes this course of action an ongoing and problematic battle for both ISPs and music industry lobbyists. Finally, the IFPI is targeting the revenue streams and business operations of websites selling or making available infringing music files. This includes online advertising (which supports free download services) and online payment processors (used when sites up-sell paid-for versions of their services or sell infringing mp3s).

Targeting pre-release groups

Pre-release piracy occurs when albums are 'leaked' to the internet (made available for download) prior to their official release date. The IFPI argues that more than 50 per cent of an album's sales are made within the first four weeks of release, so pre-release piracy can greatly affect the sales and chart potential of a record (IFPI, 2011: 21). It is also disruptive to marketing and promotional campaigns and is a high-profile way for the music pirates to assert their control of the recording industry's intellectual property. Organizations such as the IFPI and BPI target the 'release groups' that obtain and then distribute these pre-release albums, and seek to shut down the 'topsites' (internet servers) that host the infringing files.

Legal action against individuals

Music industry organizations also take or threaten legal action against individual file-sharers. This practice began in 2003 when the RIAA threatened to sue over 200 people identified using the 1998 Digital Millennium Copyright Act (which compelled ISPs to hand over the names of suspected copyright infringers). The aim of this strategy was to maximize publicity of the issue, as there are far too many people involved in downloading and uploading music to issue lawsuits against them all. It is estimated that over 30,000 lawsuits were filed by the RIAA between 2003 and 2008 (EFF, 2008), with most cases ending in out-of-court settlements. This led the RIAA to be heavily criticized by the press and public for suing its own customers. The effectiveness of this strategy for reducing online piracy is debatable, yet the threat of legal action may be a deterrent for some.

Lobbying for stronger legislation

The recording industry successfully lobbied the French government into introducing a 'graduated response' system known as HADOPI in 2009. In this system, copyright infringers are sent two warnings following which, if necessary, court action can be taken including fines and temporary suspension of internet access. In early 2012 it was reported that 833,000 initial warnings had been sent to alleged copyright infringers, with 165 cases moving towards the third stage (Pfanner, 2012). Similar systems have been introduced in New Zealand and South Korea.

In the UK, the Digital Economy Act 2010 includes the potential to introduce powers to block internet addresses, cap, filter, or limit the internet connections of persistent offenders, and to create a process for releasing the identities of persistent offenders so that legal action can be taken. This legislation has been opposed by some ISPs regarding the costs of monitoring internet traffic and by others with regard to civil liberties implications. For instance, a report by Frank La Rue (2010) for the United Nations suggests that preventing access to the internet could be a violation of international civil rights agreements and that the French and UK laws should be amended appropriately.

In the US, legislation has been proposed that seeks to provide the US government with the power to 'shutter' non-domestic websites. These include the Stop Online Piracy Act (SOPA) and the Protect IP Act (PIPA). Such laws, if passed, could effectively censor the internet for US citizens. Widespread protests in early 2012, including the 'blacking out' of Wikipedia, Wired, Reddit and other websites and opposition from internet technology firms, led to the indefinite shelving of this legislation. It is likely that other variants will be proposed in future as US copyright organizations lobby to protect their business interests.

Another legislative route is the use of international treaties that attempt to harmonize copyright laws and sanctions. For instance, the *Anti-Counterfeiting Trade Agreement* (ACTA), published in 2011, seeks to grant criminal sanctions against websites that host pirated content or are found to be 'aiding and abetting' infringement on a commercial scale. Street marches and petitions protesting the Agreement were seen across Europe in 2012 and it has been referred to the European Court of Justice prior to discussion (and potential ratification, amendment or rejection) by the European Parliament.

Educational campaigns

The ease and sheer number of potential routes for online copyright infringement mean that the recording industry is unlikely ever to completely prevent it. It is important, though, that industry organizations counter the perception that music is or should be 'free', since this could downgrade the value of their copyrights and make a sustainable online economy harder to achieve. For this reason, promotional campaigns have been created with the intent of educating the public – and children in particular – about the value of intellectual property and the legality (or otherwise) of downloading music files from the internet. Examples can be found at www.whymusicmatters.org, www.promusic.org, www. pop4schools.com and www.musicunited.org.

Promotion of legal alternatives

For the music industries to remain in control of their copyrights in the online environment, legal downloading and streaming sites must also be fostered and promoted to provide a safe, quick and easy alternative to accessing music from unlicensed sources. The IFPI *Digital Music Report 2011* suggests that there are over 400 legitimate online digital music companies around the world. Other alternatives include working with ISPs and mobile phone/device operators to offer subscription-based services and/or bundled pricing packages. For instance, the purchase price of a mobile phone handset and/or contract might include a year's subscription to a music streaming service, with a percentage of the handset/contract revenue distributed back to the music industries. It is likely that many more strategic partnerships and business ideas will emerge in the future (IFPI, 2011: 8–10).

ARTIST RESPONSES TO PIRACY

File-sharing as a marketing strategy

Top-selling artists and their recording companies often regard internet piracy as a significant threat to their earning potential, yet artists operating at a smaller scale may think differently. The latter artists are able to promote and distribute their music to a wider audience far more easily than in the past, with free music samples and file-sharing potentially helping to drive greater concert attendances, sales and the development of a fan base. For such artists, recorded music may simply be a calling card or marketing tool rather than a primary income generator (Schulenberg, 2005; David, 2010). The development of a dedicated fan base is more important than courting mass appeal, as fans can help promote the artist to others through word of mouth (or its online equivalent in chat rooms, blogs and so on). These fans will often also commercially support these artists by buying CDs, downloads and merchandise when they are made available, or by helping to fund projects (see Chapter 5).

A similar principle has long been held by 'pro-taping' (or 'tape-friendly') artists who encourage the not-for-profit trading of live concert recordings between fans (for examples, see http://etree.org/). These artists regard tape trading activities as both a marketing strategy and a way to foster a sense of community and ongoing interest between albums and tours (Anderton, 2006). The pioneer of this practice was The Grateful Dead, who felt that concert attendance and merchandising income could be increased by allowing fans to tape and swap recordings of their concerts (which often contained extended jams that differed from gig to gig). Numerous bands follow their lead today and may even set aside special taping areas in the venues that they play.

Notable successes of the 'pro-taping' approach are Phish and the Dave Matthews Band, though the practice is widespread amongst the so-called 'jam bands' that follow The Grateful Dead's practice of extended improvisation (including jazz artists such as Medeski Martin and Wood). These artists also sell CDs of studio material directly to fans through the internet, and do not condone the trading of such albums, or of any 'officially released' live concert recordings that they produce themselves. As such they generally support copyright law and the protection of intellectual property.

Creative Commons

Creative Commons (http://creativecommons.org/) is a non-profit organization established in 2002 that provides free non-exclusive licences for copyright owners who wish to adopt a 'some rights reserved' approach to their copyrights. Using these licences, musicians can allow their tracks (or samples) to be copied, distributed, edited, remixed and built upon by others so long as those others do so in accordance with the specific licence terms set out by the originator. All the licences contain an attribution clause. This specifies that credit must be given to the originator of a work whenever it is used by another, and means that the originator's moral right to be identified as such is upheld. It should also ensure that music issued under a Creative Commons licence will not become an orphan work. Internet sites like the Internet Archive (http://archive.org) and Free Music Archive (http://freemusicarchive.org) offer large libraries of public domain and Creative Commons licensed music for free download.

Creative Commons licences are useful to musicians for a number of reasons. Some artists may have full-time careers in other fields, but make music in their spare time. In such instances, the licences allow their music to be heard and distributed without completely relinquishing control. If someone does wish to use a track for a commercial purpose, they are free to negotiate a separate licence deal to do so. Other artists use the licences for marketing purposes. For instance, Nine Inch Nails issued several albums under Creative Commons licences including *Ghosts I* (2008) and *The Slip* (2008). Limited edition deluxe versions of these albums (on CD/DVD and vinyl) were also made available for fans who wanted physical merchandise, including 2,500 copies of the extended *Ghosts I–IV* box set priced at US$300 (which subsequently sold out).

Creative Commons licences have been criticized for not going far enough, since they do not seek to amend copyright law, but offer creative ways of working within it (McLeod and DiCola, 2011: 246). In addition, the organization cannot offer legal advice if a track/sample is used for a commercial purpose without permission, and has no system for ensuring that tracks/samples uploaded under a Creative Commons licence are actually the work of the uploader. Further problems include the fact that if a track incorporates music from more than one licensed source, the licence terms of the different sources might conflict with each other.

Remix culture

Remix culture refers to the use and manipulation of musical and non-musical samples from a variety of sources in order to create new tracks. In some cases, such as Girl Talk, tracks are comprised entirely of samples (sometimes looped, pitch-shifted or altered in other ways), and are issued without seeking sample clearance or licences from copyright owners (see Chapter 3). To do so would be prohibitively expensive, for instance, Girl Talk's fifth album *Feed the Animals* (released in 2008 by his label Illegal Arts) uses over 300 separate samples.

The music industries are known to be highly litigious, yet artists such as Girl Talk and Negativland have not attracted legal cases for their work in the 2000s (even when that work has been commercially released). This was not always the case. In 1991 Negativland released the single 'The Letter "U" and the Numeral "2"', which included samples of Irish rock band U2's 'I Still Haven't Found What I'm Looking For' (1987). U2's record label and publisher took legal action that cost Negativland and its label SST Records over US$90,000 (Herman and Sloop, 1998: 4). Despite this, Negativland has continued to release music without seeking clearances or licences and, with the exception of some warnings and threats, has not again faced legal action in the courts. This may be because internet piracy has become a more important target since the early 2000s or because a new legal case might prompt calls for a compulsory licensing scheme for sampling. If this was established, artists and companies could lose the right to control the use of samples of their works, and the income from such a scheme would likely be only a fraction of that obtained through the current negotiable clearance system.

CONCLUSION

This chapter has provided overviews of the copyright systems in the UK and USA, and discussed both music piracy and the responses of the music industries and artists to it. The recorded music industries seek ever stronger protection and control, yet this undermines the 'public good' justification that underlies copyright legislation. Copyright law has been slow to adapt to the challenges created by internet technologies, while the use of national laws to tackle an inherently international and cross-border technology has only added to the difficulty. Meanwhile, some artists have adapted much more quickly and have been developing ways to harness the internet for their own benefit. There is little doubt that copyright, music piracy and use of the internet will remain a fruitful area of research for many years to come, as the music industries attempt to come to terms with the online environment as it develops in the future.

FURTHER READING

For useful discussions of copyright law in the UK and US, please see Ann Harrison's *Music: the Business* (2011), Richard Schulenberg's *Legal Aspects of the Music Industry* (2005) and Simon Frith and Lee Marshall's edited collection *Music and Copyright* (2004). For music piracy and bootlegging, see Matthew David's *Peer to Peer and the Music Industry* (2010) and Lee Marshall's *Bootlegging* (2005). Finally, Lawrence Lessig's *Free Culture* (2004), Joanna Demers' *Steal this Music* (2006) and Kembrew McLeod and Peter DiCola's *Creative License* (2011) are recommended for those interested in exploring the relationship between copyright, corporate interests and musical creativity.

10

CONTRACTUAL AGREEMENTS AND RELATIONSHIPS

Contractual agreements and relationships are central to the functioning of the music industries. They detail and regulate the financial and artistic relationships of songwriters and performers with industry personnel and companies. Negotiation between the various parties involved means that each contract will be different. Nevertheless, some generic types and terms may be distinguished. This chapter will focus on three types of agreement: artist management, music publishing and music recording (including producer agreements). An understanding of the common terms and their effects is of great benefit to those wishing to study or work within the music industries, though we recommend that you obtain independent legal advice from a music industry lawyer should you be considering entering into an agreement.

KEY FINDINGS

- Artist managers represent and develop artists' careers, and an effective relationship is based on trust.
- There are no industry-standard management, publishing and recording agreements.
- Music industry agreements contain numerous clauses that need to be negotiated carefully.
- Royalty rates, advances and other terms will depend on the bargaining power of an artist, and the accountancy practices of the record company.
- Major record companies prefer multiple rights agreements.
- Music industry agreements need to adapt to take digital revenue streams into account.

ARTIST MANAGEMENT AGREEMENTS

An artist manager works not only with an act, but on behalf of an act: developing and maintaining contacts with record labels, promoters, publishers, media and many other industry firms and personnel. Managers have access to, and influence over, the business, creative and financial aspects of an act's career and are often heavily involved in contractual negotiations. As a result, artist managers are in a position of supreme trust, and management contracts are as much if not more about the management of personal relationships as they are about the fulfilment of specific rights, duties and obligations (Baskerville and Baskerville, 2010).

What artist managers are seen to do

In popular media and in everyday use, the term 'artist management' is often used as a catch-all term for the person or team of people who handle an artist's business affairs. To an extent, this is true: an effective manager will indeed be involved with every aspect of an artist's career. Yet the functions of artist management are often conflated with those of other music industry professionals such as booking agents (see Chapter 7), personal assistants (who handle the details of a performer's private and public schedules) and lawyers (who handle legal and contractual issues for an act). In some cases, managers and their firms will indeed handle these business responsibilities 'in-house', though they may still hire specialists for particular functions. For instance, if an artist is due to undertake a series of promotional concerts overseas, the artist manager may hire an experienced international tour manager to handle the administrative and day-to-day issues while the act is on the road.

The popular portrayal of artist managers in films, television programmes and books, some dating back to the era of Vaudeville and Music Hall, makes it even harder to understand their roles in reality – particularly as they have often been depicted in quite negative ways. Characters like 'Glenda Markle' in the 1957 Elvis Presley film *Loving You* and 'Mayer' in 1959's *Expresso Bongo* are two early examples of how artist managers (as well as agents) in popular music have been stereotyped as unprincipled opportunists exploiting the raw talent of naive musicians. Claims of intimidation and physical violence are also found, as noted in the biographies of managers such as Don Arden (see Rogan, 1988; Arden, 2004), who handled the Small Faces and Black Sabbath, hip hop entrepreneur Suge Knight, and Led Zeppelin's manager, Peter Grant.

What artist managers really do

The day-to-day roles and functions of artist managers are decidedly less dramatic and glamorous than those we may read about in books or see in film and television programmes. Nevertheless, they are critical to an artist's success, since all effective managers must forge opportunities and develop strategies which help their acts become successful. However, because of the unique and personal nature of the artist–manager relationship it is difficult, even unhelpful, to simply list the contractual tasks that an artist manager may perform. Imagine, for instance, how the day-to-day duties of a manager of a classical violinist might differ from those of the manager of a boy band or of a troupe of folk musicians. Instead, it is more useful to conceive of artist management as a range of varied activities and practices centred around two broad areas: artist development and artist representation.

Artist development

It is the job of the artist manager to ensure the act – as an organization – runs smoothly. Similarly, the artist manager also works to ensure that any conflicts between band members are resolved and that all members of the band are, as far as possible, happy with the general direction in which their career is progressing. Managers may negotiate, among other things, an artist's or band's image, musical style, choreography or use of media such as websites, social media and video in order to actively target and grow the act's potential audience. They should also help to promote interest and excitement about the group locally, regionally, nationally and ultimately globally, drawing on contacts in recording, publishing, marketing, media and live sectors. Those contacts must be maintained and nurtured over time so that the manager can gain access to the key decision-makers in the music and media industries who can have a positive influence over an artist's career.

Artist representation

The main reason that artists decide to take on a manager is for that manager to help the act reach a larger and more varied audience. The manager becomes the artist's key representative in external dealings and negotiations with firms and individuals who have an interest in working with an artist: concert promoters, media, record labels, publishers and the like. To that end, artist managers must have keen negotiating skills and an in-depth understanding of how the music industry works – especially of the long-term implications of signing any deals or agreements on behalf of an artist. In this way, artist managers may be described as 'gatekeepers' or intermediaries who sift through potential opportunities and developments, and determine which, if any, are appropriate for an artist. In sum, they manage business opportunities and contingencies, as well as a range of personal and professional relationships.

They also have a fiduciary duty to the artists they represent (Harrison, 2011: 45). In other words, they must act in the best interests of their artists, even though there are sometimes conflicts of interest. For instance, when negotiating a recording contract a choice needs to be made regarding whether to seek a larger advance or higher royalties. As managers are paid commission from artist income, a manager needing cash flow may prefer to negotiate a higher advance even though this may not be in the interests of the artist (Hull et al., 2011: 165). Similarly, there is the issue of 'double dipping' where, for example, a manager signs an artist to a publishing company that the manager also owns, yet still charges commission from the artists' songwriting income. In such circumstances, the manager gains 50 per cent of the music publishing income through the publishing company, plus commission on the 50 per cent earned by the artist.

Finding a manager

As artist managers are so intricately involved in all aspects of an act's career, it is important for any artist looking for a manager to find not just any manager but a manager capable of furthering the artist's career ambitions. Younger performers logically turn to family members for help in the early stages. For instance, the Jackson 5 were managed by their father Joe Jackson, Charlotte Church was initially managed by her mother, Maria, and Beyoncé's father, Mathew Knowles, handled the career of both Destiny's Child and the early stages of Beyoncé's solo career. Other family relationships may also be significant. Tom Jones has been managed by his son Mark since the 1980s, and Tony Bennett credits son Danny for the revitalization of his career in the 1990s. Most notably, Sharon Osbourne managed her husband Ozzy's solo career from the 1970s into the 2000s, and became a celebrity herself through appearances in the reality television programme *The Osbournes*.

Despite these high-profile instances, it is more usual for an act to take on a manager with industry-specific experience once a degree of success has been achieved. In such instances, artists can turn to professional organizations for assistance. In the UK for example, the Music Managers Forum (MMF) is the professional body for artist managers, and it along with the trade paper *Music Week*, regularly publish directories of artist managers. A listing in these directories is no guarantee that a manager will be right for an act, but it provides a useful first point of contact. In the USA, California and New York (and other states) have generalized regulatory policies intended to guide managers and agents in professional practice. These require potential managers to obtain a licence before embarking on a management/agent career (Baskerville and Baskerville, 2010). An alternative avenue for many artists is personal recommendation: from other bands and industry personnel such as promoters, bookers, and record label staff, or even sometimes through fan networks.

Regardless of how an artist finds a manager, it is essential that the 'fit' between the artist and the manager is appropriate. Some artists need an 'organizer' who can take creative and financial control and take decisions on every aspect of their career. Others require a manager who is less 'hands on', yet able to provide expert advice in specific business areas such as international touring or publishing. Whichever type the artist employs, the manager must be wholly trusted by all performers or members of a group to make short- and long-term decisions on their behalf.

Management styles

Chris Rojek (2011) makes a distinction between 'transactional' and 'transformational' managers. Transactional managers maintain a relatively low public profile, such as John Reid (who managed Elton John, Queen and others) and Paul McGuinness (U2). In contrast, transformational managers 'present themselves as celebrities by association with, and direct influence over, the clients whom they represent' (2011: 162). Examples include Malcolm McLaren (who managed the Sex Pistols) and Andrew Loog Oldham (who managed the Rolling Stones). These managers seek the limelight themselves or live a 'rock and roll' lifestyle similar to the acts they represent. They also expect to have a greater say in the musical and aesthetic choices of their artists and may demand higher commission rates for the vision that they bring to a project.

Rojek argues that the 1990s saw the development of a new form of transformational manager, typified by Simon Fuller (The Spice Girls, *Pop Idol* and *American Idol*) and Simon Cowell (*X Factor* and *Britain's Got Talent*). These managers understand the power of the media and cross-market artists and television shows into other areas, such as fashion, merchandising, television advertising and premium rate telephone voting. Unlike the transformational managers of the past, they operate more like 'corporate executives' than the rock and pop stars they represent, yet they still micro-manage all aspects of an artist's career and may be as or more well known than the acts they work with (Rojek, 2011: 163).

Key terms in artist management contracts

All contracts are necessarily bespoke legal documents that specify particular requirements and issues between a given artist and manager, but the clauses addressed below represent the fundamental principles found in most, if not all, artist–manager agreements.

Payment. Artist management contracts stipulate which jobs and duties a manager will perform on behalf of the artist and how much the manager will be paid in return, which is usually based on commission rather than annual salary. This means that whatever income an artist earns from any field – live performance, royalties, sponsorship and so on – the manager will receive a percentage share. That share is, on average, between 15 and 20 per cent of the gross revenue.

Exclusivity. Exclusivity means that the manager is guaranteed to be the sole provider of a range of management services and expertise, as agreed by the artist, for a specified period of time. Without the assurance of exclusivity there would be no motivation for the manager to invest time, effort and money in helping the artist achieve success, since there would be no opportunity to recoup the time and money invested.

Key-man provisions. If an artist is considering whether to sign a deal with a large management company, a 'key-man clause' may be inserted into the contract. This clause prevents the artist from being passed from one person to another, and gives legal protection against being handled by less experienced workers or by other people with whom they do not have the same level of trust or rapport. If these situations arise, the clause gives the artist the legal right to terminate the agreement. Untested and inexperienced artists may find it difficult to get a management firm to agree to a key-man clause, as it limits the availability of a firm's managers to deal with multiple clients simultaneously. Moreover, Ann Harrison (2008) notes that there are many times during an artist's career when having the undivided attention of a manager is actually unnecessary, for instance, when remixing an album or writing new material.

Term. One of the most difficult aspects to negotiate is the term, or length, of a contract between a manager and an artist. Managers generally spend the most time, and take on the most risk, in the earliest phases of an artist's career, as they attempt to progress the act from a local to a regional, national or even global level. Once sustained success is achieved, a common question arises: how long should the manager continue to earn 15 to 20 per cent commission? The manager may argue that without his or her industry knowledge, connections and expertise, the artist might never have attained success. At the same time, the artist might reason that once the manager has helped create that success, the management role changes substantially – from key decision-maker to business manager – and that the manager's commission should be adjusted accordingly. Two common ways to address this are benchmarks and sunset clauses.

Benchmarks are the specific goals that the manager agrees to achieve for an act in a limited time period and are stipulated as such in the contract, for instance, that the manager will secure a recording contract and a publishing deal within three years. If this target is not met, the artist has the right to terminate the agreement.

Sunset clauses see the manager's earnings diminish over time. For example, the contract may provide that after a specified time the initial 20 per cent commission will begin to fall incrementally to perhaps as low as 5 per cent of future income once the original contract term expires, which reflects the fact that once an act achieves a certain level of success the manager's expertise may no longer match the requirements of the artist. Thus, a sunset clause acknowledges both the short- and long-term efforts of the manager but also frees the artist from having to pay sometimes substantial monies to a manager over potentially long periods of time.

Termination. In even the best of circumstances, there will eventually come a time when the termination of an artist management contract becomes necessary. This need not indicate an acrimonious split, as there are countless reasons why either the artist or the manager may seek to do so: a band may break up, an artist may retire from the music industry, a manager may seek to move on to another group, or the relationship between them may simply have run its course, with both parties seeking to move on to new interests. Like any legal agreement, the specifications for either party to terminate the agreement must be clearly stated, with a notice of termination (perhaps 90 days) likely to be required in writing.

In other circumstances, either side may be required to prove that the other has not upheld its end of the bargain. For example, an act may seek termination if it can demonstrate that the manager has not performed the duties stipulated in the contract: booking live performance dates, securing a recording contract, organizing a national tour and the like. Similarly, a manager may seek to terminate the agreement if it can be demonstrated that the artist has wilfully turned down work or in some other way prevented the manager from fulfilling the terms of the contract. As the personal, professional and financial relationship between managers and artists is a close one its breakdown can often be highly fraught (see Box 10.1).

Box 10.1
Robbie Williams vs Nigel Martin-Smith

Robbie Williams came to prominence in the 1990s as part of boy band Take That, created by aspirant pop manager Nigel Martin-Smith. Take That went on to become one of the most successful UK pop acts of the 1990s, with several multi-platinum albums and sold-out tours, yet by 1995 personal relationships between Martin-Smith, Williams, and other band members became increasingly tense. This culminated in Williams leaving the band. He argued that the band sacked him on the advice of Martin-Smith, though Martin-Smith and the band say he left of his own accord. In 1997, Martin-Smith sued Williams for unpaid commission related to the Take That management contract. Williams alleged that Martin-Smith had advised other members of the band to sack him, and so had failed in his fiduciary duty to Williams. The court decided in favour of Martin-Smith, ruling that Williams had indeed violated the terms of the management contract (Harrison, 2011: 46). Williams subsequently appealed this decision and again lost the case. Nearly a decade later, the original lyrics of the Robbie Williams' song 'The 90's' accused Martin-Smith of stealing money from Take That. On hearing about the lyrics, Martin-Smith sued Williams and Williams amended the lyrics prior to the release of the track on the 2006 album *Rudebox*. Martin-Smith won the legal case the following year with Williams paying damages and court fees, and forced to make a public apology (MacInnes, 2007).

MUSIC PUBLISHING AGREEMENTS

As Ron Sobel and Dick Weissman (2008) note, Tin Pan Alley songwriters (see Chapter 3) sold their music and their copyrights to publishers for a one-time flat fee, in much the same way that a dealer might buy a car from a manufacturer. What this system produced, however, was a model that was decidedly unfair to composers: the publisher would receive royalties each time a piece of sheet music was sold (hence, potentially, substantial profits), while the songwriter would see no profit beyond the initial one-time fee. Over time – and through the establishment of organizations such as the American Society of Composers, Authors and Publishers (ASCAP) and Broadcast Music Incorporated (BMI) in America, and the Musicians' Union, Mechanical-Copyright Protection Society

(MCPS) and Performing Rights Society (PRS) in the UK – songwriters fought for and eventually received the opportunity to negotiate for more equitable compensation. Today, songwriters receive between 50 and 80 per cent of net income received by the music publisher, with more established songwriters achieving the higher rates. There are numerous types of agreement between songwriters and publishers, and these can be adapted to suit the requirements of any specific arrangement or relationship. The most common types are discussed below.

Exclusive publishing agreements

Exclusive publishing agreements are generally considered to be the ultimate goal of professional songwriters (Harrison, 2008). Under such agreements, a song-writer is contractually obliged to produce a specified number of songs within a specified period of time. 'Exclusivity' in this context refers to the understanding that songs produced under the contract will be controlled by the publishing com-pany. For the duration of the agreement (if not longer), the songwriter assigns copyright to the publisher in exchange for an advance, royalties and a promise that the publisher will do its best to exploit the songs to the best of its ability. Exclusive publishing agreements used to be extremely long in duration, with ten or 15 years as standard. A number of lawsuits in the UK demonstrated restraint of trade which means that today, exclusive publishing agreements are normally far shorter, perhaps just two or three years. This allows songwriters to shop around for a new and more attractive publishing deal as their circumstances and level of success dictates.

Subpublishing agreements

Subpublishing agreements are mainly concerned with the foreign exploitation of a domestic catalogue of music. A publishing firm and/or songwriter may contract with an overseas publisher for assistance in the exploitation of a song/catalogue for use in foreign films, television and advertising, or to administer and collect overseas royalties. In subpublishing deals, the foreign publisher will usually be granted a fixed-term licence to exploit a song rather than be assigned copyright. In exchange, the songwriter will be given a much smaller advance or indeed no advance at all, which reflects the fact that copyright ownership is retained.

Single-song agreements

The single-song agreement may be appropriate for songwriters who are just beginning their careers, for those who only write songs on a part-time or ad-hoc basis, or for the writers of novelty or holiday songs. Sometimes they may be a 'tester' between the songwriter and a publishing company, perhaps leading to a longer-term arrangement. In many ways, it is a smaller version of the exclusive publishing deal noted above: the songwriter will assign the copyright in a single song to a publisher in exchange for a modest advance. The publisher will then do its best to exploit the song as much as possible.

Administration agreements

Administration agreements are primarily intended for those songwriters who have a small but potentially lucrative catalogue or collection of songs (Harrison, 2008). The main difference from exclusive publishing deals is that the publisher will not normally be assigned the copyright in any songs, which remain with the songwriter. Instead, the publisher will be granted a licence to exploit a song or songs for a fixed period of time. Songwriters who sign administration deals are less concerned with the exploitation of an existing body of work, and are willing to handle the promotion and exploitation of the music personally. As there is no requirement to deliver a specific number of songs within a set timeframe, the songwriter is free to focus on the more creative aspects of music publishing, and to create a range of new material at their own pace.

Self-administration

Songwriters may also decide to deal with administration of their own copy-rights themselves by becoming individual members of royalty collection socie-ties in countries (territories) where they feel they are likely to earn income. This removes the commissions that would otherwise have been paid to a publisher or subpublisher, and allows the songwriter to receive income from each coun-try's public performance agreements (see Chapter 9). A downside is that because there is no publisher acting on behalf of the songwriter, there can be no advance against royalties and the songwriter must assume sole responsibility for promo-tion and administration of works.

Key terms in music publishing agreements

On their face, publishing agreements may seem relatively straightforward: a songwriter will sign a contract with a publisher who agrees to promote and administer songs delivered under the contract. In return, the songwriter receives at least 50 per cent of the publisher's net income. As we dig deeper into the key terms found in publishing contracts, we can see that they are seldom so simple.

Assignment and licensing of rights. Copyright ownership is central to any publishing agreement. As noted above, exclusive publishing deals provide that ownership in any song created during the term of the agreement is assigned to the publisher for the life of the copyright. If this did not happen, the songwriter could feasibly license the song to multiple publishers at the same time, or indeed exploit the song in a way that works in opposition to the goals of the publisher. In some cases, songwriters may instead offer an exclusive licence to the publisher and retain ownership of their copyrights. Here, the publisher will control and benefit in much the same way as an assignment, but their control of the song is limited merely to the duration stipulated in the contract.

Minimum commitments. Publishing agreements must specify how many songs a composer is required to deliver, and within what timeframe. A publishing deal might encompass a songwriter's entire body of work past, present and future. Or it might require the production of a certain number of new songs each year. If the songwriter also has a recording contract, the minimum commitment is likely to be based on the number of songs delivered and released. Alternatively, the agreement might be very short-term in order to 'test the waters', perhaps requiring the songwriter to deliver just one or two songs over a brief period of time: maybe 60 or 90 days. Often, agreements state that for songs to count against the minimum commitment they must be 'commercially acceptable'. This clause should be negotiated carefully to ensure that all parties agree what constitutes commercial acceptability.

Term. The term, or duration, of a publishing agreement as a whole is a critical clause to understand and negotiate. Exclusive publishing agreements are often structured in 12-month blocks with additional options available to the publisher to extend the term. This extension provision allows the publisher to maintain a relationship with a successful songwriter and to continue to gain from that relationship in the future. On first glance it may seem counter-intuitive that shorter deals are of benefit to songwriters: after all, in any other job a longer contract will guarantee a longer period of employment. However, unlike other fields, songwriting is wholly dependent on the songwriter's success, as success gives the songwriter enhanced bargaining power for future re-negotiations. On the other hand, if a particular songwriter has been unsuccessful with one publisher, the shorter term allows a better deal to be sought with another, perhaps one who can lend more support with writing and promotion so that success is more forthcoming.

Territory. Territory is another key element of the publishing agreement as it stipulates which areas of the world the agreement will cover. A large multinational publisher might have affiliate offices around the world, in which case the territory for an exclusive deal might be global. In other instances, the songwriter might be aware of a particular publisher with expertise in a relevant overseas market. In this case territory becomes important because it will determine how or even if that songwriter can work with that publisher.

Advances. An advance may be paid to a songwriter on the signing of a publishing deal or on delivery of individual songs. It is, in effect, a loan against future royalty earnings that the songwriter uses to cover living expenses. Those future royalties will only be paid to the songwriter once the advance has been repaid (known as 'recouping'). There is no set amount for a publishing advance, though they are normally substantially smaller than those seen from recording deals (discussed later). Songwriters with a substantial back catalogue of material, or those with a proven industry reputation will often see higher advances than new or untested songwriters. It is also common for advances to be split over time, such as on the initial signing of the agreement, followed by subsequent delivery and eventual release.

Accounting and administration. Accounting and administration are among the main duties carried out by a publisher so the terms that regulate these practices need to be clearly laid out in the publishing agreement. This will include details of fees paid to performing rights organizations like ASCAP, BMI, the PRS/MCPS, and to the publisher itself for the administration of a writer's works or catalogue. It will also stipulate how often a songwriter may audit the publishing company's accounts, and what steps are available if an accounting discrepancy is found. Where songs are co-written, the publishing rights for that song may be split between different publishers. In such cases, administration will be carried out by a specified company that will control how the song is exploited.

Restrictions and moral rights. It is also essential for publishing agreements to specify what cannot be done with a song. In the UK, the moral rights for a song remain with the composer, regardless of the ownership of the copyright in that song (as discussed in Chapter 9), so songwriters retain legal protection against their songs being used in any ways that may violate their personal beliefs and world view. This protection does not exist in the US, though American songwriters can ask for clauses requiring, for instance, their specific approval of any commercial and/or political uses of their songs. In practice it is common for publishers to request that the songwriter waive their moral rights, so that the publisher has freedom to place the song in as many contexts as possible.

Controlled composition clauses. A controlled composition is one where the performer of a song is also its composer, and almost all US-based recording agreements include a clause reducing the mechanical royalty on songs 'controlled' (written by) the performer to 75 per cent of the full rate. This is because the songwriter is entitled to mechanical royalties on every copy of a song (physical or digital) the record company makes. Even if the single or album is a flop, the record company will still have to pay the songwriter (who is also the artist) a considerable sum in mechanical royalties. Should the single or album be commercially successful, the record company will eventually be paying the act twice – as both songwriter and performer. In addition, US record companies often limit mechanical royalties per album to a total of ten tracks, no matter how many are actually included on the album.

Reversion of rights. Reversion of rights means that the publisher reassigns the copyright back to the songwriter at a specified point in the future. This practice is intended to protect songwriters in two key ways. First, it is a measure to ensure that publishing companies regularly and actively seek to exploit songwriters' music in a timely and effective fashion. Second, the reversion of rights after a period of time ensures that songwriters have long-term control over exploitation of the music they have written.

RECORDING AGREEMENTS

Recording agreements (also known as recording contracts or record deals) define the various obligations and promises that are made between an artist and the company that arranges for that artist's recordings to be made. In the traditional recording industry (major labels and larger independents), the artist agrees to record and deliver a minimum number of recordings to a specified company on an exclusive basis, where exclusivity means that the artist cannot record for another company whilst under contract. In return, the company pays the artist an advance: a lump-sum payment or series of payments that fund the artist's living and recording expenses.

In addition, the company agrees to pay the artist a royalty percentage (sometimes referred to as royalty points). This is calculated on net sales and ranges between 13 and 20 per cent of PPD (Hull et al., 2011: 201), where PPD stands for 'published price to dealer' and corresponds to the wholesale price charged to distributors rather than the retail price charged to consumers. In some cases royalty rates may exceed 20 per cent, but such rates are usually reserved for superstar artists or for licence deals where the record company receives a finished master recording rather than funding the recording costs (see Chapter 2). It should be noted that the advance and any other expenses agreed in the recording agreement will need to be repaid from the artist's royalties, so the artist will not actually receive a royalty payment until the advance and expenses are repaid in full (known as 'recouping'). If the advance is not recouped from artist's royalties, the artist does not have to repay the company. For this reason, Keith Negus (1992: 42) refers to the advance as 'a tax-free loan' which is only 'paid back if they [the artist] are successful'.

This process may seem fairly straightforward, but record company agreements are anything but. A number of authors, including Simon Garfield (1986) and Johnny Rogan (1988), discuss the often exploitative contracts seen in the early history of the recording industry, but as Keith Negus suggests, the majority of record companies are now much more professional in their business practices (1992: 43). Nevertheless, the language used in recording agreements, as well as the numerous clauses that they contain, mean that they must still be read and negotiated very carefully. In particular, great care must be taken when examining the artist royalty on offer, as it is actually subject to a large number of deductions and accounting practices: what may seem like a good rate may not actually be so.

Bargaining power

Experienced music industry lawyers can help an artist to gain the best possible deal, whether that artist is seeking to maximize the amount of money being offered as an advance and/or royalties, to gain reassurances as to the commitment of the record company, or to assert a strong degree of creative control (Harrison, 2008: 48). An artist's ability to achieve their goal will depend, in part, on their bargaining power. Artists who already have a proven track record of success are able to negotiate better terms than those who are starting out. Of the latter, it is those artists who have been able to create a media, industry or audience 'buzz' who can build a stronger bargaining position by generating competition between different record companies. The size of record companies is also a factor, as a smaller company is more likely to invest both time and money in a new artist, and to offer greater creative control (Harrison, 2008: 70).

Lack of standardization

There are no industry-standard agreements against which a deal may be gauged, though many record companies will begin negotiations with a version of their own in-house agreement, and the vast majority of clauses will contain variations on the same basic provisions. Whatever terms are eventually agreed, the likelihood that artists will fully recoup their advances and expenses (including recording and remixing costs, and a share of advertising, promotion and video production costs) is 'overwhelmingly small' (Schulenberg, 2005: 27): perhaps only 5 per cent of artists (one in 20) actually manage to do so (Harrison, 2008).

It is for this reason that record companies maintain the upper hand in negotiations. In simple economic terms, there is a far greater supply of potential artists than there are record deals available, leading to a 'buyer's market' (Harrison, 2008: 38). This is also why record companies ensure that they retain the copyrights of all recorded works made under their agreements – whether or not the artists manage to recoup their debt. Their justification for retaining the copyrights even after the advances and associated costs have been recouped is that they invest a substantial amount of money in the development of new talent, and that if they returned the copyrights of their successful artists, they would be unable to continue profiting from these hit songs over time. This argument has become ever more spurious in recent years as record companies have increasingly turned to licensing deals and production companies to develop new talent rather than taking on that risk themselves (Harrison, 2008: 64).

Development deals

Development deals are short-term contracts in which demo recordings are produced. They have become less common in recent years, due to A&R activities being out-sourced to production companies, yet may still be found. If a record company likes the demo recordings, it has the option to request a full album (and, potentially, subsequent albums) at regular intervals – at which point the deal turns into a full exclusive recording contract as discussed below. There is, however, no commitment by the record company to request an album, or to release the demo recordings to the public. If the company believes that the recordings have limited commercial potential, the artist will be released from the agreement. The artist is then free to seek a new recording contract elsewhere, though the demo recordings that were made remain the property of the company.

Exclusive recording contracts

Exclusive recording contracts are the most common form of contract within the traditional recording industry (major labels and large independents). Artists cannot record for another company whilst under contract, though there may be provisions allowing a band member to record as a guest or sideman on another artist's recordings. Exclusive recording contracts allow the record company to own and control master sound recordings made under the contract (whether released or not) for the full life of the copyright. This means that the artist has no control over unreleased recordings, and even if the artist recoups all advances and expenses within the life of the copyright, the record company will continue to own and control all the master recordings produced under the agreement. Exclusive contracts have a nominal term of around five years, though the actual length is ultimately determined by factors relating to delivery and acceptance.

Multiple rights contracts

Multiple rights contracts (also known as 360-degree deals) are a variant of the traditional exclusive recording agreement. Instead of relying solely on income from the sale and/or licensing of master recordings, multiple rights deals include a share of revenue derived from other sources. These additional sources include percentage shares of an artist's concert ticket income, merchandising income, sponsorship and endorsement deals, broadcast rights, internet sites and in some cases publishing rights. A number of high-profile artists signed such deals in the 2000s, including Robbie Williams, Iron Maiden, Korn, The Pussycat Dolls and Madonna. These deals recognize that record sales alone are unlikely to cover the costs associated with recording, marketing and promoting such artists in the twenty-first century. The percentages involved vary from 10 to 50 per cent of the artist's net income from each of these activities (Harrison, 2008: 68). The record company may insist on having some control over the merchandise produced or the sponsorship deals involved, as it will want to protect its investment in the artist's image, although the company might also accept its share without interference.

Multiple rights deals are clearly to the benefit of the record companies, yet artists should be careful of multiple rights deals since they cut into revenue streams that were previously retained by artists rather than shared with a record company. If an artist is one of the many who do not recoup their contractual recording and other costs from their royalties, then a multiple rights agreement will reduce the sources of income that they might otherwise have relied upon to support their living expenses.

Other types of recording agreement

While the major recording companies typically use royalty-based contracts, profit-sharing agreements may be found in the independent sector. Here, small independent companies will split any net proceeds with their artists on a 50/50 basis (or higher for more established artists) and work on short-term contractual commitments, including one-off deals for recording and releasing just one track or album. Once this commitment has been completed, the artist is free to negotiate a new contract with the same label or move to another. Online labels may be even more flexible than this by offering non-exclusive agreements. This means that an artist is not tied to releasing their work through only one label at a time. They may instead seek contracts with different companies for the release of different musical projects, or release the same recording through multiple labels (each of which may specialize in reaching a particular market).

Contractual agreements are also in place for online direct-to-fan services that help artists and small independent labels distribute and sell their products to the public. These work on a revenue-share model (for instance, Bandcamp and Topspin each take commission of between 10 and 15 per cent of sales revenue) with additional features costing more. Finally, artists may make recordings freely available to download and share through the use of Creative Commons licences (see Chapter 9).

Key terms in recording contracts

Many artists seek the financial, creative and marketing support of the larger independent and major recording companies, and so enter into often complicated royalty-based recording contracts that contain multiple clauses. These clauses are designed to address a wide range of potentialities and the language and terms differ from company to company and from contract to contract. Nevertheless, they tend to cover the same basic areas. Some of the more common clauses are identified and discussed below.

Advances. Commencement of the agreement is marked by the payment of an advance against future royalties. This is used to fund all aspects of the recording process, with a personal advance going to the artist to cover living expenses. The artist's manager earns commission on the advance, while the producer takes a fee plus a percentage royalty on sales (usually expressed as the producer's 'points'). Other expenses may also be added to the advance where they become recoupable from artist royalties, for example, for the cost of making promotional videos. It is especially important that the wording of this clause states that the advance will be recouped rather than repaid: the latter makes the contract into a personal loan, which would allow the company to demand repayment direct from the artist, rather than from royalties.

Term and options. The initial term of the recording agreement is often a period of 12 months from signing, within which the artist agrees to record and deliver a minimum number of master recordings ('masters'). The number of masters will usually equate to an album's worth of songs, though the artist should ensure that a maximum number is also detailed. If not, the company could require the artist to continue recording tracks, which could become a problem for the artist, as the costs of those recordings will be charged to them as part of their advance, recoupable from royalties and other relevant earnings.

At the end of the initial term, the record company has the option to grant a further contract period (often expressed as 12–18 months) within which the artist once again agrees to record and deliver a minimum number of masters. Note that these option decisions are made by the record company, not by the artist. In return, the company pays the artist a further advance to fund recording and living expenses. Subsequent contract periods may then be offered through the exercise of options at regular intervals, with each option affording a further advance.

Alternatively, the company may decide against exercising its option, at which time the artist may be released from the agreement, though not from the debt accrued. The artist is free to find a new contract, but this is often difficult: other companies will perceive them as a financial risk and may need to invest considerable time and money reinventing the artist's music and image in an attempt to win over the public and media (Negus, 1992: 137). In some cases, the agreement may be suspended pending the delivery of recordings which are deemed acceptable to the company. If this occurs, the artist will not be able to record elsewhere, and their career will stall unless they can support themselves through live performances.

Acceptance. One of the key issues here is 'acceptance' of the masters. Record companies may delay acceptance by rejecting recordings on the grounds of technical or commercial quality, or by requiring that artwork, sample permissions, or other materials are delivered with the masters. When negotiating the recording agreement, the artist (or their representative) should avoid subjective criteria relating to technical or commercial quality. If not, highly subjective decisions regarding a recording's 'commercial potential' could allow the company to reject the masters or demand re-recording or remixing (with financial consequences for the artist) (Harrison, 2008: 71–2).

Commitment to release. A further problem is that the A&R manager who originally signed the artist may have moved to another company by the time the masters are delivered. In such circumstances the artist may no longer have the support of the company, which may be looking to release (or 'drop') artists from its roster. The artist should protect against this by ensuring that the contract stipulates the album will be released and furthermore that such release will happen within a maximum time period from delivery and acceptance of the masters (Harrison, 2008: 77). If this clause is not present, the company has no commitment to even release the recordings that have been made.

Territory. Major label recording agreements will usually specify that the company has the right to exploit the sound recording copyright worldwide, though in some cases there may be separate deals (split-territory deals) for North America and for the rest of the world. This is because market-size in North America is significant and an artist may feel that a North American company can best represent its interests there, rather than a company based in the UK or elsewhere. Split-territory deals may also be found where an artist signs to an independent label and has licensing deals with other independents abroad, or where a non-US/UK artist with a significant national following (and deal) seeks to 'break' the US, UK or European markets.

Approval rights. The record company may seek to control the use of an artist's music, or to have control over the creative output of that artist. Artists may, in turn, seek to gain approval rights for issues like the choice of producers and remixers, the creation of promotional videos, the use of the artist's name and likeness in relation to merchandising and licensing deals, the use of the artist's music in films, television advertisements and so on rather than leave these decisions entirely in the hands of the company. Artists with strong ethical ideals may object to their music being used in certain ways and may seek a right of approval. Record companies, on the other hand, would prefer to have full control so that they can exploit the recordings through as many channels as possible.

Escalation clause. Artist royalties are a highly complicated, yet very important part of any recording agreement, and there is considerable variation in the level of royalties that a signed artist may receive. Some agreements, particularly for established artists with a track record of sales, may include an escalation clause (also known as an accelerator clause), which allows the baseline royalty rate to increase when specific contractual criteria are met, such as when an artist reaches a pre-determined sales figure.

Artist royalty deductions and other accounting practices

Whatever baseline royalty rate is being offered by a record company, it is important to consider the impacts of deductions and accounting practices found in the recording agreement. These can significantly affect how sales figures and artist royalties are calculated if they are not negotiated and amended in the best interests of an artist. The particular terms used below may not appear in the written contract, but their effect may nevertheless be realized within the detailed legal wording used. As they say – always read the small print!

Deductions to net sales. Artist royalties are calculated on the basis of net sales. Accordingly, record companies look for ways to reduce the net sales figure. For instance, some contracts still retain a 'breakage' clause – originally introduced because the shellac discs used in the early days of the industry were brittle and prone to shattering during transport. This clause can reduce the total sales figure by 10–15 per cent, meaning that the artist royalty will be calculated on only 85–90 per cent of actual sales (Schulenberg, 2005: 65–6). Another historical anachronism is a 'packaging deduction' (or 'container charge') of 20–25 per cent of sales that was originally introduced to pay for vinyl album sleeves. The clause has been dropped by some but not all labels in recent years, as it is hard to justify for digital downloads where packaging costs are essentially zero (Harrison, 2011: 102).

A 'free goods' clause may also be present, which allows the company to issue recordings royalty-free for promotional purposes. It is clearly in the artist's interest to allow this to a degree, but the level needs to be negotiated carefully. As with the breakage clause and packaging deductions, it is hard to justify this deduction in relation to digital downloads and all three should be negotiated if found in a draft contract. In addition, where the recording company is offering both physical and digital product, it might be worth seeking differing baseline royalty rates for digital versus physical sales.

Reduced royalty rates. There are a variety of ways for record companies to issue records that attract a reduced royalty. These include mail-order sales, budget price sales, television-advertised recordings, and 'premium records' (such as magazine cover-mounts, merchandising coupons, and other promotional offers). Royalties on these sales are paid at a 50 per cent or more reduction of the standard rate given in the recording agreement (Harrison, 2008: 77).

Producer's 'points'. The producer of audio recordings will normally receive a royalty, expressed as 'points', that ranges between 2 and 5 per cent of PPD. It is deducted from artist royalties, so if an artist's baseline royalty rate is 14 per cent, and the producer takes 3 points, the artist royalty will be reduced to 11 per cent. The producer will try to ensure that these points are payable from the first record sold and calculated on 100 per cent of sales and other forms of exploitation. In the UK points are often payable even if the artist's advance has not been recouped, though in the US it is more often deferred until recoupment has taken place.

Reserves. Records are distributed to wholesalers and retailers on a 'sale or return' basis. This means that any unsold stock can be returned to the record company without payment. As royalty payments are estimated on the basis of stock shipped rather than stock sold, the record company protects itself against these potential returns by withholding (reserving) 30 to 50 per cent of the artist royalties due. This 'reserves' clause may even be charged against digital sales even though there is no stock that can be returned (Hull et al., 2011: 202).

Cross-collateralization. Cross-collateralization allows unrecouped advances or other contractual debts of the artist to be repaid from past, present and future income. For instance, if an artist's first album sold poorly but the second album became a massive hit, the royalty income from the second album could be used to offset (recoup) the advances/costs of both albums. A second example is that any spending in excess of the recording budget of one album can be deducted from the advance due for the second album – before it is received. A final example, which is standard to multiple rights deals, but may also be found in some standard deals (in one form or another), is that the artist's other revenue streams such as touring, publishing, and merchandise, can be used to repay the recording advance – particularly if the artist has an agreement in these areas with a company affiliated to their recording company (Schulenberg, 2005: 101).

Digital royalties: licence vs sale. Revenues received from the digital distribution of music through legal downloading, streaming and ringtone sales may be accounted for as either sales or licences. The distinction is important since sales are accounted for through the artist royalty system noted above, while licence income is split equally. The percentage income received through licences is therefore greater than for sales, yet record companies may try to account for their licence income as sales, which has led some artists to take legal action (see Box 10.2).

Box 10.2
Digital royalties

In 2010, F.B.T. Productions, LLC (hereafter FBT), which had signed the rapper Eminem to an exclusive recording contract in 1995, took legal action against Aftermath Records (a subsidiary of the Universal Music Group). FBT had transferred its rights in Eminem's recordings to Aftermath in 1998 but was still entitled to receive a variety of royalty payments. The FBT–Aftermath deal was later renegotiated and amended but the wording regarding sales and licences was unchanged. A financial audit in 2006 found that Aftermath was treating download sales and mastertones in the same manner as physical albums for the purposes of royalty payment calculations. Consequently, FBT had received less income than if those download sales and mastertones had been treated as master licences. The legal case focused on the specific wording of the contract and found in favour of FBT. The decision was also upheld upon appeal, and has led to the filing of class action suits against Universal by attorneys working for the Estate of the deceased singer Rick James, and by Otis Williams and Ron Tyson of The Temptations. A similar case was filed in 2008 by The Allman Brothers against both Universal Music Group and Sony Music Entertainment, though it is believed that this case was settled out of court (Sources: FBT vs Aftermath, 2010; Bruno, 2011).

Record companies work with the knowledge that the majority of their artists will not recoup their advances, and so need to cover the substantial losses made by those artists who fail to do so. This is why record companies want to retain the copyrights in all of their recordings for the full term of those copyrights (irrespective of whether the advances/costs are recouped), and why they seek to maximize both their share of net sales and, where available, their share of an artist's other income streams under a multiple rights deal or cross-collateralization clause.

Richard Schulenberg (2005: 27) argues that, because of these and other accounting practices and clauses, the recording agreements of the major and large independent companies should primarily be regarded as a tool for building an artist's career, rather than a way to make artists lots of money. Higher royalty rates indicate the company's belief that the artist represents a lower level of risk to the company, so successful artists will look to renegotiate their royalty rates on renewal or expiry of their contracts in order to receive more favourable terms.

CONCLUSION

This chapter has explored three main areas of contractual agreement commonly found within the music industries. These agreements govern relationships between songwriters/performers and the managers, publishers and recording companies with which they deal. Songwriters and performers may of course opt to enter the music business on their own terms through self-management, self-publishing and self-release of albums, or they may work with friends and others without a formal contract. There may be advantages to doing this during the development phase of an act, or where an artist or band is making music for fun or for a known niche market rather than trying to 'break' into the mainstream industry. Should the songwriter or performer want to achieve a full-time career in the medium or long term, or attract a larger or more mainstream audience, it is likely that formal agreements will be required as discussed above. Employment of a strong manager and/or lawyer to represent the interests of an artist in contractual negotiations is recommended in all cases, to ensure that the terms and their implications are known and considered prior to signing.

FURTHER READING

Ann Harrison's *Music: the Business* (2011) is a highly readable text that examines music industry contracts and copyrights in the UK and discusses a number of legal cases that have driven changes in sector practices. In-depth coverage of US law related to management, publishing and recording agreements is available in Richard Schulenberg's *Legal Aspects of the Music Industry* (2005). For an excellent discussion of music publishing, see Sobel and Weissman's *Music Publishing: the Roadmap to Royalties* (2008).

CONCLUSION

The purpose of this book has been to provide a framework for achieving a deeper understanding of how the music industries operate in the twenty-first century; of how they connect with culture, technology, politics, and international and local economies; and how they shape the ways we encounter and experience music. Embarking on a study of the music industries at a time of significant change and upheaval is a challenging and rewarding activity. While there are several seminal and influential works that provide a strong theoretical basis for further research, the complexity and fluidity of the field mean that it is wide open for analysis and interpretation. The possibilities for the creation and discovery of new knowledge in the field make it a rich area for research and a fascinating subject for theorists and practitioners alike.

COMPLEXITY AND SYMBIOSIS

This book has provided some structural and intellectual frameworks within which such an investigation can take place, and has examined what are generally considered to be the key components of the music industry ecosystem. It should be noted that while these components have been separated out for our study here, all of the parts are actually interconnected and to some extent symbiotic. Nevertheless, by tackling each of them individually it is possible to step back and understand how these parts integrate into a coherent though complex form.

To that end, we have outlined some of the key research approaches through which the music industries have been studied and understood by scholars, and investigated the operations of the dominant sectors of the music industries (the publishing, recording and live music businesses). We have also explored the relationships between the composition, production, distribution, promotion and consumption of music, and the ways that these complicated and discursive practices are inscribed by the economic, political, technological and cultural contexts within which they are situated. We have discussed the current legal framework that guides the ownership, remuneration and use of musical intellectual property and pointed to the philosophical, political and historical bases on which those legal frameworks are legitimized. Throughout, we have underscored the fact that all of these things have been, and continue to be, subject to change.

BE WARY OF METANARRATIVES

And while we have discussed the profound effect that the past 20 years of digitalization has had on the music industries, what we have resisted throughout is the temptation to predict the future. There is no shortage of commentary online and in contemporary books that claims to describe 'the future of music' (Kusek and Leonhard, 2005) or confidently predict a world of 'music in the cloud' (Wikström, 2009), yet a more reflective analysis of the music industries shies away from such grand unified theories (metanarratives – see Chapter 1) and sweeping prognostication. The music industries encompass such a wide range of practices, discourses, activities, genres, professions, motivations and gratifications that the future of music is undoubtedly as complex and interesting as its present and past.

The profound impacts of the many music industry innovations that have been seen over the past 100 years and more have been not only unforeseen, but also unforeseeable. This brings to mind Marshall McLuhan's (1964) work in which he talks about the unanticipated consequences of new technologies: that they may be not be used in the ways that their designers had intended, or that when viewed in retrospect their effects were more far-reaching than first imagined.

For instance, the introduction of audio recording and radio broadcasting in what we might call the electric age (see Chapter 1) radically changed almost every aspect of the music industries in ways that the dominant industry of the time could not have anticipated. The printing of sheet music became a marginal activity when it had formerly been the principal way to make money from music. This did not mean the 'death of' sheet music as an industry, since it is still possible to walk into a store and buy a printed score; however, this is no longer the main route through which music industry revenues are generated. In the early twenty-first century, live music and music synchronization together exceed the annual revenues generated from selling recordings of music, while printed sheet music barely registers on the chart. Nevertheless, most predictions of the future of music involve an assumption that recordings will remain economically dominant; that it is only how those recordings are distributed and consumed that will change.

Essentialism and totalizing theories abound when it comes to discourses on the future of the music industries. Not only are we supposedly witnessing 'the death of' all manner of things, but 'in the future, we will all ...' behave and use music in certain ways, such as streaming from subscriber services, sharing music via social networks or doing everything on our mobile phones. However, while fairly common behaviours today, they are neither universal nor unproblematic. They tend not to account for differences in demographics, genre tastes, or the legislative frameworks of different countries. These developments are not insignificant, of course, but they are neither 'the future of music', nor likely to be completely true.

DIVERSITY AND REORGANIZATION

What is perhaps more interesting than inventing ultimate destinies for the music industries, based on contemporary trends, is to contemplate and examine how the diversity and complexity of those music industries are altering, and then to reflect upon the meanings and implications of those changes. We are not migrating from one simple system to another, but expanding and rearranging a set of complex business and consumer practices.

Meanwhile, it is important to consider that the most profound future developments in the music industries may well be innovations that we have not, as yet, encountered or imagined. While many of the most important developments for the music industries might seem retrospectively obvious and part of an ongoing continuum of progress (or decline, depending on your perspective), the significant thing is that these developments were invented. The many and varied technologies that are changing the business and consumer practices of the music industries are creative, socially negotiated and innovative responses to the potential of digital technology and the interconnectivity of the internet. These range from YouTube, Bandcamp, Spotify, and podcasts, to BitTorrent, *Guitar Hero*, ringtones, and online ticketing, and from Pay What You Want album sales, mash-ups, and crowdfunding to mobile apps, music blogs and print-on-demand merchandise (amongst many others).

Likewise, it is a fair assumption that any future developments for the music industries will neither be universally adopted, nor a simple case of consumers doing more of something they were already doing. There will almost certainly be no 'death of' any currently existing behaviours (though the marginalization of current practices and products is statistically likely – as with printed sheet music in the twentieth century), and neither will a single model emerge which 'solves' the music industry for any particular party.

Finally, it is worth noting that the economic weight of the music industries has fundamentally shifted. Technology companies such as Apple and Amazon, and super-retailers like Walmart and Tesco, are significantly larger in economic terms than any of the major record labels or traditional music retail outlets. At the same time, small and innovative independent companies and entrepreneurial organizations are making the most of the upheavals, uncertainties and new opportunities that digital technologies have contributed to. Whether the legal and political frameworks within which these innovative practices must establish themselves will be conducive to this kind of creative response or overtly conservative and restrictive is a moot point. It is of course to the benefit of major music industry organizations to retain the status quo, which is why we have seen legal action and lobbying for legislation with regards to music copyright and control of the online environment.

WHERE NEXT?

Scholars of the music industries have the luxury of stepping back, of taking in the broader picture. They can examine what is going on; ask why it is going on, and why in this particular time, at this particular place and in this particular way. Through thoughtful reflection, they can understand how things came to be the way that they are (and in whose interests). They can adopt a questioning approach that can imagine other ways in which the music industries might be configured. They can become invaluable thinking practitioners and managers within the sector, and use their critical position to contribute to the unexpected, innovative and creative future of the business of music. We offer this book as a starting point on this journey.

GLOSSARY

360-degree deal. A recording contract in which the label gains a share of an artist's broad revenue streams (such as from recording, touring and merchandising).

A&R (Artist & Repertoire). Record company department which seeks, signs and develops new artists.

A2IM (American Association of Independent Music). A non-profit corporation representing the American independent recording industry.

Advance. Monies paid under a publishing or recording contract to a songwriter or recording artist which are to be recouped from any royalties earned from the songs or recordings delivered under that contract (and other income sources if a 360 deal is in place).

AIF (Association of Independent Festivals). A non-profit trade association representing independent music festivals.

AIM (Association of Independent Music). A non-profit trade association representing independent record companies and distributors in the UK.

Ancillary income. Revenues earned from business activities which lie adjacent to the core business; for instance, car-parking fees and food and drink sales at live concert venues.

App. A specialized program designed to be downloaded and used on mobile digital devices.

ASCAP (American Society of Composers, Authors and Publisher). An American performing rights organization.

Assignment. Where control or ownership of a contract or copyright is signed over to another person or organization.

Berne Convention. The Berne Convention for the Protection of Literary and Artistic Works (originally signed in 1886) is an international trade agreement related to authors' (songwriters and publishers) rights. It includes clauses related to moral rights and reciprocal treatment.

Bit Torrent. A peer-to-peer file distribution system which connects multiple internet users in a network; pieces of files are simultaneously uploaded and downloaded from individual computers in the network, which are then compiled into completed files.

Blanket licence. Commonly issued by performing rights organizations, these grant permission for the use of music catalogues in return for negotiated fees.

Blog. Short for 'web log', a blog is a website that is updated in the manner of an online journal or diary.

BMI (Broadcast Music Inc.). An American performing rights organization.

Booking agent. Finds or brokers work at live music venues and events on behalf of artists.

BPI (British Phonographic Industry). A non-profit trade association representing the British recorded music industry.

CD. Compact (audio) disc.

Collection society. Another term for a performing rights organization.

Compulsory licence. One determined by copyright law rather than by negotiation; for instance, once a song has been recorded and distributed to the public, any artist may record it so long as they pay a fixed royalty as determined by applicable copyright law.

Controlled composition clause. Contractual wording between a record company and a composer/artist which demands a reduced mechanical royalty be payable by the record company on any works controlled (i.e. written) by that recording artist.

Co-publishing. Two or more people or companies owning a share of the publishing rights in a song.

Copyright. Grants the owner legal rights over a song or sound recording, such as the right to reproduce, distribute and publicly perform the work.

Copyright infringement. Reproducing, adapting, distributing, performing publicly or displaying a copyrighted work without permission of the copyright owner.

Cover, cover song, cover record. A new recording of a song which was previously recorded and released by another artist.

Cross-collateralization. Contractual wording in a recording contract which allows unrecouped monies incurred by one project/release to be recouped from the earnings of another.

Cross-over artist/recording. An artist or song that is successful in one genre format or market segment that becomes successful in one or more others.

Cultural capital. A sociological term associated with the work of Pierre Bourdieu that refers to non-financial cultural and intellectual knowledge that provides enhanced status in society.

Cultural industries. A collective term for businesses involved in the creation and distribution of goods or services which are predominantly cultural or artistic in nature and which are protected by intellectual property rights such as copyrights.

Cyberlocker. An online site providing digital storage space. Users upload files that can be accessed and downloaded by multiple other users. They have many legitimate uses, but have also been used to transfer music and video files and artwork without permission from, or payment to, copyright owners.

D2C (direct-to-consumer). Distribution of goods or services directly to consumers, rather than through intermediaries such as record companies.

Demo. A 'demonstration' recording of a song, or series of songs, not intended for official release, but to attract the attention of promoters, agents, publishers and record companies.

Development deal. Financial support for the creation of demo recordings or artistic development; the financing company usually has first option of signing the artist to a recording deal or of brokering a recording deal with another company.

Digital aggregator. A company that distributes digitized music to online retailers.

DJ (disk jockey). Someone who chooses and plays a sequence of pre-recorded music to an audience on the radio or internet, or at venues such as bars, clubs and festivals.

DVD-A. DVD-Audio offers higher quality audio resolution and playing time than the compact disc and supports surround sound reproduction. The discs are usually backwards-compatible so that they may be played on DVD players.

Dynamic pricing. A pricing structure determined by levels of demand, where concert ticket prices are varied to maximize attendance and profit.

EPK (electronic press kit). A promotional package for an artist or event which is presented in digital form. EPKs include a range of information and parts including press releases, photographs, biographies/histories and audio/visual media. The term has also been used to refer to short promotional documentary films as well as audio only interviews.

Exploit. To use intellectual property for financial or promotional gain, such as sales, licensing, and marketing tie-ins.

File-sharing. Sharing of digital files through the internet; where conducted without permission of copyright owners, it is referred to as illegal file-sharing.

Fixed costs. Business expenses which are not dependent on the quantity of sales achieved; for instance, the recording costs of an album, or staging costs of an event.

FLAC (free lossless audio codec). A digital audio file format which compresses audio files without losing any of the original audio information (hence lossless).

Freelancer. Someone who is self-employed.

Gatekeeper. A term derived from communication studies, a gatekeeper is someone who decides which messages are passed on. For instance, a radio station programme director is a gatekeeper, as he/she decides which recordings will be playlisted.

Gig. Commonly used to refer to music jobs undertaken by performers/musicians, such as concerts and paid recording sessions.

Harry Fox Agency. An American organization which collects and pays royalties to songwriters and publishers when their songs are manufactured by a record company onto any format.

Heritage act. An artist with a substantial long-term following and career.

Horizontal integration. Investing in companies which are in the same line of business, such as when one record company purchases another.

IASPM (International Association for the Study of Popular Music). An international organization founded in 1981 which promotes the academic analysis of popular music.

IFPI (International Federation of the Phonographic Industry). A not-for-profit organization which represents the worldwide recorded music industry.

Independent record label (or 'indie'). Typically a small record label which operates independently of the major transnational recording companies (the 'majors'). Many are, however, distributed by major-label owned distribution companies and, in some cases, the majors may also finance or part-own the indie.

ISP (internet service provider). Companies which provide computer and mobile device users with access to the internet.

ISRC (International Standard Recording Code). An internationally recognized method of identifying sound recordings and music video recordings.

Key man clause. A provision which may be negotiated into artist contracts, whereby the artist is free (i.e. no contractual reprisals) to follow a 'key person' (agent, manager, producer and so on) should that person leave the employment of the company to which the artist is contracted.

Library music. Collections of music which are created for sale (usually for a one-off flat fee) to users such as radio, television, and film, rather than to the general public.

Long-tail theory. A theory developed by Chris Anderson which suggests that the low costs of digital music distribution, together with the unlimited shelf space of the online retail environment, may allow niche artists and labels to sell their music profitably.

LP (Long Play). An analogue storage and distribution medium based on twelve-inch vinyl records played at 33 1/3 rpm. LPs were the backbone of recorded music industry profits in the 1970s, but were displaced by the compact disc in the 1980s and 1990s.

Major label. A transnational recording company which controls its own distribution and holds more than 5 per cent of the global consumer sales market.

Marginal cost. Business costs which are dependent on the quantity and type of product produced. Digital music files have very low marginal costs, whereas vinyl album production costs are higher (due to the costs associated with pressing, packaging, storing and distributing physical products).

Mash-up. A music track created by blending two or more pre-existing sound recordings which are played at the same time, such as a vocal track taken from one source overlaid on top of an instrumental track taken from another source.

Master. A sound recording from which copies are made.

Maven. An individual with a respected knowledge of a scene, and recognized as a taste-maker or opinion leader within a social or community group.

MCPS (Mechanical-Copyright Performance Society). A British organization, now part of PRS for Music, which collects and pays royalties to songwriters and publishers when their songs are manufactured by a record company onto any format.

Mechanical licence. Record companies are required to obtain a mechanical licence from songwriters or publishers when creating and duplicating sound recordings of their songs.

Mechanical royalties. Standardized financial payments (as set by copyright law or copyright tribunal) which are paid by record companies to songwriters and publishers pursuant to a mechanical licence.

MIDI (Musical Instrument Digital Interface). A technological standard used for exchanging or communicating musical instructions between or to electronic musical instruments which can understand, reproduce or act upon those instructions.

MP3. A digital audio file format which compresses audio information in order to reduce the size of the file for easier storage and transfer. It is referred to as 'lossy' because some audio information is lost during compression.

Napster. Originally a peer-to-peer file-sharing website of the mid- to late-1990s which allowed users to illegally share music with each other. It was closed down after legal action by the music industries, and later re-launched as a legitimate downloading store.

Neighbouring (or related) rights. Rights which belong to performers, broadcasters and producers rather than to songwriters and sound recording copyright holders.

Niche market. A specialized consumer segment based on demographics (such as age, location and socio-economic group) and/or psychographics (musical tastes, lifestyle choices and personality traits).

Option. A contractual provision which gives a record company or publisher the right to renew (or not) the term (length) of a recording or publishing agreement.

Overdubbing. The recording of additional tracks (music or sounds) to a pre-existing sound recording.

P&D deal (pressing and distribution deal). A contractual agreement in which a record company or distributor will manufacture and distribute the product of an independent record label or artist in return for a percentage of the revenue achieved.

P2P (peer-to-peer). A computer program which allows users to download music files from other people's computers, rather than from a centralized store.

Payola. Illicit financial payments and gifts/services offered in return for obtaining radio airplay.

Pay to play. In order to secure a performance at a particular venue an artist will, under this business agreement, purchase tickets from the venue then re-sell them to their fans to make their money back.

Performance right. Copyright owners have the exclusive right to authorize the public performance of their works.

Performing rights organizations. Organizations which administer the performance rights of copyright holders by issuing public performance licences to music users such as radio and television stations and by collecting and distributing income received.

Piracy. A catch-all term used to describe various forms of unauthorized copying and distribution of copyrighted works.

Playlist. A list of songs (updated at least weekly) played regularly by a radio station.

PPD (published price to dealers). The price paid by distributors for record company products.

PPL (previously known as Phonographic Performance Limited). A British performing rights organization (or collection society) which also administers International Standard Recording Codes (ISRCs) in the United Kingdom.

Producer. A person who works with artists, recording engineers and record labels to create a music recording.

PRS for Music. A British performing rights organization (or collection society) which also issues mechanical licences (administered through MCPS).

Public domain. Different kinds of cultural works (such as music, lyrics and sound recordings) are granted copyright protection for maximum periods of time; when that time period has passed, the copyright expires and the works may be used by anyone without seeking permission from, or making payment to, the original copyright owner. At this point the works are said to be in the public domain.

Recording contract. A contractual agreement between a recording company and an artist.

Recouping. When an advance which is paid under a recording or publishing contract is repayable from royalties earned by the artist or songwriter.

Remix. An alternative version of a song, created from the component elements of an original audio recording, sometimes with additional recordings (such as drum loops, sound effects and so on).

Revenue stream. Any source of income due to the exploitation of copyrights, or income from other sources, such as merchandising sales.

Reversion clause. A contractual provision in a music publishing agreement which stipulates that the rights in a song may be returned to the songwriter if the song is not recorded or otherwise exploited in the manner detailed in the agreement.

RIAA (Recording Industry Association of America). A trade organization representing the American recording industries.

Rider. A contractual provision related to live music which details the artists' personal and technical requirements for a concert appearance.

Ringback tones. Sounds or music heard by a telephone caller while they wait for their call to be answered.

Ringtone. Sounds or music played by a telephone to indicate that someone is calling.

Roster. A list of artists signed to a recording, publishing or production company.

Royalty. Monies earned by a songwriter or recording artist under a royalty-based contractual agreement; often expressed as a percentage of the retail or wholesale price. Royalties are used to recoup any contractual advances which have been received.

Royalty escalation clause. A contractual term which increases the royalty percentage received by a songwriter or recording artist when certain preset criteria are achieved, such as specific sales figures.

RPM (revolutions per minute). RPM refers to the speed that various physical recorded media are played to give correct sound reproduction; for instance, LPs typically rotate at 33 1/3 rpm.

SACD. Super audio compact discs are favoured by some audiophiles as they allow a greater frequency and dynamic range than standard CD. They can store surround sound recordings, and if used primarily for stereo recordings can have a playing time of four hours or more. However, a specialist SACD player is required.

Sample clearance. When sampling a pre-existing song recording for use in a new piece of music, permission (and usually payment) is required from the copyright's owners (for both the music publishing and the sound recording). Sample clearance is the name given to the process involved.

Sampling. The practice of using (usually) short clips of pre-existing sound recordings in the creation of a new recording; sampled elements may be used in unchanged form or manipulated using a synthesizer, computer program or other equipment.

Single. Commonly used term for 45 rpm vinyl discs which typically feature just one song per side, but also used to refer to the sale and download of individual tracks from internet music stores.

SESAC (formerly Society of European Stage Authors & Composers). An American performing rights organization.

Smartphone. A mobile phone which has additional computing features such as access to the internet and built-in or downloadable software applications (data storage, gaming, photography, music player and so on).

Street team. A promotional team which works on behalf of an artist, record company or event to create awareness and interest amongst a target market. Street teams may be paid or voluntary, and may also exist online.

Subcultural capital. Non-financial cultural and intellectual knowledge that provides enhanced status within a group, subculture or scene of people with similar interests.

Sunset clause. A contractual provision which specifies that an agreement will come to an end or be modified under specific future circumstances.

Synchronization right. The right to use music with film, television or video.

Taste-maker. Someone who influences popular music tastes or fashions, such as a high-profile blogger or journalist.

Territory. A grouping of countries which share characteristics of some kind, and are dealt with as singular units for business and marketing purposes.

Tin Pan Alley. Nickname for an area of New York that was central to the music publishing and songwriting business from the 1920s to the 1950s. Tin Pan Alley pop songs are simple commercially motivated songs in which the chorus predominates.

Track. Individual sound recordings of songs on an album; alternatively, all of the individual components of a sound recording: for instance, the drum parts, vocal parts and so on of a song are typically recorded separately in a multi-track recording studio before being combined into a final stereo product.

Upstreaming. A contractual arrangement between a major recording company and an independent record company in which the major has the option to take over an artist's recording contract should that artist prove commercially successful.

Vertical integration. Purchasing or investing in companies which are involved in the production, marketing or use of a product; for example, Sony Music is part of a vertically integrated conglomerate (Sony Corporation) which also includes radio, television, and film companies, and telecommunications and gaming companies which make use of music.

VPL (Video Performance Limited). Part of PPL, this organization grants licences for the public performance of music videos.

Weasel. A music company employee that covertly uses message boards and blogs to drive grassroots conversations about artists and products.

Work for hire. A contractual agreement in which the rights to a song or recording are to be owned by an employer, rather than by the composer or performer; hence no royalty payments are due to the composer or performer, who instead receives a flat fee or regular salary.

REFERENCES

Adorno, Theodore (1990) 'On Popular Music', in Simon Frith and Andrew Goodwin (eds), *On Record: Rock, Pop, and the Written Word*. London: Routledge, pp. 301–19.

Adorno, Theodore and Horkheimer, Max (2002) *Dialectic of Enlightenment*. Tr. Edmund Jephcott. Stanford: Stanford University Press.

Allen, Paul (2010) 'Charts, airplay, and promotion', in Tom Hutchison, Amy Macy, and Paul Allen (eds), *Record Label Marketing*, 2nd ed. Burlington, MA and Oxford: Focal Press, pp. 187–206.

Allen, Paul and Hutchison, Tom (2010) 'Grassroots marketing', in Tom Hutchison, Amy Macy, and Paul Allen (eds), *Record Label Marketing*, 2nd ed. Burlington, MA and Oxford: Focal Press, pp. 287–98.

Anderson, Chris (2006) *The Long Tail: Why the Future of Business is Selling Less of More*. New York: Hyperion.

Anderson, Chris (2009) *Free. The Future of a Radical Price*. London: Random House Business Books.

Anderton, Chris (2006) 'Beating the bootleggers: fan creativity, "lossless" audio trading, and commercial opportunities', in Michael D. Ayers (ed.), *Cybersounds. Essays on Virtual Music Culture*. New York: Peter Lang, pp. 161–84.

Anderton, Chris (2007) '(Re)Constructing Music Festival Places'. PhD dissertation, Swansea University.

Anderton, Chris (2009) 'Commercializing the Carnivalesque: the V Festival and Image/Risk Management', *Event Management*, 12(1): 39–51.

Anderton, Chris (2011) 'Music festival sponsorship: between commerce and carnival', *Arts Marketing* 1(2): 145–58.

Arden, Don (2004) *Mr. Big: Ozzy, Sharon and My Life as the Godfather of Rock*. London: Robson Books.

Ashworth, Eddie (2009) 'The post-millennial DIY explosion and its effects on record production', *Proceedings of the fifth annual Art of Record Production conference*, 13–15 November. Available at: http://www.artofrecordproduction.com/content/view/220/114/ (accessed 4 December 2011).

Atton, Chris (2001) 'Living in the past? Value discourses in progressive rock fanzines', *Popular Music*, 20(1): 29–46.

Atton, Chris (2009) 'Writing about listening: alternative discourses in rock journalism', *Popular Music*, 28(1): 53–67.

Auslander, Philip (2008) *Liveness. Performance in a Mediatized Culture*, 2nd ed. London & New York: Routledge.

Azerrad, Michael (2001) *Our Band Could Be Your Life*. New York: Little Brown.

Baringer, Sandra (2004) *The Metanarrative of Suspicion in Late Twentieth Century America*. New York & London: Routledge.

Barker, Hugh and Taylor, Yuval (2007) *Faking It: The Quest for Authenticity in Popular Music*. New York: W.W. Norton and Co.

Baskerville, David and Baskerville, Tim (2010) *Music Business Handbook and Career Guide*, 9th ed. Los Angeles: Sage.

Baudrillard, Jean (1994) *Simulacra and Simulation*. Tr. Sheila F. Glaser. Ann Arbor, MI: University of Michigan Press.

Belk, Russell W. (2001) *Collecting in a Consumer Society*, 2nd ed. London: Routledge.

Bennett, Andy (1999) 'Subcultures or neo-tribes? Rethinking the relationship between youth, style and musical taste', *Sociology*, 33(3): 599–617.

Bernier, Ivan (2003) 'Local content requirements for film, radio, and television as a means of protecting cultural diversity: theory and reality (Section I)'. *Cultural Diversity*, November–December. Available at: http://www.diversite-culturelle.qc.ca/fileadmin/documents/pdf/update031112section1.pdf (accessed 4 April 2012).

Blake, Andrew (2007) *Popular Music: The Age of Multimedia*. Middlesex: Middlesex University Press.

Booms, Bernard H. and Bitner, Mary J. (1980) 'Marketing strategies and organisation structures for service firms', in James H. Donnelly and William R. George (eds), *Marketing of Services*. Chicago: American Marketing Association, pp. 47–51.

Bourdieu, Pierre (1984) *Distinction: A Social Critique of the Judgement of Taste*. Tr. Richard Nice. Cambridge, MA: Harvard University Press.

BPI (2006a) *BPI Guidelines on Bar Coding*. Available at: http://www.bpi.co.uk/assets/files/BPI_Guidelines_on_Bar_Coding.pdf (accessed 25 April 2011).

BPI (2006b) *Numbering Systems and Codes used in the Record Industry: A Guide for Beginners*. Available at: http://www.bpi.co.uk/assets/files/Numbering_Systems_and_Codes.pdf (accessed 25 April 2011).

Brabazon, Tara (2011) *Popular Music: Topics, Trends & Trajectories*. London: Sage.

Brackett, David (1995) *Interpreting Popular Music*. Cambridge: Cambridge University Press.

Braheny, John (2006) *The Craft and Business of Songwriting*, 3rd ed. Cincinnati, OH: Writer's Digest Books.

Brassington, Frances and Pettitt, Stephen (2006) *Principles of Marketing*, 4th ed. Harlow: Pearson Education Ltd.

Brennan, Matt (2006) 'The rough guide to critics: musicians discuss the role of the music press', *Popular Music*, 25(2): 221–34.

Brennan, Matt (2010) 'Constructing a rough account of British concert promotion history', *Journal of the International Association for the Study of Popular Music,* 1(1): 4–13.

Brown, Mark (2008) 'The Guardian profile: Cathy Dennis', *The Guardian*, 15 August. Available at: http://www.guardian.co.uk/theguardian/2008/aug/15/popandrock (accessed 4 April 2012).

Bruno, A. (2011) 'Rick James' Estate Files Class Action Suit Against UMG in Wake of Eminem Verdict', *Billboard.biz*, 4 April 2011. Available at: http://www.billboard.biz/bbbiz/industry/record-labels/rick-james-estate-files-class-action-suit-1005110602.story (accessed 24 March 2012).

Bull, Michael (2000) *Sounding Out the City: Personal Stereos and the Management of Everyday Life*. London: Berg.

Bull, Michael (2005) 'No dead air! The iPod and the culture of mobile listening', *Leisure Studies*, 24(4): 343–55.

Bull Michael (2007) *Sound Moves: iPod Culture and Urban Experience*. London: Routledge.

Burnett, Robert (1996) *The Global Jukebox. The International Music Industry*. London & New York: Routledge.

Butler, Judith (1999) *Gender Trouble: Feminism and the Subversion of Identity*, rev. ed. London: Routledge.

Cardew, Ben (2010) 'Live and kicking: concert clout revealed by survey', *Music Week*, 14 August, p. 4.

Caulfield, Keith (2012) 'Adele rules 2011 with top selling album & song', *Billboard.com*, 4 January. Available at: http://www.billboard.com/news/adele-rules-2011-with-top-selling-album-1005784152.story#/news/adele-rules-2011-with-top-selling-album-1005784152.story (accessed 26 March 2012).

Celma, Oscar (2010) *Music Recommendation and Discovery. The Long Tail, Long Fail, and Long Play in the Digital Music Space*. Berlin: Springer-verlag.

Chapple, Steve and Garofalo, Reebee (1977) *Rock 'n' Roll is Here to Pay: the History and Politics of the Music Industry*. Chicago: NelsonHall.

Cloonan, Martin (2010) 'Live music and music policy: some initial thoughts', *Journal of the International Association for the Study of Popular Music*, 1(1): 14–23.

CMU (2012a) 'AEG Live signs Saint Saviour to 360 deal', 4 April. Available at: http://www.thecmuwebsite.com/article/aeg-live-signs-saint-saviour-to-360-deal/ (accessed 30 April 2012).

CMU (2012b) 'American radio royalties up for debate in Congress', 8 June. Available at: http://www.thecmuwebsite.com/article/american-radio-royalties-up-for-debate-in-congress/ (accessed 12 June 2012).

Collin, Matthew and Godfrey, John (1997) *Altered State: the Story of Ecstasy Culture and Acid House*, 2nd ed. London: Serpent's Tail.

Collins, Karen (ed.) (2008) *From Pac-Man to Pop Music: Interactive Audio in Games and New Media*. Aldershot: Ashgate.

Connell, John and Gibson, Chris (2003) *Sound Tracks. Popular Music, Identity and Place*. London and New York: Routledge.

Cunningham, Mark (1999) *Live & Kicking. The Rock Concert Industry in the Nineties*. London: Sanctuary Publishing Limited.

Curran, James (1999) 'The impact of advertising on the British mass media', in Paul Marris and Sue Thornham (eds), *Media Studies: a Reader*, 2nd ed. Edinburgh: Edinburgh University Press, pp. 710–26.

David, Matthew (2010) *Peer to Peer and the Music Industry. The Criminalization of Sharing*. London: Sage.

Demers, Joanna (2006) *Steal this Music. How Intellectual Property Law Affects Musical Creativity*. Athens, GA: University of Georgia Press.

Devine, Sean (2009) MA Songwriting Question and Answer Session, Bath Spa University, 24 November.

Dhar, Vasant and Chang, Elaine (2007) 'Does chatter matter? The impact of user-generated content on music sales', *CeDER Working Papers, New York University*. Available at: http://hdl.handle.net/2451/23783 (accessed 15 April 2012).

Dockwray, Ruth and Moore, Allan (2010) 'Configuring the sound-box 1965–1972', *Popular Music*, 29(2): 181–97.

Dring, Christopher (2011) 'Xbox signs Kylie Minogue', *MCV UK*, 17 February. Available at: http://www.mcvuk.com/news/read/xbox-signs-kylie-minogue (accessed 20 February 2011).

Duncombe, Stephen (1997). *Notes from Underground: Zines and the Politics of Alternative Culture*. London: Verso.

Echo Nest (2012) 'EMI partnership', Available at: http://developer.echonest.com/sandbox/emi/ (accessed 20 May 2012).

EFF (2008) 'RIAA v. the People: Five Years Later', September. Available at: http://www.eff.org/wp/riaa-v-people-years-later (accessed 5 August 2011).

Expresso Bongo (1959) Directed by Val Guest. UK: Val Guest Productions.

Fabbri, Franco (1982) 'A theory of musical genres: two applications', in David Horn and Philip Tagg (eds), *Popular Music Perspectives*. Gothenburg and Exeter: IASPM, pp. 52–81.

FBT vs Aftermath (2010) *F.B.T. Productions, LLC v. Aftermath Records, 09-55817* (9th Cir. 3 September). Available at: http://www.ca9.uscourts.gov/datastore/opinions/2010/09/03/09-55817.pdf (accessed 24 March 2012).

Fiske, John (1992) 'The cultural economy of fandom', in Lisa A Lewis (ed.), *The Adoring Audience: Fan Culture and Popular Media*. London: Routledge, pp. 30–49.

Fonarow, Wendy (2001) *Empire of Dirt: the Aesthetics and Rituals of British Indie Music*. New York: Little Brown.

Forde, Eamonn (2001) 'From polyglottism to branding. On the decline of personality journalism in the British music press', *Journalism*, 2(1): 23–43.

Frascogna, Xavier M. Jr and Hetherington, H. Lee (2004) *This Business of Artists Management*, 4th ed. New York: Billboard Books.

Frith, Simon (1981) *Sound Effects: Youth, Leisure, and the Politics of Rock*. London: Constable.

Frith, Simon (1987) 'Why Do Songs Have Words?', in Simon Frith (ed.) (2007), *Taking Popular Music Seriously: Selected Essays*. Aldershot: Ashgate, pp. 209–38.

Frith, Simon (1992) 'The industrialization of popular music', in James Lull (ed.), *Popular Music and Communication*, 2nd ed. London: Sage, pp. 49–74.

Frith, Simon (1996) 'Music and identity', in Stuart Hall and Paul du Gay (eds), *Questions of Cultural Identity*. London: Sage, pp. 108–27.

Frith, Simon (2002) 'Fragments of a sociology of rock criticism', in Steve Jones (ed.), *Pop Music and the Press*. Philadelphia: Temple University Press, pp. 235–46.

Frith, Simon (2007) 'Live music matters', *Scottish Music Review*, 1(1): 1–17.

Frith, Simon (2010) 'Analysing live music in the UK: findings one year into a three-year research project', *Journal of the International Association for the Study of Popular Music*, 1(1): 1–3.

Frith, Simon and Goodwin, Andrew (1998) *On Record: Rock, Pop, and the Written Word*. London: Routledge.

Firth, Simon and Marshall, Lee (eds) (2004) *Music and Copyright*, 2nd ed. Edinburgh: Edinburgh University Press.

Garfield, Simon (1986) *Expensive Habits. The Dark Side of the Music Industry*. London: Faber & Faber.

Garofalo, Reebee (1999) 'From music publishing to MP3: music and industry in the twentieth century', *American Music*, 12(3): 318–54.

Getz, Donald (2002) 'Why Festivals Fail', *Event Management*, 7(4): 209–19.

Gillett, Charlie (1988) *Making Tracks: Atlantic Records and the Growth of a Multi-Billion-Dollar Industry*. London: Souvenir Press.

Gladwell, Malcolm (2000) *The Tipping Point. How Little Things can make a Big Difference*. London: Little, Brown.

Godrich, Nigel (n.d.) *Nigel Godrich: Bio*. Available at: http://www.nigelgodrich.com/bio.htm (accessed 16 April 2011).

Hall, Stuart and Jefferson, Tony (eds) (1976) *Resistance Through Rituals: Youth Subcultures in Post-War Britain*. London: Hutchinson.

Harrison, Ann (2008) *Music: the Business. The Essential Guide to the Law and the Deals*, 4th ed. London: Virgin Books.

Harrison, Ann (2011) *Music: the Business. The Essential Guide to the Law and the Deals*, 5th ed. London: Virgin Books.

Healey, Jon (2011) 'EMI and Echo Nest create a 'sandbox' for app developers', *LA Times*, 2 November. Available at: http://latimesblogs.latimes.com/technology/2011/11/emi-and-the-echo-nest-create-a-sandbox-for-app-developers.html (accessed 20 May 2012).

Health and Safety Executive (1999) *The Event Safety Guide. A Guide to Health, Safety and Welfare at Music and Similar Events.* Norwich: HSE Books.

Hebdige, Dick (1979) *Subculture: the Meaning of Style.* London: Methuen.

Hendy, David (2000) 'Pop music in the public services: BBC Radio One and new music in the 1990s', *Media, Culture & Society*, 22(6): 743–61.

Herman, Andrew and Sloop, John M. (1998) 'The politics of authenticity in postmodern rock culture: the case of Negativland and "The Letter 'U' and the Numeral '2'"', *Critical Studies in Mass Communication*, 15(1): 1–20.

Hesmondhalgh, David (1998) 'Post-Punk's attempt to democratize the music industry: the success and failure of Rough Trade', *Popular Music*, 16(3): 255–74.

Hesmondhalgh, David (2007) *The Cultural Industries*, 2nd ed. Los Angeles & London: Sage.

Hesmondhalgh, David and Baker, Sarah (2011) *Creative Labour: Media Work in Three Cultural Industries.* London: Routledge.

Heylin, Clinton (1994) *Bootleg. The Secret History of the Other Recording Industry.* New York: St Martin's Griffin.

Hirsch, Paul M. (1990) 'Processing fads and fashions: an organization-set analysis of cultural industry systems', in Simon Frith and Andrew Goodwin (eds), *On Record. Rock, Pop, and the Written Word.* London & New York: Routledge, pp. 127–39.

Hodgkinson, Will (2007) *Song Man: A Melodic Adventure or My Single-Minded Approach to Songwriting.* London: Bloomsbury.

Holman, Tomlinson (2008) *Surround Sound. Up and Running*, 2nd ed. Burlington, MA & Oxford: Focal Press.

Hornby, Nick (1996) *High Fidelity.* London: Indigo.

Howard, George (2005) *Music Publishing 101.* Boston, MA: Berklee Press.

Howard, George (2011) 'How to get your song on commercial radio', *TuneCore blog*, 15 September. Available at: http://blog.tunecore.com/2011/09/how-to-get-your-song-on-commercial-radio.html (accessed 28 March 2012).

Hull, Geoffrey, Hutchison, Thomas and Strasser, Richard (2011) *The Music Business and Recording Industry*, 3rd ed. New York & London: Routledge.

Huq, Rupa (2006) *Beyond Subculture: Pop, Youth and Identity in a Postcolonial World.* London: Routledge.

Hutchison, Tom and Allen, Paul (2010) 'Publicity of recorded music', in Tom Hutchison, Amy Macy, and Paul Allen (eds), *Record Label Marketing*, 2nd ed. Burlington, MA & Oxford: Focal Press, pp. 207–28.

Hutchison, Tom, Macy, Amy, and Allen, Paul (2010) *Record Label Marketing*, 2nd ed. Burlington, MA & Oxford: Focal Press.

IFPI (n.d.) 'What is copyright?', *International Federation of the Phonographic Industry.* Available at: http://www.ifpi.org/content/section_views/what_is_copyright.html (accessed 27 March 2009).

IFPI. (2001) *Recording industry world sales 2000.* Available at: http://www.ifpi.org/content/library/worldsales2000.pdf (accessed 22 November 2009).

IFPI (2006) *The Recording Industry 2006: Piracy Report. Protecting Creativity in Music.* Available at: http://www.ifpi.org/content/library/piracy-report2006.pdf (accessed 15 September 2009).

IFPI. (2008) *Recorded music sales 2007 (physical, digital and performance rights revenues).* Available at: http://www.ifpi.org/content/library/Recorded-music-sales-2007.pdf (accessed 22 November 2009).

IFPI (2011) *Digital Music Report 2011.* Available at: http://www.ifpi.org/content/library/DMR2011.pdf (accessed 5 August 2011).

Informa Telecoms and Media (2011) 'Universal Music Group reasserts its recorded-music dominance in 2010', *Music & Copyright's Blog*, 23 March. Available at: http://musicandcopyright.wordpress.com/2011/03/23/universal-music-group-reasserts-its-recorded-music-dominance-in-2010/ (accessed 1 April 2011).

Inglis, Ian (ed.) (2006) *Performance and Popular Music: History, Place and Time*. Aldershot: Ashgate.

IQ (2011) 'Ticketing report 2011', Vol. 35, May. Available at: http://issuu.com/gregiq/docs/iq_issue_35_1/ (accessed 10 June 2011).

James, Martin (1997) *The Prodigy: Adventures with the Voodoo Crew*. London: Ebury Press.

James, Martin (2001) *Moby: Replay: His Life and Times*. London: Independent Music Press.

James, Martin (2003) *French Connections: From Discotheque to Discovery*. London: Sanctuary.

James, Martin (2004) *Dave Grohl: Nirvana, Foo Fighters and Other Misadventures*. Church Stretton: Independent Music Press.

Jenkins, Henry (2006) *Confessions of an Aca-Fan: the Official Weblog of Henry Jenkins*. Available at: http://henryjenkins.org/ (accessed 22 April 2011).

Jennings, David (2007) *Net, Blogs and Rock'n'Roll*. London: Nicholas Brealey.

Jenson, Joli (1992) 'Fandom as pathology: the consequence of characterization', in Lisa A. Lewis (ed.), *The Adoring Audience. Fan Culture and Popular Media*. London: Routledge, pp. 9–29.

Jones, Graham (2010) *Last Shop Standing: Whatever Happened to Record Shops?* London: Proper Music Publishing.

Jones, Mike (2006) Interview with Andy West, 7 April.

Jones, Steve (2002) *Pop Music and the Press*. Philadelphia: Temple University Press.

Katz, Mark (2010) *Capturing Sound: How Technology has Changed Music*, 2nd ed. Berkeley & London: University of California Press.

Kelleher, Caren (2011) 'The lessons I learned from a $10,000 Kickstarter campaign…', *Digital Music News*, 8 June. Available at: http://www.digitalmusicnews.com/stories/060811funding (accessed 23 March 2012).

Kelly, Kevin (2008) *1,000 True Fans*. Available at: http://www.kk.org/thetechnium/archives/2008/03/1000_true_fans.php (accessed 22 April 2011).

Klavens, Kent J. (1989) *Protecting Your Songs & Yourself*. Cincinnati: Writer's Digest Books.

Knopper, Steve (2010) 'Live Nation and Ticketmaster merge, creating music-industry superpower', *Rolling Stone* 1098, 18 February, pp. 14–15.

Kurkela, Vesa and Väkevä, Lauri (2009) *De-Canonizing Music History*. Cambridge: Cambridge Scholars Publishing.

Kusek, David and Leonhard, Gerd (2005) *The Future of Music: Manifesto for the Digital Music Revolution*. Boston, MA: Berklee Press.

Laing, Dave (1985) *One Chord Wonders: Power and Meaning in Punk Rock*. Milton Keynes: Open University Press.

Laing, Dave (2004a) 'The three Woodstocks and the live music scene', in Andy Bennett (ed.), *Remembering Woodstock*. Aldershot: Ashgate, pp. 1–17.

Laing, Dave (2004b) 'Copyright, politics and the international music industry', in Simon Frith and Lee Marshall (eds), *Music and Copyright*, 2nd ed. Edinburgh: Edinburgh University Press, pp. 70–85.

Lamere, Paul (2009) 'The loudness war analyzed', *Paul Lamere's Music Machinery Blog*, 23 March. Available at: http://musicmachinery.com/2009/03/23/the-loudness-war/ (accessed 4 December 2011).

La Rue, Frank (2010) *Report of the Special Rapporteur on the Promotion and Protection of the Right to Freedom of Opinion and Expression*. UN General Assembly, 1 June. Available at: http://www.unhcr.org/refworld/publisher,UNGA,,,4d6e48c12,0.html (accessed 14 March 2012).

Lee, Stephen (1995) 'Re-examining the concept of the independent record company', *Popular Music*, 14(1): 13–31.

Leonard, Marion (2007) *Gender in the Music Industry. Rock, Discourse and Girl Power.* Aldershot: Ashgate.

Lessig, Lawrence (2004) *Free Culture*. New York: The Penguin Press.

Levine, Robert (2007) 'The death of high fidelity', *Rollingstone.com*, 26 December. Available at: http://web.archive.org/web/20100410062131/http://www.rollingstone.com/news/story/17777619/the_death_of_high_fidelity (accessed 20 January 2012).

Leyshon, Andrew (2001) 'Time-space (and digital) compression: software formats, musical networks, and the reorganisation of the music industry', *Environment and Planning A*, 33(1): 49–77.

Leyshon, Andrew (2009) 'The Software Slump?: digital music, the democratisation of technology, and the decline of the recording studio sector within the musical economy', *Environment and Planning A*, 41(6): 1309–31.

Lieberman, Robbie (1995) *My Song is My Weapon: People's Songs, American Communism and the Politics of Culture 1930–1950*. Urbana & Chicago: University of Illinois Press.

Lindberg, Ulf, Gudmundsson, Gester, Michelson, Morten and Weisethaunet, Hans (2005) *Rock Criticism from the Beginning: Amusers, Bruisers and Cool-Headed Cruisers*. New York: Peter Lang.

Long, Paul (2011) 'Student Music', *Arts Marketing*, 1(2): 121–35.

Lopes, Paul D. (1992) 'Innovation and diversity in the popular music industry, 1969 to 1990', *American Sociological Review*, 57(1): 56–71.

Loving You (1957) Directed by Hal Kanter. USA: Paramount Pictures.

Lyotard, Jean-François (1984) *The Postmodern Condition: a Report on Knowledge*. Tr. Geoff Bennington and Brian Massumi. Ann Arbor, MI: University of Minnesota Press.

M Magazine (2011) 'I wrote that: Can't get you out of my head', *M Magazine*, 26 September. Available at: http://www.m-magazine.co.uk/featuresinterviews/interviews/i-wrote-that-cant-get-you-out-of-my-head/ (accessed 20 March 2012).

Machin, David (2010) *Analysing Popular Music: Image, Sound, Text.* London: Sage.

MacInnes, Paul (2007) 'Robbie Williams apologises to ex-manager for not keeping his Rudebox shut', *The Guardian*, 5 December. Available at: http://www.guardian.co.uk/music/2007/dec/05/1 (accessed 24 March 2012).

Maffesoli, Michel (1996) *The Time of the Tribes: the Decline of Individualism in Mass Society.* Tr. Don Smith. London: Sage.

Malbon, Ben (1999) *Clubbing: Dancing, Ecstasy and Vitality*. London: Routledge.

Marr, Andrew (2004) *My Trade: A Short History of British Journalism*. London: Macmillan.

Marshall, Lee (2005) *Bootlegging. Romanticism and Copyright in the Music Industry.* London: Sage.

Masson, Gordon (2011) 'Investment: Live music festivals targeted by VCTs', *Music Week*, 29 January, p. 12.

McCarthy, E. Jerome (1960) *Basic Marketing. A Managerial Approach.* Homewood, Il: Richard D. Irwin.

McKay, George (2000) *Glastonbury: A Very English Fair.* London: Victor Gollancz.

McLaren, Malcolm (2009) 'Fast Forward: Will the Next Decade Prove to be as Groundbreaking for the Music Industry as the Noughties?', *M Magazine*, Issue 34, December.

McLeod, Kembrew and DiCola, Peter (2011) *Creative License. The Law and Culture of Digital Sampling*. Durham & London: Duke University Press.

McLuhan, Marshall (1964) *Understanding Media. The Extensions of Man.* New York: McGraw-Hill.

Millard, Andre (1996) *America on Record: A History of Recorded Sound.* New York: Cambridge University Press.

Milner, G. (2009) *Perfecting Sound Forever. An Aural History of Recorded Music.* New York: Faber and Faber Inc.

Mitchell, Tony (1997) *Popular Music and Local Identity: Rock, Pop and Rap in Europe and Oceania.* London: Leicester University Press.

MobiThinking (2012) 'Global mobile statistics 2012', *MobiThinking*, February. Available at: http://mobithinking.com/mobile-marketing-tools/latest-mobile-stats (accessed 22 March 2012).

Moore, Allan F. (2001) *Rock: the Primary Text. Developing a Musicology of Rock*, 2nd ed. Aldershot: Ashgate.

Moore, Allan (2002) 'Authenticity as authentication', *Popular Music*, 21(2): 209–23.

Morley, Paul (2009) 'Look Back in Anger: Can a Song Change the World?', *M Magazine*, Issue 34: December.

Mueller, Andrew (1999) *Rock in Hard Places.* London: Virgin.

Muggleton, David and Weinzierl, Rupert (eds) (2003) *The Post-Subcultures Reader.* Oxford: Berg.

Murphy, Ralph. (2007) MA Songwriting Guest Lecture, Bath Spa University, 12 October.

Negroponte, Nicholas (1995) *Being Digital.* New York: Alfred A. Knopf.

Negus, Keith (1992) *Producing Pop: Culture and Conflict in the Popular Music Industry.* London: Arnold.

Negus, Keith (1996) *Popular Music in Theory. An Introduction.* Cambridge: Polity Press.

Negus, Keith (1999) *Music Genres and Corporate Cultures.* London: Routledge.

Nicholson, Stuart (2006) 'Amy Winehouse, Back to Black', *The Observer*, 15 October. Available at: http://www.guardian.co.uk/music/2006/oct/15/shopping.popandrock1 (accessed 22 January 2012).

Nielsen Music (2011) 'Digital music consumption and digital music access', *Nielsen white paper produced for MIDEM*, January.

NPD (2011) 'With Limewire shuttered, peer-to-peer music file sharing declines precipitously', press release dated 23 March. Available at: https://www.npd.com/press/releases/press_110323.html (accessed 20 March 2012).

Official Chart Company (2011) 'The biggest selling vinyl albums of 2011 revealed', *Official Chart Company*, 19 October. Available at: http://www.officialcharts.com/chart-news/the-biggest-selling-vinyl-albums-of-2011-revealed/ (accessed 20 March 2012).

Ogg, Alex (2009) *Independence Days. The Story of UK Independent Record Labels.* London: Cherry Red Books.

Orman, John M. (1980) *The Politics of Rock Music.* Chicago: NelsonHall.

Page, Will (2007) 'Economics. Time to face the music', *Music Ally*, 18 October, pp. 7–8.

Page, Will and Carey, Chris (2009) 'Adding up the music industry for 2008', *Economic Insight* 15. Available at: http://www.prsformusic.com/creators/news/research/Pages/default.aspx (accessed 20 May 2011).

Page, Will and Carey, Chris (2010) 'Adding up the UK music industry for 2009', *Economic Insight* 20. Available at: http://www.prsformusic.com/creators/news/research/Pages/default.aspx (accessed 20 May 2011).

Page, Will and Carey, Chris (2011) 'Adding up the UK music industry 2010', *Economic Insight* 23. Available at: http://www.prsformusic.com/creators/news/research/Pages/default.aspx (accessed 18 August 2011).

Paine, Andre (2010) 'Mute goes indie again, EMI keeps Depeche Mode', *Billboard.biz*, 22 September. Available at: http://www.billboard.biz/bbbiz/content_display/industry/e3ied4f9346f54dc08e9dfca2b9c594a1f0 (accessed 20 December 2011).

Palmley, Greg (2011) 'Talent's got Britain', *IQ Magazine*, July, pp. 38–46.

Passman, Donald S. (2009) *All You Need to Know About the Music Business*, 7th ed. New York: Free Press.

Pearce, Susan (ed.) (1997) *Experiencing Material Culture in the Western World*. London & Washington DC: Leicester University Press.

Perpetua, Matthew (2011) 'U2 to sell 360 tour "claw" as permanent venue', *Rolling Stone*, 28 June. Available at: http://www.rollingstone.com/music/news/u2-to-sell-360-tour-claw-as-permanent-venue-20110628 (accessed 20 December 2011).

Perry, Mark (2000) *Sniffin' Glue: the Essential Punk Accessory*. London: Sanctuary.

Peterson, Richard A. and Berger, David G. (1990) 'Cycles in symbol production: the case of popular music', in Simon Frith and Andrew Goodwin (eds), *On Record. Rock, Pop, and the Written Word*. London & New York: Routledge, pp. 117–33.

Pfanner, E. (2012) 'Copyright Cheats Face the Music in France', *The New York Times*, 19 February. Available at: http://www.nytimes.com/2012/02/20/technology/20iht-piracy20.html?pagewanted=all (accessed 24 March 2012).

Reinartz, Joe (2010) 'Top tours 2010', *Pollstar.com*, 29 December. Available at: http://www.pollstar.com/blogs/news/archive/2010/12/29/751701.aspx (accessed 30 June 2011).

Roberts, Rebecca (2009) 'Jill Sobule: with a little help from her fans', *NPR Music*, 11 April. Available at: http://www.npr.org/templates/story/story.php?storyId=103013140 (accessed 20 March 2012).

Rodman, Gilbert B. and Vanderdonckt, Cheyanne (2006) 'Music for nothing or, I want my MP3. The regulation and recirculation of affect', *Cultural Studies*, 20(2–3): 245–61.

Rogan, Johnny (1988) *Starmakers and Svengalis*. London: Futura.

Rojek Chris (2005) 'P2P leisure exchange: net banditry and the policing of intellectual property', *Leisure Studies*, 24(4): 357–69.

Rojek, Chris (2011) *Pop Music, Pop Culture*. Cambridge: Polity Press.

Rose, Kara (2011) 'Cassette tapes see new life after MP3s', *USA Today*, 10 March. Available at: http://www.usatoday.com/life/music/news/story/2011-10-02/mp3s-cassette-tapes-vinyl-albums/50639144/1 (accessed 15 April 2012).

Ross, Peter G. (2005) 'Cycles in symbol production research: foundations, applications and future directions', *Popular Music and Society*, 28(4): 473–87.

Sanjek, Russell (1988) *American Popular Music and its Business: The First Four Hundred Years, Vol. 3*. New York: Oxford University Press.

Schulenberg, Richard (2005) *Legal Aspects of the Music Industry. An Insider's View*. New York: Billboard Books.

Shelton, Robert (2003) *No Direction Home: the Life and Music of Bob Dylan*. New York: Da Capo Press.

Shepherd, Ian (2008) 'Metallica "Death Magnetic" – Stop the loudness wars', *Ian Shepherd's Mastering Media Blog*, 16 September. Available at: http://mastering-media.blogspot.com/2008/09/metallica-death-magnetic-stop-loudness.html (accessed 4 December 2011).

Shuker, Roy (2001) *Understanding Popular Music Culture*. London: Routledge.

Shuker, Roy (2010) *Wax Trash and Vinyl Treasures: Record Collecting as a Social Practice*. Farnham: Ashgate.

Shuker, Roy (2012) *Popular Music Culture: the Key Concepts*, 3rd ed. London: Routledge.

Simon, Ralph (2011) 'Another BRICA in the wall', *IQ – Live Music Intelligence*, Vol. 35: 15.

Singerman, Robert and Lockshin, Miriam (2007) *US Market Guide and Contacts*. Available at: http://www.scribd.com/doc/16203733/Us-Guide (accessed 26 April 2011).

Smith, Jay (2010) '2010 by the numbers (so far)', *Pollstar*, 9 July. Available at: http://www.pollstar.com/blogs/news/archive/2010/07/09/731238.aspx (accessed 10 July 2011).

Smith, Jay (2011) '2011 by the numbers (so far)', *Pollstar*, 8 July. Available at: http://www.pollstar.com/blogs/news/archive/2011/07/08/773926.aspx (accessed 10 July 2011).

Sobel, Ron and Weissman, Dick (2008) *Music Publishing: The Roadmap to Royalties*. New York: Routledge.

Sparrow, Andrew (2006) *Music Distribution and the Internet. A Legal Guide for the Music Business*. Aldershot: Gower Publishing Limited.

Statham, Paul (2009) MA Songwriting Question and Answer Session, Bath Spa University, 20 October.

Stein-Sacks, Shelley (Brock & Chaloux Group Inc.) (2012) *On Quotas as they are Found in Broadcasting Music*. Report prepared for the Canadian Radio-television and Telecommunications Commission, 9 February. Available at: http://www.crtc.gc.ca/eng/publications/reports/rp120309c.htm (accessed 4 April 2012).

Stephens, John and McCallum, Robyn (1998) *Retelling Stories, Framing Culture: Traditional Story and Metanarratives in Children's Literature*. London: Routledge.

Sterne, Jonathan (1999) 'Thinking the Internet: cultural studies versus the millennium', in Steve Jones (ed.), *Doing Internet Research: Critical Issues and Methods for Examining the Net*. London: Sage, pp. 257–88.

Stokes, Simon (2005) *Digital Copyright. Law and Practice*, 2nd ed. Oxford and Portland, Oregon: Hart Publishing.

Strachan, Robert (2007) 'Micro-independent record labels in the UK: discourse, DIY cultural production and the music industry', *European Journal of Cultural Studies*, 10(2): 245–65.

Straw, Will (1997) 'Sizing up record collections: gender and connoisseurship in rock music culture', in Sheila Whiteley (ed.), *Sexing the Groove: Popular Music and Gender*. London: Routledge, pp. 3–16.

Talbot, Martin (2002) 'Putting a price on independence', *Music Week*, 25 May.

Talbot, Mary (2007) *Media Discourse: Representation and Interaction*. Edinburgh: Edinburgh University Press.

Tavern, M. (2011) Email interview with Andrew Dubber, 13–14 April.

Taylor, Timothy D. (1997) *Global Pop: World Music, World Markets*. London: Routledge.

Tessler, Holly (2008) 'The new MTV? Electronic Arts and "playing" music', in Karen Collins (ed.), *From Pac-Man to Pop Music: Interactive Audio in Games and New Media*. Aldershot: Ashgate, pp. 13–26.

Tham, David C. (2010) 'New music audiences: the generative impulse', conference paper given at *The 2010 Communications Policy & Research Forum*, 15 November. Available at: http://www.slideshare.net/nanoKnowledge/tham-generative-music-audiences (accessed 15 April 2012).

Thornton, Sarah (1990) 'Strategies for reconstructing the popular past', *Popular Music*, 9(1): 87–95.

Thornton, Sarah (1995) *Club Culture: Music, Media, and Subcultural Capital*. London: Polity Press.

Tomlinson, John (1991) *Cultural Imperialism: A Critical Introduction*. London and New York: Continuum.

Tschmuck, Peter (2006) *Creativity and Innovation in the Music Industry*. Dordrecht, The Netherlands: Springer.

TSG. (2008) 'Van Halen's legendary M&M's rider', 11 December. Available at: http://www.thesmokinggun.com/documents/crime/van-halens-legendary-mms-rider (accessed 2 February 2012).

Turner, Victor (1969) *The Ritual Process: Structure and Anti-Structure.* London: Routledge and Kegan Paul.

Turner, Victor (1982) *From Ritual to Theatre. The Human Seriousness of Play.* New York: PAJ Publications.

Vauxhall (2010) 'Introducing Katie Melua, our new brand ambassador', 15 November. Available at: http://www.vauxhall.co.uk/about-vauxhall/archive/2010/November/katie-melua-brand-ambassador.html (accessed 4 April 2012).

Vision One (2009) 'InStore Music. Maximising the impact of music to enhance shopper experience & sales', Case Study No.5. Available at: http://www.visionone.co.uk/files/png/Vision_One_-_In_Store_Music_(Heartbeat)_-_Case_Study.pdf (accessed 4 April 2012)

Waddell, Ray (2011) 'U2's 360 Tour gross: $736,137,344', *Billboard.biz*, 29 July. Available at: http://www.billboard.biz/bbbiz/others/u2-s-360-tour-gross-736-137-344-1005298062.story (accessed 10 August 2011).

Wald, Elijah (2009) *How the Beatles Destroyed Rock 'n' Roll: an Alternative History of American Popular Music.* New York: Oxford University Press.

Wall, Tim (2003) *Studying Popular Music Culture.* London: Arnold.

Wall, Tim and Long, Paul (2009) 'Jazz Britannia: mediating the story of British jazz's past on television', *Jazz Research Journal*, 3(2): 145–70.

Wallman, Ian (2011) Email interview with Andrew Dubber, 16 April.

Waltz, Mitzi (2005) *Alternative and Activist Media.* Edinburgh: Edinburgh University Press.

Watson, Nessim (1997) 'Why we argue about virtual community: a case study of the phish.net fan community', in Steven G. Jones (ed.), *Virtual Culture: Identity and Communication in Cybersociety.* London: Sage, pp. 102–32.

Weinstein, Deena (2006) 'Rock protest songs: so many and so few', in Ian Peddie (ed.), *The Resisting Muse: Popular Music and Social Protest.* Aldershot: Ashgate, pp. 3–16.

West, Andy (2007) *Developing Pedagogical Tools for the Teaching of Songwriting at Postgraduate Level.* Available at: http://www.heacademy.ac.uk/assets/documents/subjects/palatine/developing-pedagogical-tools-creating-an-ma-in-songwriting.pdf (accessed 8 February 2012).

Wikström, Patrik (2009) *The Music Industry: Music in the Cloud.* Cambridge: Polity Press.

Williamson, John and Cloonan, Martin (2007) 'Rethinking the music industry', *Popular Music*, 26(2): 305–22.

Willis, Paul (1978) *Profane Culture.* London: Routledge and Kegan Paul.

Worthington, Andy (2004) *Stonehenge: Celebration and Subversion.* Loughborough: Alternative Albion.

Yalch, Richard and Spangenberg, Eric (1990) 'Effects of store music on shopping behavior', *Journal of Services Marketing*, 4(1): 31–9.

Zollo, Paul (2003) *Songwriters on Songwriting*, 4th ed. Cambridge, MA: Da Capo Press.

INDEX

CPSIA information can be obtained
at www.ICGtesting.com
Printed in the USA
BVHW070726150722
641819BV00004B/51

9 781446 207956